Learn to Create WordPress Themes by Building 5 Projects

Master the fundamentals of WordPress theme development
and create attractive WordPress themes from scratch

Eduonix Learning Solutions

BIRMINGHAM - MUMBAI

Learn to Create WordPress Themes by Building 5 Projects

First published: December 2017

Production reference: 1271217

Published by Packt Publishing Ltd.
Livery Place
35 Livery Street
Birmingham
B3 2PB, UK.
ISBN 978-1-78728-664-1

www.packtpub.com

Credits

Author
Eduonix Learning Solutions

Project Editor
Suzanne Coutinho

Acquisition Editor
Dominic Shakeshaft

Content Development Editor
Deepti Thore

Technical Editors
Gaurav Gavas
Bhagyashree Rai

Copy Editor
Tom Jacob

Proofreader
Safis Editing

Indexer
Tejal Daruwale Soni

Graphics
Tom Scaria

Production Coordinator
Melwyn Dsa

About the Author

Eduonix Learning Solutions creates and distributes high-quality technology training content. Our team of industry professionals have been training manpower for more than a decade.

We aim to teach technology the way it is used in the industrial and professional world. We have a professional team of trainers for technologies ranging from mobility and web, to enterprise, database, and server administration.

Customer Feedback

Thanks for purchasing this Packt book. At Packt, quality is at the heart of our editorial process. To help us improve, please leave us an honest review on this book's Amazon page at http://www.amazon.com/dp/1787286649.

If you'd like to join our team of regular reviewers, you can email us at customerreviews@packtpub.com. We award our regular reviewers with free eBooks and videos in exchange for their valuable feedback. Help us be relentless in improving our products!

www.PacktPub.com

For support files and downloads related to your book, please visit www.PacktPub.com.

Did you know that Packt offers eBook versions of every book published, with PDF and ePub files available? You can upgrade to the eBook version at www.PacktPub.com and as a print book customer, you are entitled to a discount on the eBook copy. Get in touch with us at service@packtpub.com for more details.

At www.PacktPub.com, you can also read a collection of free technical articles, sign up for a range of free newsletters and receive exclusive discounts and offers on Packt books and eBooks.

https://www.packtpub.com/mapt

Get the most in-demand software skills with Mapt. Mapt gives you full access to all Packt books and video courses, as well as industry-leading tools to help you plan your personal development and advance your career.

Why subscribe?

- Fully searchable across every book published by Packt
- Copy and paste, print, and bookmark content
- On demand and accessible via a web browser

Table of Contents

Preface

Throughout this book, we will build 5 different WordPress themes from start to finish. We will look at all the fundamental concepts that are needed to start building great themes.

To get through the book, you should have some experience in HTML/CSS and PHP. You will also need to have a general idea of what WordPress is—it's installation and WordPress website management—and a basic understanding of some programming fundamentals, for example, arrays, variables, loops, statements, and so on. The projects are mainly based around HTML5, CSS3, and PHP.

Apart from these, there are some other technologies and concepts that we will be looking at throughout the book. These include WordPress post loops, which is the main loop that grabs database to WordPress, hooks/actions, the `functions.php` file where we put our dynamic code for our WordPress theme, widgets, WP_queries, and theme customizer. Also, we'll be using a range of frameworks such as Bootstrap, Foundation, and W3 CSS, which is a fairly new framework.

So, let's dive in and start building the cool themes.

What this book covers

Chapter 1, *Creating a Simple Theme with WordPress*, is an introductory project chapter. We'll discuss about the files which we need to create for our theme, the syntax, and the dynamic snippets.

Chapter 2, *Building a WordPress Theme*, is a project chapter that goes in depth and uses advanced concepts to build a WordPress theme, including custom template and home pages, archived pages, and post formats.

Chapter 3, *Building a WordPress Theme for Photo Gallery*, is about a project to build a WordPress theme for a photo gallery. We're going to use the w3.CSS framework and also some simple animations to build the theme.

Chapter 4, *Building a Twitter Bootstrap WordPress Theme*, is a project chapter that explains integration of Bootstrap with WordPress. This is going to be our chapter to use Wordstrap for our Twitter Bootstrap to implement our WordPress theme. We are also going to use WP nav walker, which is a class we can have for drop-down menus.

Chapter 5, *The Foundation E-Commerce Theme*, is about building an e-commerce theme using the foundation framework, which is similar to the Bootstrap framework.

What you need for this book

You will need the following to work through the projects in this book:

- HTML5/CSS3
- PHP
- WordPress
- W3.CSS framework

Who this book is for

If you are a blogger or a WordPress user who wants to learn how to create attractive, eye-catching WordPress themes, this book is for you. A basic understanding of HTML5, CSS3, PHP, and some creativity is all you need to get started with this book.

Conventions

In this book, you will find a number of styles of text that distinguish between different kinds of information. Here are some examples of these styles, and an explanation of their meaning.

Code words in text, database table names, folder names, filenames, file extensions, path names, dummy URLs, user input, and Twitter handles are shown as follows: Code words in text are shown as follows: "The single.html file is going to represent the single image."

A block of code is set as follows:

```
<!DOCTYPE html>
<html>
<head>
  <title></title>
</head>
<body>
</body>
</html>
```

When we wish to draw your attention to a particular part of a code block, the relevant lines or items are set in bold:

```
<!DOCTYPE html>
<html>
<head>
  <title>PhotoGenik</title>
</head>
<body>
</body>
</html>
```

New terms and important words are shown in bold. Words that you see on the screen, in menus or dialog boxes for example, appear in the text like this: "To upload a file, we'll click on the **Select Files** button."

Warnings or important notes appear in a box like this.

Tips and tricks appear like this.

Reader feedback

Feedback from our readers is always welcome. Let us know what you think about this book—what you liked or may have disliked. Reader feedback is important for us to develop titles that you really get the most out of.

To send us general feedback, simply send an e-mail to feedback@packtpub.com, and mention the book title via the subject of your message.

If there is a topic that you have expertise in and you are interested in either writing or contributing to a book, see our author guide on www.packtpub.com/authors.

Customer support

Now that you are the proud owner of a Packt book, we have a number of things to help you to get the most from your purchase.

Downloading the example code

You can download the example code files for this book from your account at `http://www.packtpub.com`. If you purchased this book elsewhere, you can visit `http://www.packtpub.com/support` and register to have the files emailed directly to you. You can download the code files by following these steps:

1. Log in or register to our website using your email address and password.
2. Hover the mouse pointer on the **SUPPORT** tab at the top.
3. Click on **Code Downloads & Errata**.
4. Enter the name of the book in the **Search** box.
5. Select the book for which you're looking to download the code files.
6. Choose from the drop-down menu where you purchased this book from.
7. Click on **Code Download**.

Once the file is downloaded, please make sure that you unzip or extract the folder using the latest version of:

- WinRAR / 7-Zip for Windows
- Zipeg / iZip / UnRarX for Mac
- 7-Zip / PeaZip for Linux

The code bundle for the book is also hosted on GitHub at `https://github.com/PacktPublishing/Learn-to-Create-WordPress-Themes-by-Building-5-Projects`. We also have other code bundles from our rich catalog of books and videos available at `https://github.com/PacktPublishing/`. Check them out!

Downloading the color images of this book

We also provide you with a PDF file that has color images of the screenshots/diagrams used in this book. The color images will help you better understand the changes in the output. You can download this file from `https://www.packtpub.com/sites/default/files/downloads/LearntoCreateWordPressThemesByBuilding5Projects_ColorImages.pdf`.

Errata

Although we have taken every care to ensure the accuracy of our content, mistakes do happen. If you find a mistake in one of our books-maybe a mistake in the text or the code-we would be grateful if you could report this to us. By doing so, you can save other readers from frustration and help us improve subsequent versions of this book. If you find any errata, please report them by visiting http://www.packtpub.com/submit-errata, selecting your book, clicking on the **Errata Submission Form** link, and entering the details of your errata. Once your errata are verified, your submission will be accepted and the errata will be uploaded to our website or added to any list of existing errata under the Errata section of that title. To view the previously submitted errata, go to https://www.packtpub.com/books/content/support and enter the name of the book in the search field. The required information will appear under the **Errata** section.

Piracy

Piracy of copyrighted material on the internet is an ongoing problem across all media. At Packt, we take the protection of our copyright and licenses very seriously. If you come across any illegal copies of our works in any form on the internet, please provide us with the location address or website name immediately so that we can pursue a remedy. Please contact us at copyright@packtpub.com with a link to the suspected pirated material. We appreciate your help in protecting our authors and our ability to bring you valuable content.

Questions

If you have a problem with any aspect of this book, you can contact us at questions@packtpub.com, and we will do our best to address the problem.

1
Creating a Simple Theme with WordPress

Welcome to the WordPress Themes Project book! In this book, we will build 10 WordPress themes from scratch. We will look at all of the fundamental knowledge that is needed to build great themes.

In this first chapter, we will create a very simple project. We will not really focus on creating an awesome design; the chapter is more about explaining the files that we need to create for our theme, the syntax, the dynamic snippets, and related topics.

Installing and setting up WordPress

This project will be a little different from the rest because it's going to be sort of an introductory project. We will see how to install and set up WordPress, so that you can have a fresh installation to work with. We will create a theme, but we'll be focusing more on the code and the overall look and style. We'll create files and folders, add PHP code, and related things. First, I want to get you familiarized with PHP code, and then we can add some simple style.

With respect to an environment, there are a lot of different ways you can run WordPress. You may have your own server set up; if you don't, you can use something like AMPPS, which is what I'll be using. It gives you an Apache server, PHP, and MySQL all on your local machine. You could also use XAMPP, which is very similar, or WAMP; there's also MAMP for Mac. There are lot of different choices, but if you want to use AMPPS, you can go to `https://ampps.com/` and download it. It's available for Windows, Mac, and Linux, and it is pretty easy to get set up.

Now, let's see how to install WordPress. Most of you probably already know how to do this:

1. Go to the link `https://wordpress.org/download/` and click on the **Download WordPress** button:

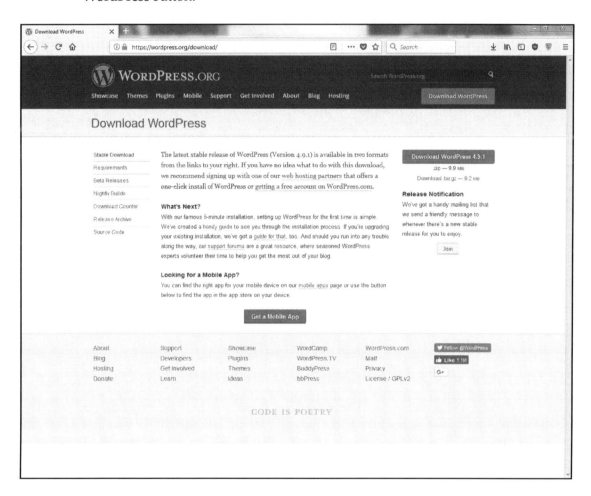

2. Download the package and go to your server root folder, as shown here:

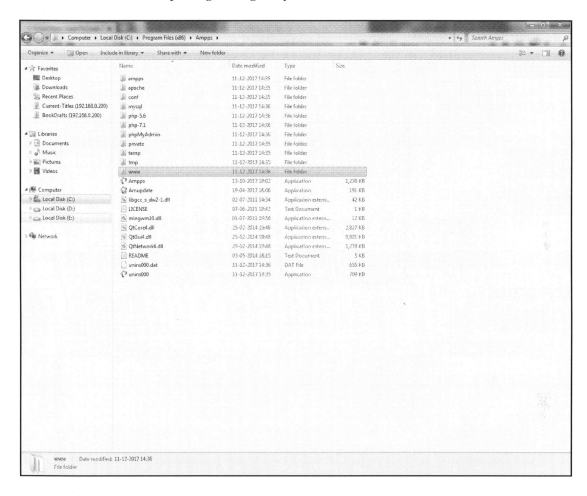

If you're using AMPPS, the package should be in your C:\ drive or in your route drive. In the Ampps folder, you'll find a www folder; this is the hosting root, as shown in the preceding image. In most cases, the default folder will be Program Files in the C:\ drive.

3. Create a folder called wpthemes; this is where we will install WordPress.

4. Go to the `Downloads` folder and open the WordPress package. Next, extract all the files into the project folder, `wpthemes`. Before we proceed, we need a database, a MySQL database, and if you installed AMPPS or if you're using XAMPP or something similar, then you most likely have **phpMyAdmin**, as shown as follows; this is what we'll be using.

5. Now, go to `http://localhost/phpmyadmin`:

6. Next, go to the **Databases** tab to create a new database called `wpthemes` and click on **Create**. We will see an empty database.

7. We'll go back to the files we created or brought over from the WordPress package. You will see the **wp-config-sample.php** file. We'll rename this to just `wp-config`, and get rid of the `-sample`.

8. Open the `wp-config` file using Sublime Text as the editor. You can use whichever editor you feel comfortable with.

9. Now, in this editor, we will change or add some information:

```
/** The name of the database for WordPress */
define('DB_NAME', 'wpthemes');

/** MySQL database username */
define('DB_USER', 'root');

/** MySQL database password */
define('DB_PASSWORD', '123456');
```

We will add DB_NAME, as shown here, which in this case is wpthemes, then DB_USER, which in this case is root, and then DB_PASSWORD—you need to enter whatever the password is for your database. The rest can stay the same.

10. We'll go ahead and save the entered information, and then we should be able to go to localhost/wpthemes:

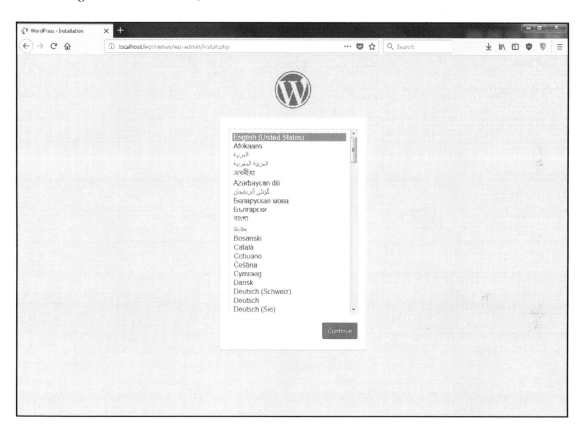

11. We can now go ahead and run the installation. As shown in the following screenshot, we will enter **Site Title** as WordpressDEV and **Username** as admin. Next, you need to enter the password; I'm using a very weak password here. After you enter the email address, click on **Install WordPress**:

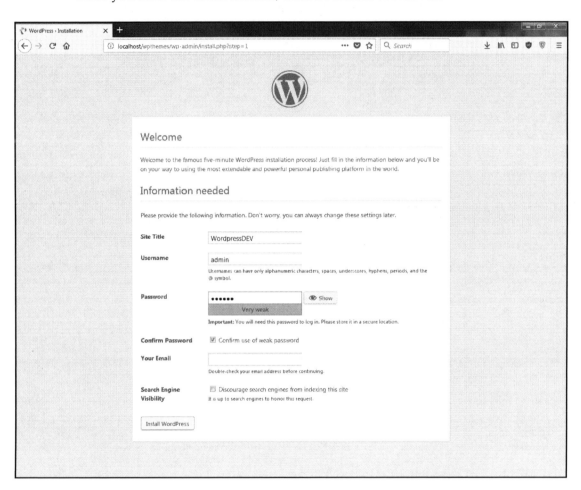

You can see that **WordPress has been installed**.

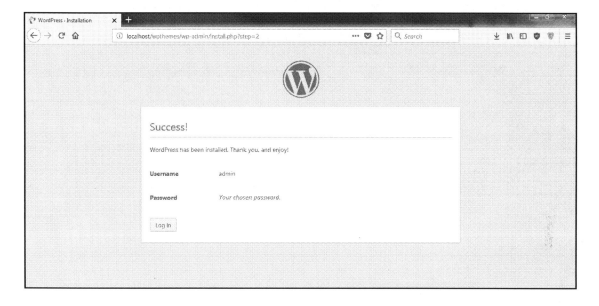

12. Now, click on **Log In**, and this will take us to the admin login. Go ahead and put your username and password in, and it'll take you to your backend:

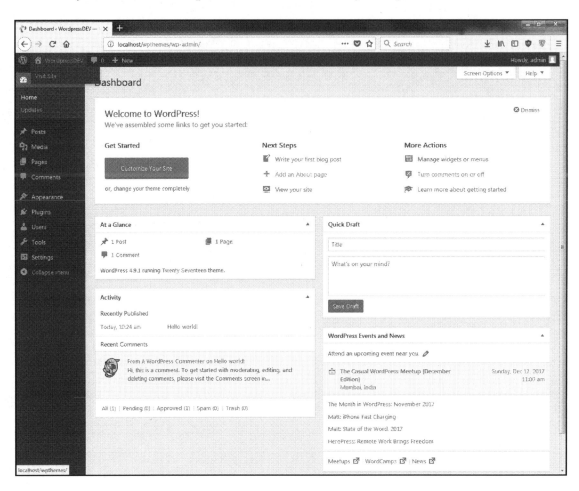

13. Now we can click on **Visit Site**, as shown in the preceding image. Open this in a new tab, and you'll see that we have a brand new WordPress site:

This is what we'll be working with.

I'm sure a lot of you have experience with WordPress.

On the `localhost/wpthemes/wp-admin/` WordPress page, we have our **Posts** area, where we can create and manage posts:

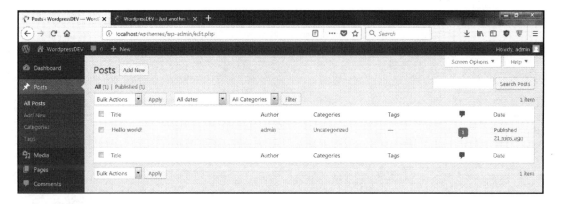

We can have **Categories**, as shown in the following screenshot:

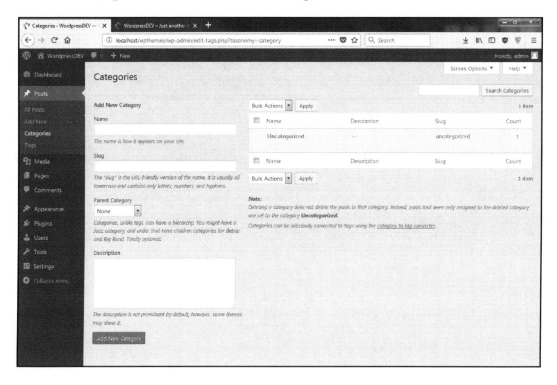

We can also see **Pages**:

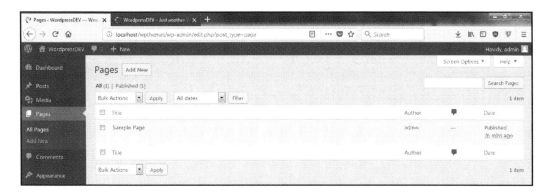

Website pages such as About Us, or Services, would go on **Pages**. If we go to **Appearance**, and click on **Themes**, it will show us the installed themes, as shown in the following screenshot:

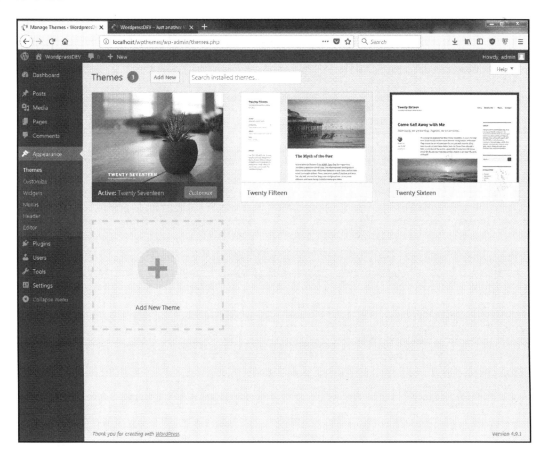

By default, we have **Twenty Seventeen**, **Twenty Fifteen**, and **Twenty Sixteen**, but we will be creating a new theme in the next section.

Creating and enabling themes

In this section, we'll see how to create our theme files and enable a theme. We'll use Sublime Text and add the project folder, so that we can access the files easily:

1. Go to C:\Ampps\www\wpthemes.
2. The folder in which you want to create your theme is going to be themes, which is within the wp-content folder:

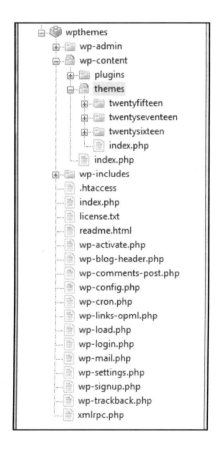

You can see here that we have the three themes that come with WordPress already installed, namely `twentyfifteen`, `twentyseventeen`, and `twentysixteen`.

3. We'll create a new folder and call it `simple`. This is going to be the name of our theme:

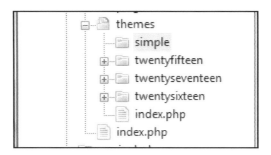

There are two files that you absolutely need in order to enable your theme: one will be `style.css`, and the other will be `index.php`. Now, the reason we need `style.css` is because that's where all of our declarations, such as theme name and the descriptions, go.

4. We'll open up a comment block and enter the fields, shown as follows:

 You can refer to the documentation at `https://codex.wordpress.org/Theme_Development`, which shows all the different fields that you can use. We'll not use all of them as they're not required. `Theme Name` is all that's required, but it's good to have some other information as well.

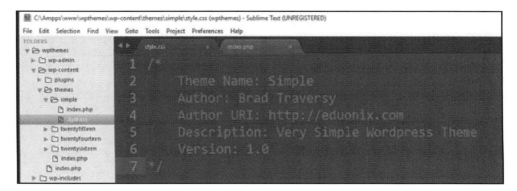

5. We will enter the `Theme Name` as `Simple`. We also need to have an `Author`; you can put your own name there if you'd like. We'll also have `Author URI`. If you are creating themes for clients, you'd probably want to put your company's website there. We can have a `Description`. We'll enter `Very Simple Wordpress Theme`, and then enter `Version: 1.0`. Let's save this. Now, just having this information will allow WordPress to see your theme.

6. Now let's go back into our `localhost/wpthemes/wp-admin/themes.php` backend, and go to **Appearance** and then **Themes**; you can see the **Simple** theme, and we can actually activate it:

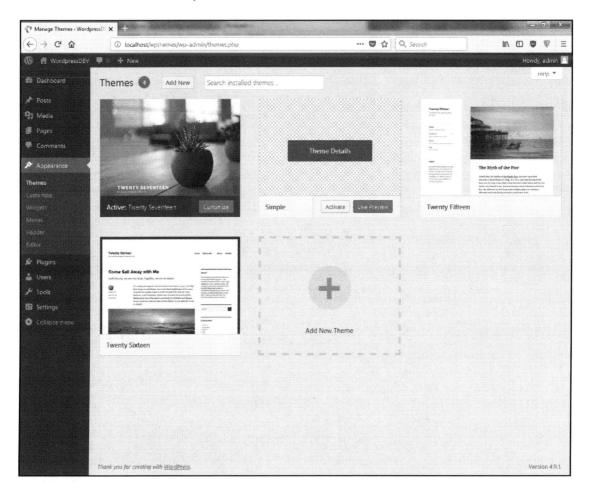

7. Now, in order for a screenshot to show in the **Simple** theme, we need to put an image in the root of the theme folder and call it `screenshot.png`:

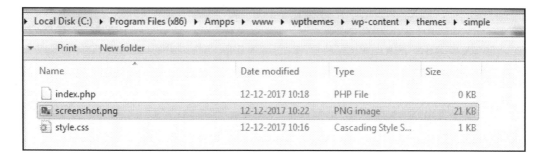

8. Let's create a sample screenshot using Photoshop, which just says **SimpleTheme**, and place that in our `theme` folder, as shown in the preceding screenshot. Go to the server root, `www\wpthemes\wp-content\themes`, and then `simple`. We'll just paste that screenshot in there. Now if we go back to the backend and reload, you can see that we have a screenshot, as shown here:

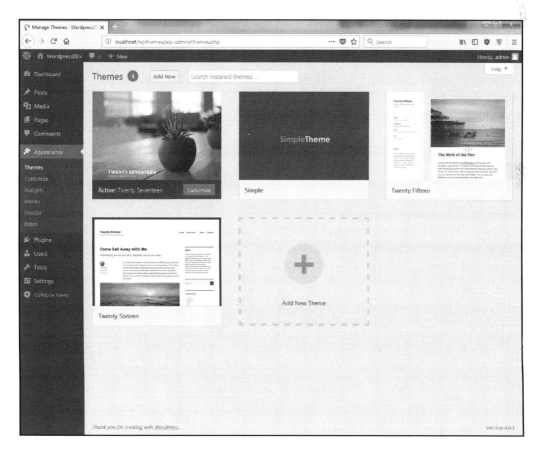

Well, it's not really a screenshot but it's an image.

9. Now if we go ahead and activate our theme for this, and go to our frontend and reload—we get absolutely nothing because we haven't added any code yet:

Our theme just contains nothing, it's completely blank.

10. Now let's open the `index.php` file and enter TEST, then save and reload; we can see that we get TEST on our frontend too:

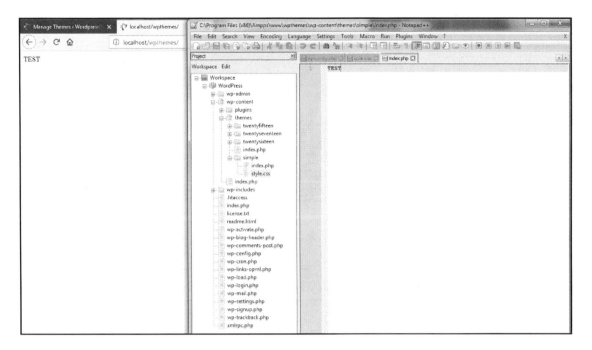

Basically, it's reading our `index.php` file by default.

Creating an HTML structure

1. Now let's create our HTML structure. We will put in some core HTML tags, as shown here:

```
<!DOCTYPE html>
<html <?php language_attributes(); ?>>
<head>
    <title><?php bloginfo('name'); ?></title>
```

As you can see, we have DOCTYPE, an html, head, body, and title tags. Now, if you consider starting at the top, we have our <html> tags; sometimes, you want to include a language here, and WordPress has a function that we can actually include in this file to make it dynamic. We can add php language_attributes, which is a function that will determine the language we want the theme to display. You probably want to make your title dynamic, or you want to add your site name; to do that, we can say php and use a function called bloginfo, as shown in the preceding code block. This is really useful because it has a bunch of things that you can get, such as the site name, the description, the character set, URLs, and the list goes on. You can actually look at the documentation to see exactly what it includes. However, what we'll use is name.

2. Once you save this, you can go back and reload the page. You can see that the title says **WordpressDEV**, as shown here:

If you remember, this is what we named the site.

3. Let's go back to our head tag and continue. We'll need a character set, so we'll enter meta charset. Then, we can use bloginfo here as well, and just pass in charset:

```
<!DOCTYPE html>
<html <?php language_attributes(); ?>>
<head>
    <meta charset="<?php bloginfo('charset'); ?>">
    <title><?php bloginfo('name'); ?></title>
```

4. Let's save this, and take a look at our source code. Using *Ctrl + U*, you can look at both the language attributes; it says that we're using English US and the character set is **UTF-8**, as shown here:

These things can now be controlled from within WordPress.

Working with the style sheet

The next thing we will do is include our style sheet:

1. Open the `style.css` file and enter the following code:

```
body{
    background:#000;
}
```

2. Save this and reload; we'll not get a black background as the style sheet is not being read:

3. In order for that style sheet to be seen, we'll enter the following code:

```
<!DOCTYPE html>
<html <? php language_attributes(); ?>>
<head>
    <meta charset="<?php bloginfo('charset'); ?>">
    <title><?php bloginfo('name'); ?></title>
    <link rel="stylesheet"
     href="<?php bloginfo('stylesheet_url'); ?>">
```

The preceding code will get the style sheet from the correct location.

4. Save this code and reload. We can now see a black background:

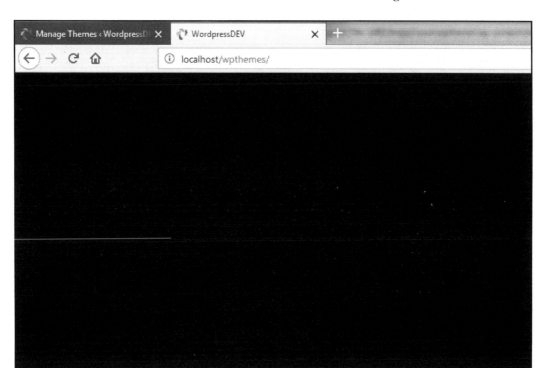

So whatever we put in our style sheet will now be registered.

Adding a function in the head tag

We will next see how to enter a function called `wp_head()` in the `<head>` tag. This puts any additional information that is needed into the `head` tag. For example, when you install a plugin and, let's say, it needs to include a style sheet, or it needs to do something in the head, to do this we need to enter the following code. So when you create plugins, you can have stuff pop out right in the head:

```
<!DOCTYPE html>
<html <? php language_attributes(); ?>>
<head>
    <meta charset="<?php bloginfo('charset'); ?>">
    <title><?php bloginfo('name'); ?></title>
    <link rel="stylesheet" href="<?php bloginfo('stylesheet_url'); ?>">
    <?php wp_head(); ?>
```

In the following source code, we have a bunch of other stuff now, and this is all coming from that `wp_head()` function:

If I go ahead and take the `wp_head()` function out, and then go back and reload, it just gives us what we have in the `index.php` file. So we're going to need the `wp_head()` function:

In the next section, we'll start to build out the body. We will see how to grab posts, create menus, and so on.

Building the HTML body

We will now see how to add basic HTML tags in the body:

1. We'll create a `<header>` tag, which is an HTML5 tag. We will enter an `<h1>` tag, and in this tag we will add the website name:

```
<header>
    <h1><?php bloginfo('name'); ?></h1>
</header>
```

2. We can actually take the dynamic code from the `<title>` tag, which we saw earlier, and put that in `<h1>` as well. Now if we save that and look at our frontend, we get **WordpressDEV**:

3. Now, if we wanted to change the frontend output, we could go to **Settings**, and change **Site Title** to `My Website`:

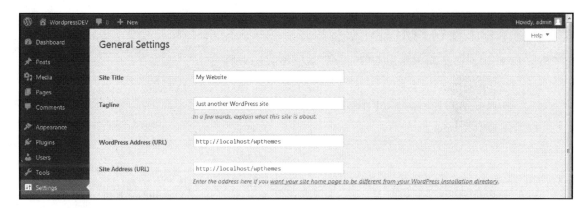

4. Save the settings. Now, we can see the change.
5. In addition to the name, we can also include a **Tagline**. To do this, we will enter the `<small>` tags, but instead of using `name`, we will use `description`, as shown in the following code block:

```
<header>
    <h1><?php bloginfo('name'); ?></h1>
    <small><?php bloginfo('description'); ?></small>
</header>
```

6. When you reload it, you can see that we get **Just another WordPress site**:

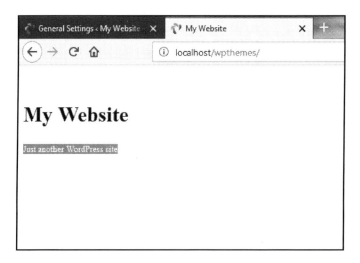

7. We can make the changes in the settings. We'll enter `The Best Website Ever` in the **Tagline** textbox:

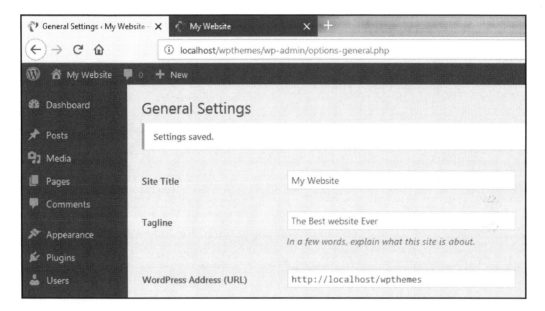

8. Save the changes and put `description` in the `span` tag, as shown in the following code block:

```
<h1><?php bloginfo('name'); ?></h1>
<span><?php bloginfo('description'); ?></span>
```

9. When we reload, we get this:

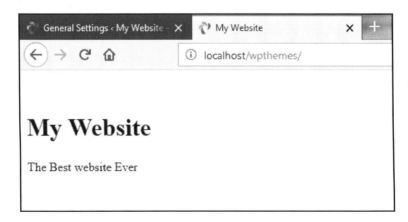

10. Now let's add more HTML tags, as shown in the following code block:

```
<header>
    <h1><?php bloginfo('name'); ?></h1>
    <span><?php bloginfo('description'); ?></span>
</header>

<div class="main">
<?php if(have_posts()) : ?>
    post found
<?php else : ?>
    <?php echo wpautop('Sorry, No posts were found'); ?>
<?php endif; ?>
</div>
</body>
</html>
```

Here, we go under the <header> tag and enter the div class as main. We'll fetch our blog posts; WordPress uses something called the loop, or the main loop, which will fetch every blog post that you have, regardless of the category or whatever it may be. Without specifying any restrictions, it's going to get every post. So, the first thing we'll do is check to see whether there are any posts. We'll use an if statement for that, and then use the shorthand. We will use the syntax that will help us go quickly in and out of php. We'll then use if(have_posts) to see whether there are any posts in WordPress. We'll also put an else statement here, so that if there are no posts, then we just want to let the user know that. Now, instead of just spitting out text, we'll use a function. We'll say echo wpautop; what this does is that it takes double line breaks and automatically makes them into paragraphs. It's a good function to use when you just want to output text. We'll say, Sorry, No posts were found. Then, inside if(have_posts), we'll use post found. Let's go and reload, and you can see that we get **post found**:

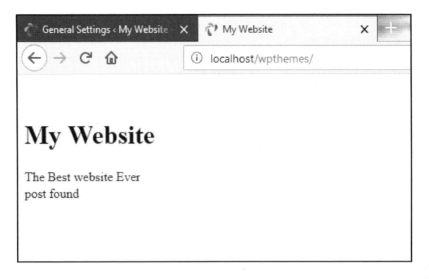

11. Let's go back to our backend and go to **Posts**; you can see that we have **Hello world**. We will move that to Trash, and if we now go back and reload, we get **Sorry, No posts were found**, as shown in the following screenshot:

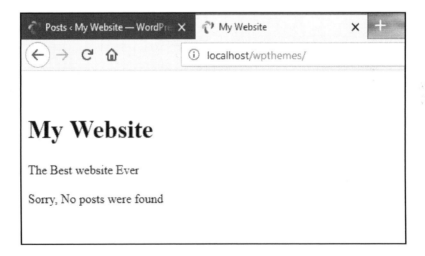

12. Now let's go to **Trash** and restore it. We will see that the post can be seen again. We will now see how to display these posts. We'll delete `post found` within the `if` statement and we'll use a while loop for this with a `php` tag. We'll use `while(have_posts)`. Now, with WordPress, we have to use this thing called `the_post()`, so we'll use `the_post()`, which is a little weird as far as a syntax is concerned. I've never really seen this anywhere else apart from WordPress, but just know that you need to have this as well. Then, we'll use `endwhile`; again, this is just using shorthand syntax, so you could just use the curly braces. But what we'll do here is when it finds a post, we want to get the title. So, in an `<h3>` tag, we'll use `<?php the_title(); ?>`, which is a function:

```
<div class="main">
<?php if(have_posts()) : ?>
    <?php while(have_posts()): the_post(); ?>
        <h3><?php the_title(); ?></h3>
    <?php endwhile; ?>
<?php else : ?>
    <?php echo wpautop('Sorry, No posts were found.'); ?>
<?php endif; ?>
```

13. Let's go and reload, and now you can see that it's getting the **Hello world!** title:

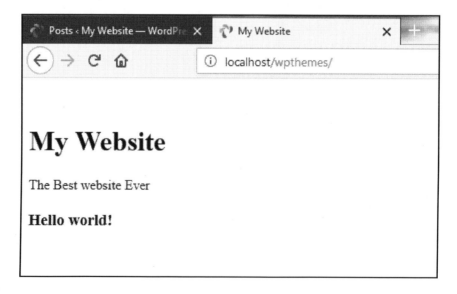

14. Now, let's go ahead and create a post as an example. We will name it `My Blog Post`, and let's just get some sample text. I have taken some text from the `www.lipsum.com` website:

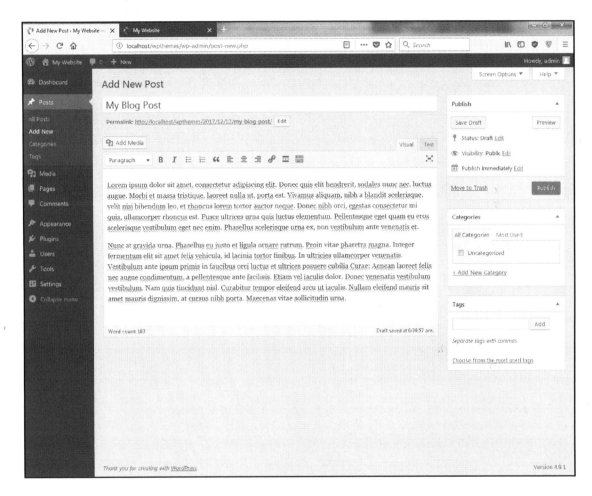

We will add a couple of paragraphs and publish it.

15. Now let's reload; you can see that it gives us **My Blog Post**:

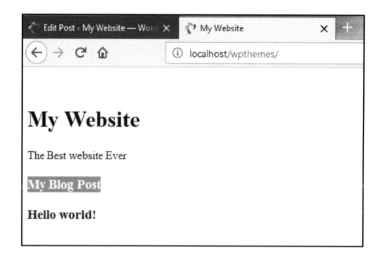

16. Now, to get the actual content, we'll go right to the <h3> tag and enter <?php the_content(); ?>. As you can see, WordPress makes it really easy in terms of the names of the functions:

```
<div class="main">
<?php if(have_posts()) : ?>
   <?php while(have_posts()): the_post(); ?>
      <h3><?php the_title(); ?></h3>
      <?php the_content(); ?>
   <?php endwhile; ?>
<?php else : ?>
   <?php echo wpautop('Sorry, No posts were found'); ?>
<?php endif; ?>
</div>
```

So now, this gets us the content from each blog post and displays it:

17. There are different things that we can display with the posts: the date, author, categories, and so on. Let's go right under the title and add the following code block:

```
<h3><?php the_title(); ?></h3>
<div class="meta">
Created By <?php the_author(); ?>
</div>
<?php the_content(); ?>
<?php endwhile; ?>
```

Here, we added `Created By` along with the author's name.

18. When we reload, we can see the following output:

In this case, **admin** is the username of the person who created the post.

19. Now, if you want the date, you can add this code:

```
Created By <?php the_author(); ?> on <?php the_date(); ?>
```

20. When we reload, we get **Created By admin on December 12, 2017**; basically, it gives us the date:

> **My Website**
>
> The Best website Ever
>
> **My Blog Post**
>
> Created By admin on December 12, 2017

21. We will now see how to format the date. You can format the date in a lot of different ways; if you know PHP and you've worked with the date function, you know that there's a lot of different formatting options.
We will take a look at one such example from
`php.net/manual/en/function.date.php`:

```
Created By <?php the_author(); ?> on <?php the_date('l jS \of F
    Y h:i:s A'); ?>
```

22. Let's see what that gives us. You can see the format, shown in the following screenshot, with the day, date, time, and PM or AM:

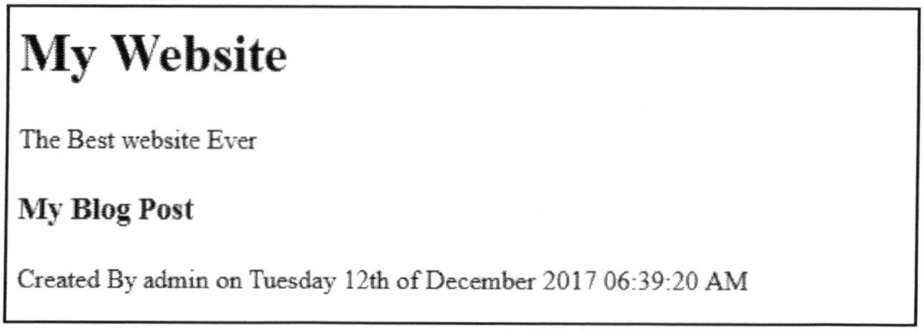

> **My Website**
>
> The Best website Ever
>
> **My Blog Post**
>
> Created By admin on Tuesday 12th of December 2017 06:39:20 AM

One thing that I like to do is to use the time instead of the date:

```
Created By <?php the_author(); ?> on <?php the_time(); ?>
```

This will give you just the time; it doesn't give you the date, but you can actually format it to give you the date:

```
Created By <?php the_author(); ?> on <?php the_time('F j, Y g:i a'); ?>
```

If we take a look at this, it gives us the date and the time:

```
My Website

The Best website Ever

My Blog Post

Created By admin on December 12, 2017 6:39 am
```

So it's all up to you, it all depends on your preferences.

Now, let's do a little bit of styling. We will see how to add a `<footer>` tag at the bottom, and a paragraph to make it dynamic. We can put a copyright symbol, and then for the year, instead of just typing in the year, we can use `the_date()`, and then just pass in as a parameter, `Y`, as shown in the following code:

```
<footer>
    <p>&copy; <?php the_date('Y'); ?></p>
</footer>
```

So we get © **2017**:

```
Hello world!

Created By admin on December 11, 2017 10:24 am

Welcome to WordPress. This is your first post. Edit or delete it, then start writing!

© 2017
```

Then, if we want the site name, we can just say `bloginfo` and pass in `name`:

```
<footer>
    <p>&copy; <?php the_date('Y'); ?> - <?php bloginfo('name'); ?></p>
</footer>
```

So now we have a dynamic footer.

Base styling

Now let's add some base styling. To do this, we will work with the style sheet. Now, the idea of this whole project actually is not to create some great-looking theme, I just want you to get familiar with the PHP code and how themes are set up.

1. Let's enter the following code:

```
body{
    font-family: Arial;
    font-size:15px;
    color:#333;
    background:#f4f4f4;
    margin:0;
    padding:0;
    line-height: 1.7em;
}

header{
    background: #393939;
    color:#fff;
    padding:20px 10px;
}

header h1{
    color:#fff;
    margin:0;
}
```

2. Save the code and reload. You will get the following result:

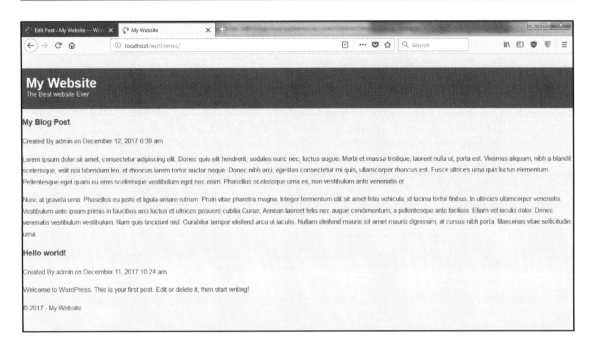

You can see the empty space at the top; this is because we're logged in as an admin, so even on the frontend it knows that, and it's trying to display the admin bar. Now, it's not displaying the admin bar because we don't have the special function to display it.

3. Let's go to `index.php`, and before the ending body, we'll add `<?php wp_footer(); ?>`:

```
<footer>
    <p>&copy; <?php the_date('Y'); ?> - <?php bloginfo('name'); ?>
    </p>
</footer>

<?php wp_footer(); ?>
</body>
</html>
```

4. Save this and reload. You can see that we have the admin bar:

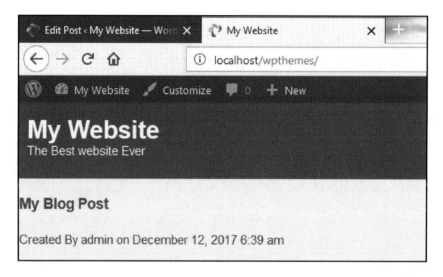

5. We will add a little padding to `h1` at the bottom:

```
header h1{
    color:#fff;
    margin:0;
    padding:0;
    padding-bottom: 10px;
}
```

6. We will also add a `container` div to the code, as shown here:

```
.container{
    width:1020px;
    margin:0 auto;
    overflow: auto;
}
```

We have set `width` to `1020 px`, `margin` to `0 auto`, and `overflow` to `auto`.

7. We will now go to `index.php`, to the `<header>` tag, and enter this code:

```
<header>
    <div class ="container">
    <h1><?php bloginfo('name'); ?></h1>
    <span><?php bloginfo('description'); ?></span>
    </div>
</header>
```

8. We'll add the same code to `main`:

```
<div class="main">
    <div class="container">
<?php if(have_posts()) : ?>
```

9. Also, for `footer`, it would be the same:

```
<footer>
    <div class="container">
        <p>&copy; <?php the_date('Y'); ?> - <?php bloginfo('name'); ?>
        </p>
    </div>
</footer>
```

10. When you reload, you can see that everything's moved to the middle.

11. Let's add a little bit of styling to `footer`. Just copy what we have in the header. We'll also align the text to the center:

```
footer{
    background: #393939;
    color:#fff;
    padding:10px 10px;
    text-align: center;
}
```

12. Next, we will add `margin` to the `main` div:

```
.main{
    margin:15px 0;
}
```

13. Let's reload and this is what we get:

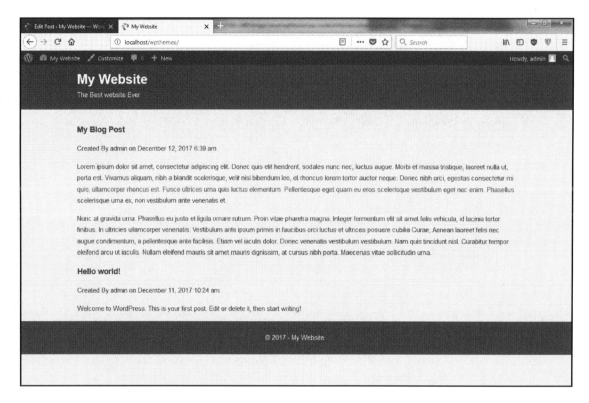

You can see that we have our header and main area, where we're looping through the posts and displaying them, and we have our footer area.

Now, common practice in WordPress is to break the header and footer into their own files and then include them in the index.

14. To do this, we will now create a new file, call it `header.php`, and then create a new file called `footer.php`.

15. Let's go to the `index.php` file and cut the portion of code, as shown in the following code block:

```
<!DOCTYPE html>
<html <?php language_attributes(); ?>>
<head>
    <meta charset="<?php bloginfo('charset'); ?>">
    <title><?php bloginfo('name'); ?></title>
    <link rel="stylesheet"
      href="<?php bloginfo('stylesheet_url'); ?>">
```

```
    <?php wp_head(); ?>
</head>
<body>
    <header>
        <div class="container">
            <h1><?php bloginfo('name'); ?></h1>
            <span><?php bloginfo('description'); ?></span>
        </div>
    </header>
```

16. We'll replace the highlighted portion with php get_header:

```
<?php get_header(); ?>
```

17. Go into header.php and paste the previous code which was cut, and save it.
18. We will now do the same thing with footer:

```
<footer>
    <div class="container">
        <p>&copy; <?php the_date('Y'); ?> - <?php bloginfo('name');
            ?>
        </p>
    </div>
</footer>

    <?php wp_footer(); ?>
</body>
</html>
```

19. We will cut the code shown in the preceding code block and replace it with php get_footer(), as shown in the following code block:

```
<?php get_footer(); ?>
```

20. Paste the footer code that was cut in *step 18* and place that in the footer file. The output will look the exact same.

Next, we will see how just a click on these posts will take us to the actual individual post page.

Single posts and thumbnails

Now we'll take a look at the single post page. Right now, we have this roll of posts from our site, but that's it; we can't click on it and go to the individual post, where we would have our comments and things like that. So let's go ahead and work on that:

1. Let's go to the `index.php` file and make the title clickable. We'll add a link to the title. To do this, let's go to the `<h3>` tag, as shown in the following code; add the `<a>` tag, and wrap that around the `<title>` tag:

```php
<?php get_header(); ?>
    <div class="main">
        <div class="container">
            <?php if(have_posts()) : ?>
                <?php while(have_posts()): the_post; ?>
                    <h3>
                    <a href="<?php the_permalink(); ?>">
                        <?php the_title(); ?>
                    </a>
                    </h3>
                    <div class="meta">
                    Created By <?php the_author(); ?> on <?php the_time('F
                        j, Y g:i a'); ?>
                    </div>
                    <?php the_content(); ?>
                <?php endwhile; ?>
            <?php else : ?>
                <?php echo wpautop('Sorry, No posts were found.'); ?>
            <?php endif; ?>
        </div>
    </div>
    <?php get_footer(); ?>
```

2. Let's save it and reload:

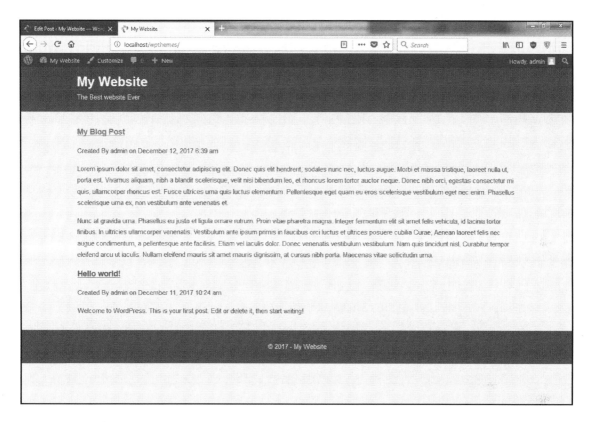

Now you'll see we have a link on the titles. For example, when we click on **My Blog Post**, it takes us to the post.

3. Let's add a little bit of style to the links. I don't like the color of the links; I also want to make the description bold so that it stands out. It is good to wrap each post in its own div. Where we have `while`, we'll put it in `<article>`, as shown in the following code:

```php
<?php get_header(); ?>
    <div class="main">
        <div class="container">
            <?php if(have_posts()) : ?>
                <?php while(have_posts()): the_post(); ?>
                    <article class="post">
                        <h3>
                        <a href="<?php the_permalink(); ?>">
```

```
                <?php the_title(); ?>
            </a>
            </h3>
            <div class="meta">
            Created By <?php the_author(); ?> on
            <?php the_time('F j, Y g:i a'); ?>
            </div>
            <?php the_content(); ?>
        </article>
        <?php endwhile; ?>
    <?php else : ?>
        <?php echo wpautop('Sorry, No posts were found'); ?>
    <?php endif; ?>
    </div>
</div>
```

4. Then, in our style sheet, let's add the color:

```
a{
    color:#333;
}
```

The color will be just the same as the text.

5. Now we will just add a border at the bottom using this code:

```
article.post{
    border-bottom:1px #ccc solid;
}
```

6. When you reload you can see the border at the bottom:

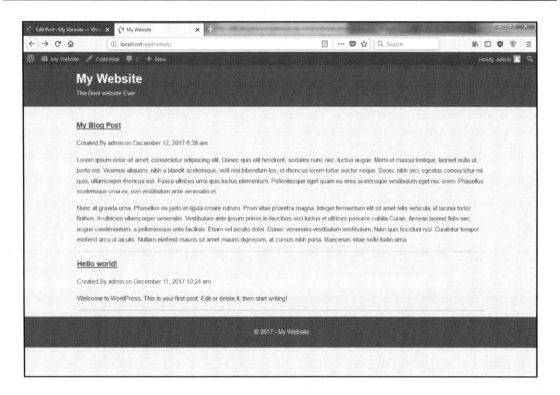

7. Now we have the title. The title has a link, but we'll usually see some kind of Read More button as well, so let's go ahead and add that. All we have to do is just add the code, shown in the following code block. We'll say `Read More` and give it the class of a button:

```
Created By <?php the_author(); ?> on <?php the_time(
  'F j, Y g:i a'); ?>
</div>
<?php the_content(); ?>
</article>
<br>
<a class="button" href="<?php the_permalink(); ?>">
  Read More
</a>
```

8. Now, we should have a link for `Read More`. To do that, we will add the following code block:

```
article.post{
    border-bottom:1px #ccc solid;
    overflow:hidden;
```

```
}

article.post a.button{
    display:inline-block;
    background:#333;
    color:#fff;
    padding:10px 5px;
    margin-bottom: 10px;
    text-decoration: none;
}
```

9. We can now go to the single page, as shown in the following screenshot:

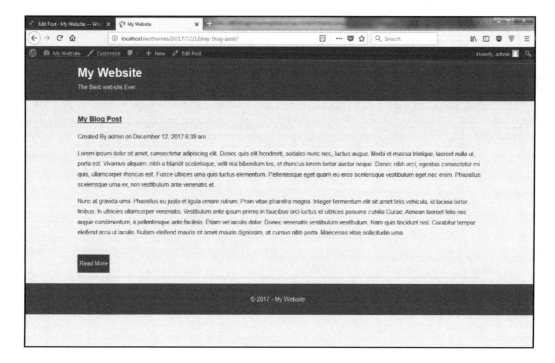

10. Now, in the single page, we don't want **My Blog Post** to be a link; that's kind of silly, so we want to change that. Also, there's going to be other things we want. We'll want a comment form as well, so we need to have a special page for single posts.

11. So we'll create a new file in our theme, and we'll just call it `single.php`, and let's just say TEST.

12. If we go back to the single page and reload, we get **TEST**. If we go back to our main website, which is our main post roll, it is the same as before, but if we go to a single page we get **TEST** only, because it's automatically looking at the `single.php` file. So what we can do is copy the code from `index.php`, and we can use this code as a starting point. If we paste that in `single.php` and save, it'll show us the same result. Now we can change whatever we want in the `single.php` file, and it will only take effect on the single page.

13. We can get rid of the link and `Read More` in the code; we're obviously not going to want that. So now we have a single page:

14. Let's add a little bit of style to our single page. To do that, we will make `meta`, as shown here:

```
.meta{
    background:#333;
    color:#fff;
    padding:5px;
}
```

As you can see here, I have also added some padding at the bottom of the post.

I'm not trying to go nuts with the styling, because like I said, I just want you to kind of learn the code rather than learn how to create a great design; we'll be getting into that later.

Adding an image to the post

Now, if we go to the form shown here to add a post, and you look on the right-hand side, you don't see a **Featured Image** box, which you may have seen in other WordPress themes or on other WordPress websites. The reason for that is we didn't include that functionality:

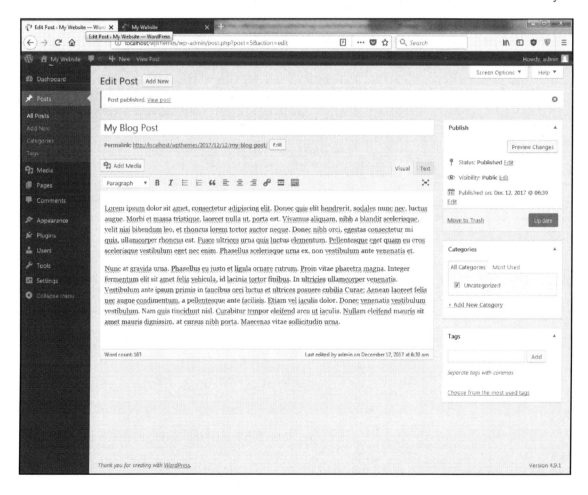

1. Let's go into our `themes` folder, and we'll create a file and save it as `functions.php`. Now, this is where we can put a custom function; this is where we can hook into certain parts of the code, register widgets, and do all that—basically, anything dynamic.

2. Here, we'll create a setup function. To do this, we will add the following code block:

```php
<?php
function simple_theme_setup(){
    // Featured Image Support
    add_theme_support('post-thumbnails');
}
add_action('after_setup_theme', 'simple_theme_setup');
```

Here, we have added a comment, `Featured Image Support`, followed by a function called `add_theme_support`. Now this function isn't going to run if we leave it just like this. So, we have used `add_action` and certain hooks that we can hook into and run this function. The one that we want is called `after_setup_theme`. Then, the second parameter will be the name of the function. We will save it and then run it.

3. Let's go back and reload this page:

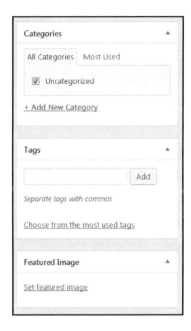

Now you'll see down at the bottom that we have the **Featured Image** box. If we click on that, we can go ahead and upload files, as shown here:

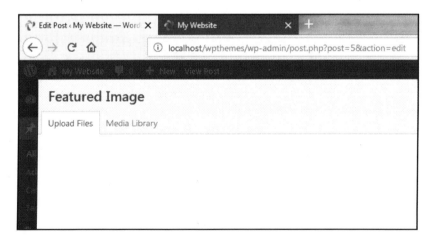

4. Now, I'll choose an image and save it so that you can see it's inserted, and we can then click on **Update**:

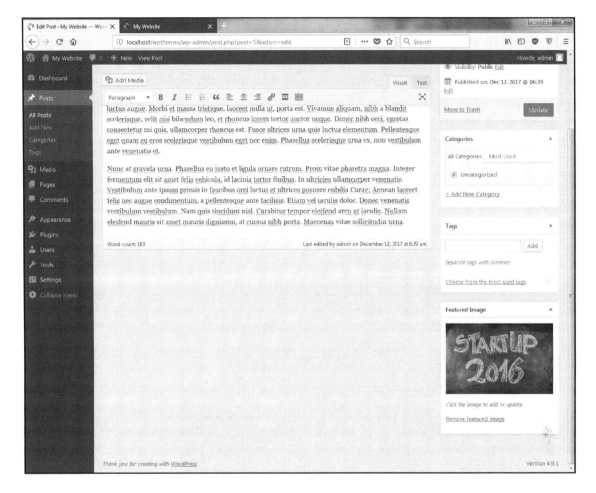

Now, if we go to the frontend and reload, we'll not see it yet, because we didn't add it to our `index.php` file.

5. Let's go to the `index.php` file. You don't have to show the image in the index. You can just show it in single page if you want, but usually you want it to be shown on both pages. So, in `index.php`, let's just add the image right below `meta`, as shown here:

```
<div class="meta">
Created By <?php the_author(); ?> on <?php the_time(
  'F j, Y g:i a'); ?>
</div>
<?php if(has_post_thumbnail()) : ?>
```

```
<div class="post-thumbnail">
<?php the_post_thumbnail(); ?>
</div>
<?php endif; ?>
```

At first, it's not going to look too great, but we'll fix that later on. In the preceding code, we have first checked to see if there's an image using an `if` statement. If there's a thumbnail, then we'll create a `<div>` tag. We'll give it a class of `post-thumbnail` and then add `php the_post_thumbnail`, as shown in the preceding code block.

6. Let's save it, go back, and reload. You will get the following result:

Now, it looks a little out of the way because it's not reaching 100% across the page, but we're actually going to put a sidebar in a little bit, when we get to the widgets, so that it looks a lot better. However, I am going to add a width of `100%` in the CSS, where we have this post, `this class="post-thumbnail"`.

7. Let's go into our style sheet and add the following code block:

```
.post-thumbnail img{
    width:100%;
    height:auto;
}
```

For the image, we want the width to be 100% and we can keep `height:auto`.

8. When we reload, we can see that it reaches across the whole page:

I know that's really big, but like I said, we'll get a sidebar in there, and it'll shrink that a little bit.

9. Now we also want the image on the single post page. So we'll copy the code from `index.php` and paste it in the `single.php` file, right under `meta`:

```
<div class="meta">
Created By <?php the_author(); ?> on <?php the_time(
  'F j, Y g:i a'); ?>
</div>
<?php if(has_post_thumbnail()) : ?>
   <div class="post-thumbnail">
      <?php the_post_thumbnail(); ?>
   </div>
<?php endif; ?>
```

Now we'll get the same image on the single page as well.

As you can see, in the posts on the index page, it shows the whole content, but we want just a piece of the content to show.

10. To do that, let's go to the `index.php` file, and instead of saying `the_content`, we can actually say `the_excerpt`, as shown in the following code:

```
<?php the_excerpt(); ?>
```

What this will do is, it will cut the content to around 55 words. You can actually customize that and make it as long or as short as you want, and that's actually really easy.

11. Go to the `functions.php` file and create a custom function, as shown here:

```
<?php
function simple_theme_setup()>{
    // Featured Image Support
    add_theme_support('post-thumbnails');
}

add_action('after_setup_theme', 'simple_theme_setup');

// Excerpt Length
function set_excerpt_length(){
    return 25;
}

add_filter('excerpt_length', 'set_excerpt_length');
```

We'll just say `set_excerpt_length`, and all we need to do here is just return a number, so let's say we wanted it to be `25`. Then, what we can do is, instead of `add_action`, we'll say `add_filter`, because `add_action` is usually used to add something or create something; `add_filter` is usually used to change something. The filter we want to hook into here is called `excerpt_length`. Then, we just want to put in the name of our function, which is `set_excerpt_length`.

12. If we go back and reload, we can see that it's only 25 words long. If you want it a little longer, let's say return 60. I just wanted to show you that it's possible.

So we have our index page set up, and we have our single post page set up, apart from the comments, which we'll do a little later. However, in the next section, we will see how we can create a menu and start dealing with pages as well as posts.

Pages and menus

In this section, we'll start looking at pages and menus. In addition to creating posts in WordPress, we can also create pages:

1. If we go to the backend and click on **Pages**, you'll see we have a **Sample Page**:

2. Let's create a new one, and we'll just call it `About page`. Then we'll just grab some content, say two paragraphs. Let's just click on **Publish**:

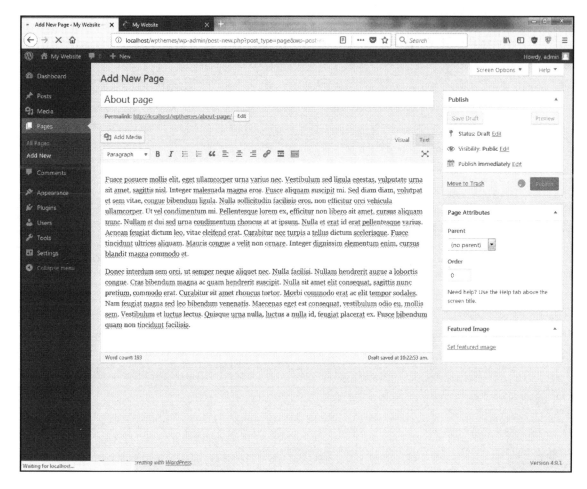

3. So we have an `About` page, and we have a `Sample Page`. Let's create one more and call it `Services`. Now we need some kind of navigation. Let's go ahead and do that.

4. In order to use the menu system, we need to edit the `functions.php` file, because right now, if we go to **Appearance**, there's no **Menus** option. So let's open up `functions.php` and enter the following code:

```
<?php
function simple_theme_setup(){
```

```
//Featured Image Support
add_theme_support('post-thumbnails');

//Menus
register_nav_menus(array(
    'primary' => __('Primary Menu')
));
}

add_action('after_setup_theme', 'simple_theme_setup');
```

In this `simple_theme_setup` function that we created, we will add `register_nav_menus`. Then we will pass in an array, and to do that, we will set the primary and then the readable version. We'll use the double underscore function; we don't need quotes here, though. It is a localization function, and it has to do with using multiple languages in your theme. So we'll enter `Primary Menu` and then save it.

5. Now, if we go to the backend, reload, and go to **Appearance**, you'll see we have this **Menus** option:

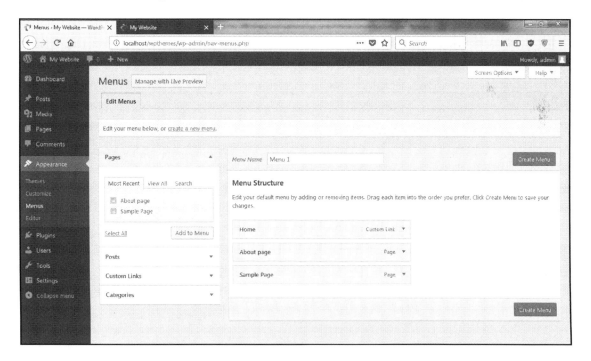

6. If we click on **Create Menu**, now you can see that by default it has all the pages on the site and you can remove some if you want:

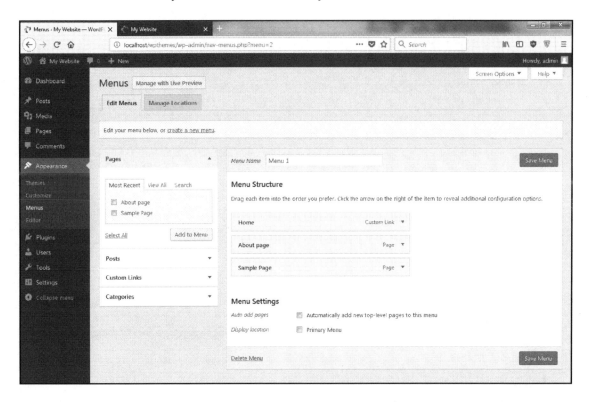

If you want to add pages, you can easily do it; click on **Add to Menu**. We'll just keep what we have here, and then we need to make sure to choose **Primary Menu**, where it says **Theme locations**. We'll save this.

7. Now, if we go to the frontend and reload, we'll not see anything yet because we haven't included it in our header file; this is where we want to add the menu, because we want it on every page.

8. Let's go right underneath the `<header>` tag and create a `<nav>` tag, as shown here:

```
<!DOCTYPE html>
<html <?php language_attributes(); ?>>
<head>
    <meta charset="<?php bloginfo('charset'); ?>">
    <title><?php bloginfo('name'); ?></title>
    <link rel="stylesheet"
     href="<?php bloginfo('stylesheet_url'); ?>">
    <?php wp_head(); ?>
</head>
<body>
    <header>
        <div class="container">
            <h1><?php bloginfo('name'); ?></h1>
            <span><?php bloginfo('description'); ?></span>
        </div>
    </header>
    <nav class="main-nav">
        <div class="container">
            <?php
                $args = array(
                    'theme_location' => 'primary'
                );
            ?>
<?php wp_nav_menu($args); ?>
</div>
</nav>
```

We'll add a class of main-nav, then we'll wrap it in a container. Then, all we have to do is open up some php tags and create a variable called args. This is just going to hold an array of arguments; we only need one for now, and that'll be theme_location. We're basically specifying what menu we want to put here, and that'll be primary, which is the only one we have. Then, what we can do is, we can call a function called wp_nav_menu and just pass in that args variable. Let's save this.

9. Go to the frontend, reload, and there's our menu:

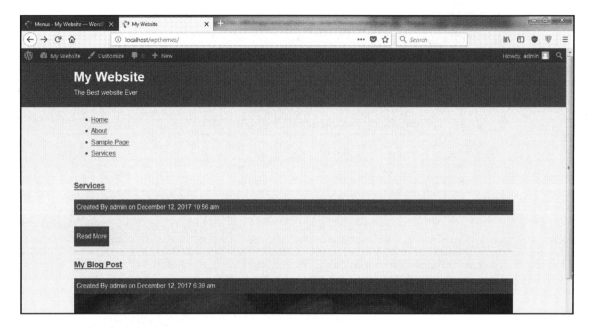

The menu has all the pages that we created.

10. If we want to remove one, go to **Menus**, select `Sample Page` we want to remove, save, reload, and now that's gone:

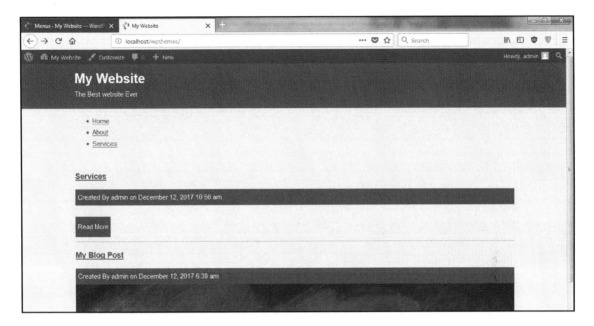

11. Just to style this a little bit, let's go to `style.css` and add this code:

```
.main-nav{
    background:#000;
    color:#fff;
    padding:5px;
}

.main-nav ul{
    margin:0;
    padding:0;
}

.main-nav li{
    list-style:none;
    float:left;
    padding-right:15px;
}

.main-nav a{
    color:#fff;
    text-decoration:none;
}
```

We'll add `main-nav` and give it a background; we'll add a black background and white color for text. To style the list items, we will add `main-nav li`; first we want to remove the bullet, so we'll say `list-style: none`, and then we want to float these menu to the left. We will also add `padding-right:15px`, and then we will add the links; make sure that they are white, and remove the text decoration as well. Next we will add `ul`, and we will remove the default margin and padding. Then we'll add some padding to `main-nav`, say `5px`.

12. When we reload, we have a little navigation menu:

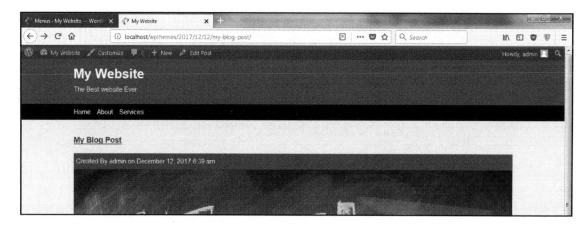

13. If we click on **About**, it'll take us to the About page, and it's the same with **Services**. Now you will notice that when we go to **About**, it has been formatted the exact same way as the `index.php` page, as if it was a post—but it's not, it's a page:

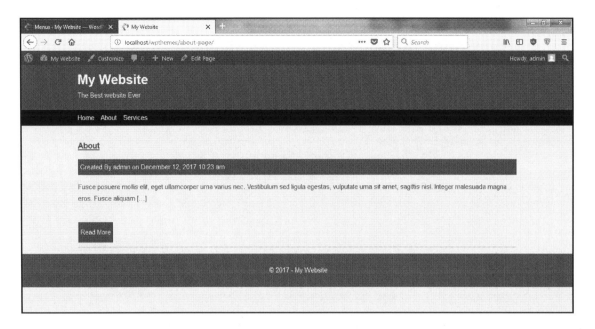

We'll not need the metadata or the **Read More** link. So what we need to do is add another page to our theme.

14. Let's create a new file and save it as `page.php`.

15. Now if I go back and reload, it's blank because it's looking at the empty file. So what we can do is copy the code that's in `index.php` and use it in `page.php`.

16. Here are few changes that we will do in the code:

```php
<?php get_header(); ?>
    <div class="main">
        <div class="container">
            <?php if(have_posts()) : ?>
                <?php while(have_posts()): the_post(); ?>
                    <article class="post">
                        <h3>
                            <?php the_title(); ?>
                        </h3>
                        <?php if(has_post_thumbnail()) : ?>
                            <div class="post-thumbnail">
                                <?php the_post_thumbnail(); ?>
                            </div>
                        <?php endif; ?>
                        <?php the_content(); ?>
                        <br>
```

```
        </article>
    <?php endwhile; ?>
  <?php else : ?>
      <?php echo wpautop('Sorry, No posts were found.'); ?>
  <?php endif; ?>
 </div>
</div>

<?php get_footer(); ?>
```

The first thing we'll do is remove the link from the title, because we don't want to go anywhere else. Also, we can get rid of `Read More` completely. It also has an excerpt, and we don't want that; we want the whole thing, so we'll change that to `the_content()`. Then, in `meta`, we can get rid of the whole div and save it; let's take a look:

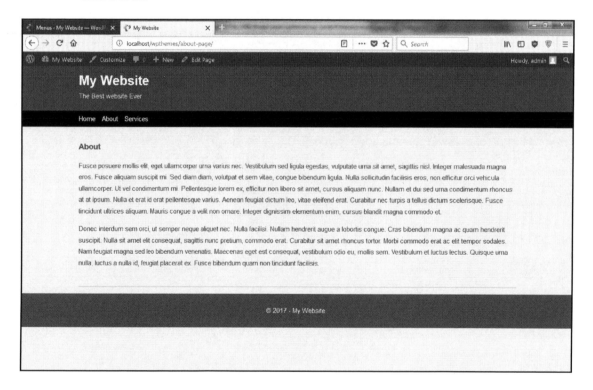

Now it looks more like a regular web page. We'll do the same thing with **Services**. This is how you can create pages and how you can target the markup for that page. You can also create custom pages and custom templates; you can kind of have different layouts for different pages, but we'll get into that in the next project. There's a lot more to building a theme. There's a lot more you can do that we're not going to get into in this project, but I just want to cover the basics in this project. We now have pages and a menu. In the next section, we'll get into widget locations, because now we want to be able to have a sidebar with widgets.

Widget locations and comments

Now I'll show you how to create a widget location in the theme. We'll have one widget location, and that'll be in the sidebar. Let's get started!

Working with widgets

1. Let's take a look at `index.php`, where we have this `<div>` tag with the class of `main`. What we want to do is go right between `main` and the ending `</div>` tag. We'll create a `<div>` tag with the class of `sidebar`, as shown in the following code:

```
<div class="sidebar">
TEST
</div>
```

We have also added `TEST` in the next line, which shows up as follows:

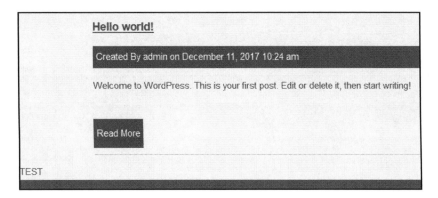

Now we want to float the main `<div>` and set a width, and then have the sidebar float to the right.

2. Let's go to the style sheet, where we have main with margin:15px, both at the top and bottom. Let's go ahead and float this to the left, and let's set a width of 68%, as shown in the following code block:

```
.main{
    margin:15px 0;
    float:left;
    width:68%;
}

footer{
    background:#393939;
    color:#fff;
    padding:10px 10px;
    text-align:center;
}
```

Let's see what that gives us:

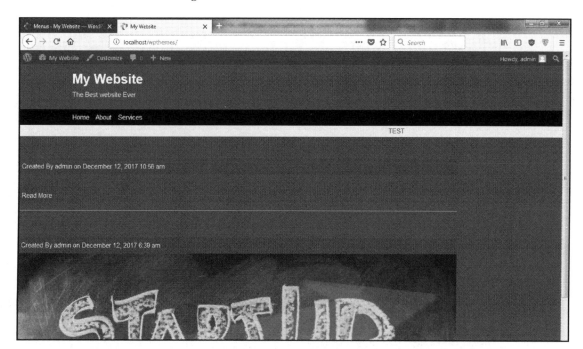

The reason that this looks really weird is because we didn't clear the float.

3. So what we'll do is go under the `sidebar` div and enter `<div class="clr">`:

```
<div class="sidebar">
TEST
</div>

<div class="clr"></div>
```

4. Now, we'll go to our CSS, add a class called `clr`, and we'll just say `clear:both;`:

```
.clr{
    clear:both;
}
```

5. Then let's add the `sidebar` class; that's going to float to the right, and we'll set a width of `28%`, as shown in the following code:

```
.sidebar{
    float:right;
    width:28%;
}
```

6. Now, we'll want to put a container around both of the files—`index.php` and `style.css`, because right now, `main` has a container inside of it, but what we want is to remove that and put it above `main`, as shown in the following code:

```
<?php get_header(); ?>

<div class="container">
    <div class="main">
```

We will end it here:

```
    <div class="sidebar">
    TEST
    </div>

    <div class="clr"></div>
</div>
<?php get_footer(); ?>
```

Now, let's run this:

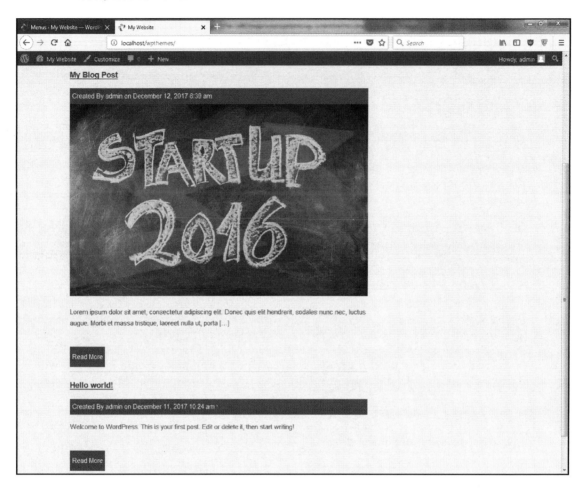

7. So now we have the main area and a sidebar.

8. Next, we will see how to add widgets, and to do that, we'll go to functions.php. Here, we can actually use widgets and define what location we want the widgets to be allowed in. We'll go down to the very bottom of the file and create a function, as shown in the following code block. We'll call it init_widgets, and that'll take in id, and we'll call it register_sidebar. Now we will create a sidebar widget, but just know that no matter where you put it, register_sidebar is the function that we'll use, even if it's not a sidebar—if it's down below, or in the header, or wherever it may be, this is what's used to actually register widget locations. Now, that's going to take in an array, and it's going to take a name; let's set that to Sidebar, and then the ID, which is usually the same, just lowercase and no spaces. You can use hyphens if there's more than one word. Then, we can also use before_widget. We can also use <div class="side-widget">, and then we can add after_widget; that's going to be the ending </div> tag. Then, we can also add before_title and after_title for the widget, as shown in the following code block. We want an <h3> tag before the title. Now, this code isn't going to run yet. We need to perform add_action, and the hook we want is called widgets_init; we want to put in our function name, which is init_widgets:

```php
//Excerpt Length
function set_excerpt_length(){
    return 60;
}

add_filter('excerpt_length', 'set_excerpt_length');

//Widget Locations
function init_widgets($id){
    register_sidebar(array(
        'name' => 'Sidebar',
        'id' => 'sidebar',
        'before_widget' => '<div class="side-widget">',
        'after_widget' => '</div>',
        'before_title' => '<h3>',
        'after_title' => '</h3>'
    ));
}

add_action('widgets_init', 'init_widgets');
```

9. Now we'll save the code. If we go back and reload, we get this:

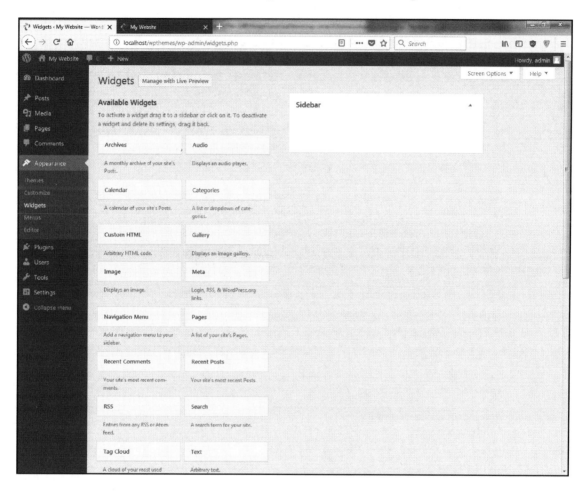

We have a **Widgets** item at the side and a **Sidebar** location.

10. Let's drag the **Categories** widget and bring that over to the **Sidebar**. We will also bring **Recent Posts**:

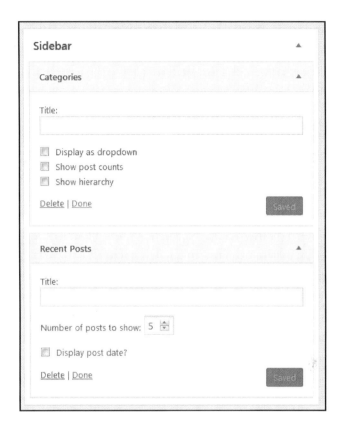

Save and go to the frontend; if we reload now, we'll not see anything because we need to add it to our template.

11. Let's go down to where we have the sidebar in the index.php file, and we'll first check for the widget using the following code:

```
<div class="sidebar">
    <?php if(is_active_sidebar('sidebar')) : ?>
        <?php dynamic_sidebar('sidebar'); ?>
    <?php endif; ?>
</div>
```

We'll check whether it'll be a function called `is_active_sidebar()`, and like I said before, even if it's not a sidebar, this is still going to work. We will also add our location, which happens to be sidebar. We will also add a `dynamic_sidebar()` function, and then the ID of the widget again is sidebar.

12. Save it, reload, and take a look at it:

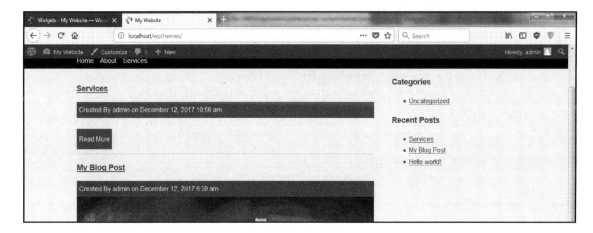

We get our two widgets: **Categories** and **Recent Posts**.

13. Now, remember that we put the `side-widget` class in the `function.php` file so that we can style widgets using the `style.css` file, as shown in the following code block:

```
.side-widget{
    border:1px #ccc solid;
    padding:10px 10px;
    margin-bottom:20px;
    margin-top:20px;
}
```

We have added `side-widget` with a border and padding of `10px 10px`. We have added `margin-bottom`. Now if we reload, you can see that they have a border. Therefore, we will add `margin-top` too. We'll say `margin-top:20px`.

14. To make this look a little better, we will use the following code:

```
.Side-widget li{
    list-style: none;
    line-height:2.2em;
    border-bottom:dotted 1px #ccc;
}

.Side-widget a{
    text-decoration: none;
}
```

Here, we have taken away `text-decoration`.

15. When you save and reload, you get this:

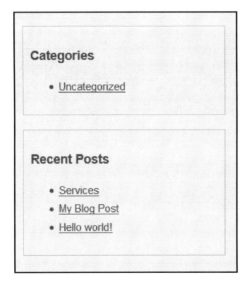

So this looks good.

16. We can see that the pages will be messed up now:

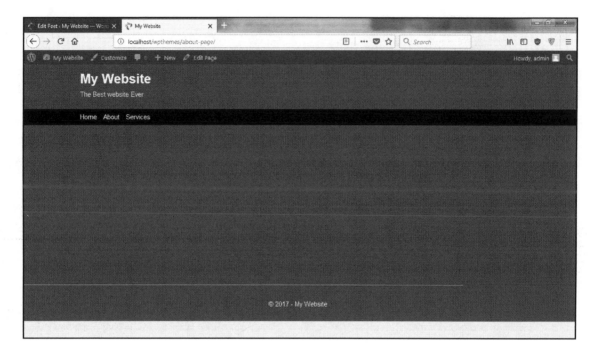

This is because in `page.php`, we still have the `container` class inside of `main`.

17. What we want to do is just copy what we did in `index.php`:

```
<div class="sidebar">
  <?php if(is_active_sidebar('sidebar')) : ?>
    <?php dynamic_sidebar('sidebar'); ?>
  <?php endif; ?>
</div>

<div class="clr"></div>
</div>
<?php get_footer(); ?>
```

We need to add the sidebar after main ends, and then we actually want to take the container out and put that above `main`. We'll need to make sure to take the ending `</div>` tag and put that on the outside down.

18. Let's go ahead and check that out:

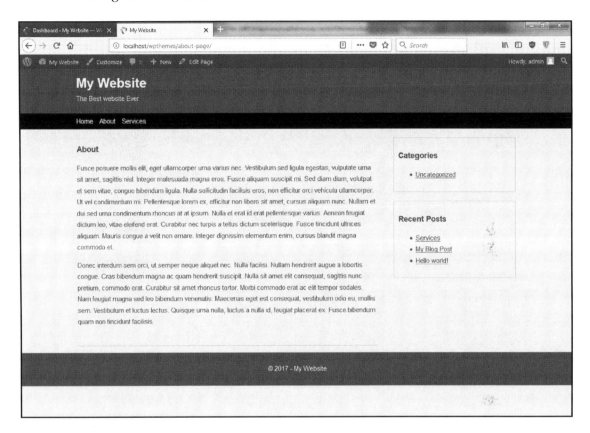

So this looks good.

19. We will repeat the same thing with `Single.php`, and we will get the following result:

So all the different formats and all the different pages are all set; they have the sidebar implemented. And, of course, if you didn't want the sidebar on one of those, you don't have to have it. If we want to kind of minimize the code a little bit, we can put the following code inside the `footer.php`:

```
<div class="sidebar">
<?php if(is_active_sidebar('sidebar')) : ?>
    <?php dynamic_sidebar('sidebar'); ?>
<?php endif; ?>
</div>

<div class="clr"></div>
</div>
```

20. We can cut and save, and then add that code in `footer.php` at the top, as shown here:

```
<div class="sidebar">
    <?php if(is_active_sidebar('sidebar')) : ?>
        <?php dynamic_sidebar('sidebar'); ?>
    <?php endif; ?>
</div>
<div class="clr"></div>
</div>

<footer>
    <div class="container">
        <p>&copy; <?php the_date('Y'); ?> - <?php bloginfo('name'); ?>
        </p>
    </div>
</footer>

<?php wp_footer(); ?>
</body>
</html>
```

21. Save, and then get rid of the following code from `page.php` and `index.php`, because it's now in `footer.php`:

```
<div class="sidebar">
<?php if(is_active_sidebar('sidebar')) : ?>
    <?php dynamic_sidebar('sidebar'); ?>
<?php endif; ?>
</div>

<div class="clr"></div>
</div>
```

Our frontend should look the exact same way. So that's good, that's widgets.

Adding the comment functionality

1. Now, the one thing that is left is comments—we want the comment functionality. This is actually really easy; all we have to do is go to our `single.php` file and see where we want the comment, which is right under the end `</div>` tag, as shown in the following code block:

```php
<?php endif; ?>

<?php comments_template(); ?>
</div>
```

2. We can save the code and reload. Here is the output:

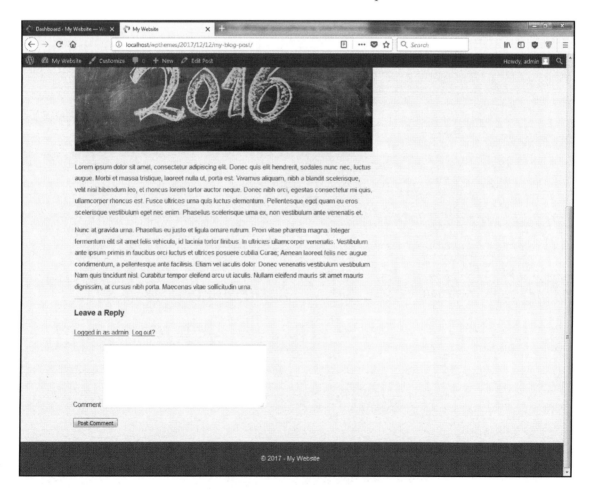

3. We can now see the comment functionality. Let's add `Great Post!` and then click on **Post Comment**.

Here is what we get:

4. We can see that it has an avatar, the username, date, and also a reply link. Now you'll realize that this doesn't look like the best comments section you've ever seen, but that's just because it's the default design.

5. If we take a look at the markup, we can see that they separate everything so you can style:

Here, we have `ol commentlist`; each `<li>` has a class of comments, and we have classes around the author, around `vcard`, and around the reply. You can style this however you like.

Now you can actually replace this whole template by creating a `comments.php` file; we'll get into that later on. I don't want to do it in this chapter because this is just a very basic introductory theme.

Since the comments are working, we'll not go ahead and create a custom comment template or anything like that. I think that's pretty much it. Like I said, there's more we could do; we could create a separate template for archived posts.

Actually, what I want to do real quick is to make the author's name a link, so that you can click on it and see all of the author's posts.

6. Let's go to `index.php` and go to where we have the author, and enter following highlighted code:

```
Created By
<a href="<?php get_author_posts_url(
    get_the_author_meta('ID')); ?>">
```

```php
<?php the_author(); ?>
</a>
on <?php the_time('F j, Y g:i a'); ?>
</div>
<?php if(has_post_thumbnail()) : ?>
```

As shown here, we'll just add a link around that.

7. Let's reload, and now **admin** is a link; I need to change its style because we can't see it. Open `style.css`. Go to `meta` and add the following code:

```css
.meta{
    background:#333;
    color:#fff;
    padding:5px;
}

.meta a{
    color:#fff;
}
```

8. We can see the author in white now:

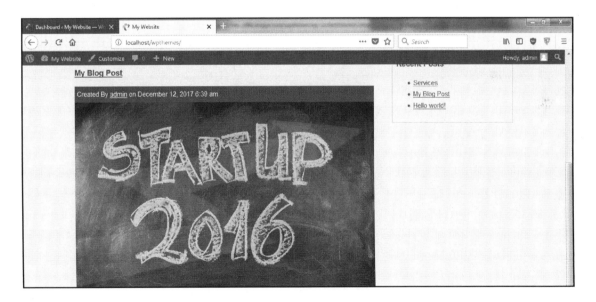

9. If I click on admin now, it shows us all the posts by admin, but if there were multiple users—multiple authors—this would allow us to see all the posts from that particular author.

10. We'll wrap this up here. You may realize that this isn't the greatest design you've ever seen, but the point of this project was to get you familiar with not just the code but also the structure of the theme and what files are included. As we saw, there are certain names that we need for the files such as `page` and `single.php`.

Summary

Hopefully, you enjoyed this chapter.

In this chapter, we started off by installing and setting up WordPress. We moved on to create and enable themes. We also created an HTML structure and body, and applied some base styling to it. We dealt with single posts, thumbnails, pages, and menus. Later, we saw how we could add images and links to the post. In the end, we saw how to create a widget location in the theme and how to add the comments functionality to the widgets.

We'll be using what you've learned in this project and applying it in the future projects. You'll also learn more as we go.

In the next chapter, we will see how to build a WordPress theme.

2

Building a WordPress Theme

In this chapter, we'll jump into more details and get our feet wet. In the previous chapter, we covered the basics, but now we'll use some of the more advanced concepts to build a WordPress theme. Here we will cover the following concepts:

- Custom template pages
- Archived pages
- Post formats
- Custom home pages

Let's take a quick look at the project:

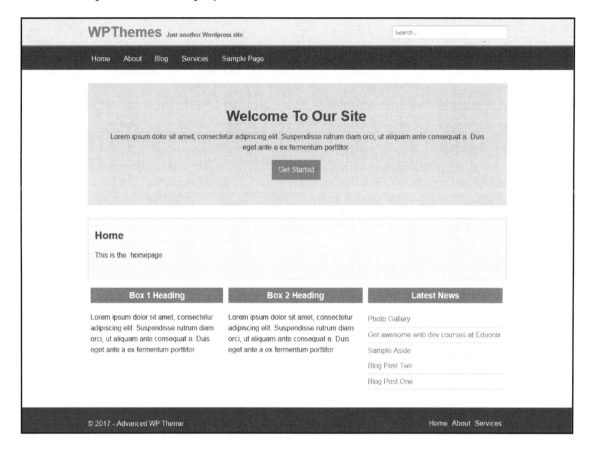

In the preceding image, you can see the **WordpressDev** home page with some widgets that we'll implement, such as the showcase. You can also see three box widgets.

Post formats

When you visit the blog page, you can see we have multiple post types:

- Gallery posts
- Linked posts
- A-side posts
- Regular blog posts

In the following screenshot, you can see Gallery post and the linked posts:

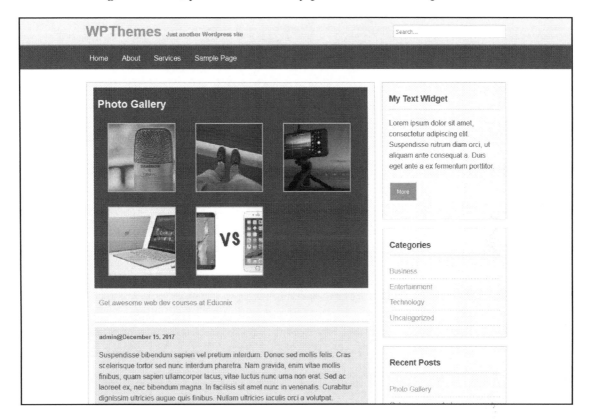

This is how the A-side post looks:

This is what a regular blog post looks like:

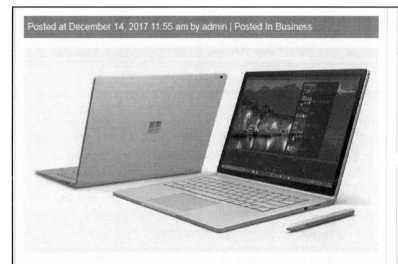

Posted at December 14, 2017 11:55 am by admin | Posted In Business

Sed nec interdum nunc. Nullam tellus augue, ornare sed velit a hello, euismod feugiat nisi. Ut a ligula nec sapien auctor finibus. Mauris fermentum ante in massa convallis, et ultrices justo commodo. Donec ligula dolor, euismod eu cursus sit amet, porta eu libero.

Lorem ipsum dolor sit amet, consectetur adipiscing elit. Suspendisse rutrum diam orci, ut aliquam ante consequat a. Duis eget ante a ex fermentum porttitor. Quisque sed massa mattis, fermentum justo eu, elementum odio. Quisque eu ipsum vel lectus imperdiet faucibus et sed lorem. Praesent laoreet eros a justo consequat, ac euismod libero dignissim. In ultrices suscipit varius. Suspendisse urna nisi, mollis at condimentum pulvinar, convallis quis odio.

Lorem ipsum dolor sit amet, consectetur adipiscing elit. Suspendisse rutrum diam orci, ut aliquam ante consequat a. Duis eget ante a ex fermentum porttitor.

More

Categories

Business

Entertainment

Technology

Uncategorized

Recent Posts

Photo Gallery

Get awesome web dev courses at

Eduonix

When we click on **Read More**, it takes us to a single page where we have our comment form and the customized comments interface, as shown in the following image:

We will now see how to create custom layouts; for instance, the **About** page, shown in the following screenshot, is in a layout called Company, where we have the phone number displayed in a `div` class:

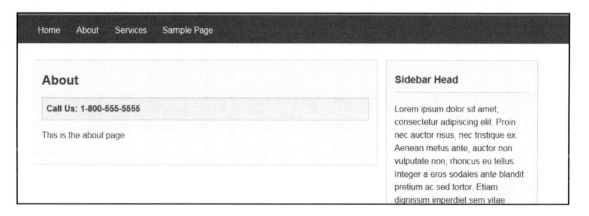

Now let's click on **Posts** or **Pages** and then on **About**:

You'll see that we have **Default Template** and **Company Layout** in the **Template** option:

Now we will see how to create a submenu for pages that have parents; for instance our **About** page has two children, **FAQ** and **Our Team**, as shown in the following screenshot:

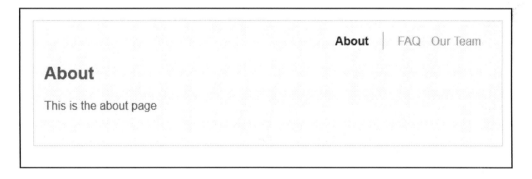

Now let's take a look at an archive listing. Go to the blog page and click on one of categories such as **Technology**:

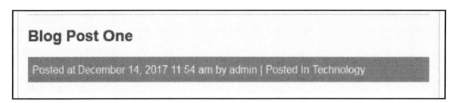

We can see that the page displays all the posts in **Technology.** Also, if we go to the username and click on that, it'll show you posts by that author, and as you can see in the following image, it's a custom layout for the archive pages:

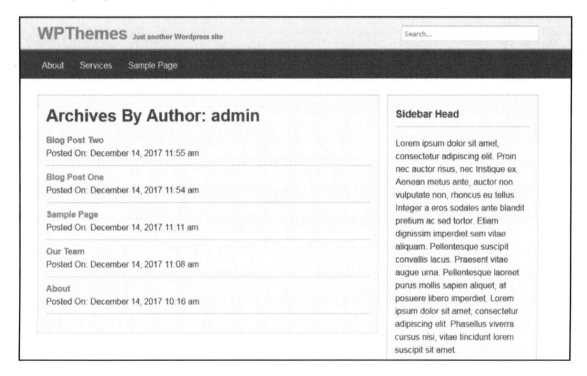

Let's go ahead and search. We have a special theme or a special layout for that, as you can see in the following screenshot:

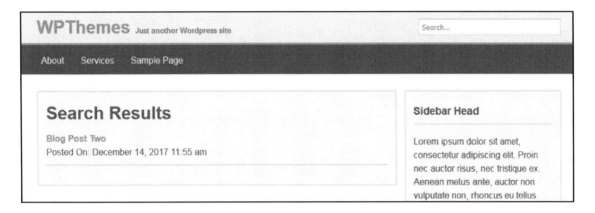

We'll get in a little deeper than we did in the first chapter.

Creating a design using HTML and CSS

Let's see how to create our theme, but before we get into WordPress, we'll first map out and just create the design using HTML and CSS.

Usually, when we build a WordPress theme, or a Drupal or Joomla theme, you can usually create the design first using just static HTML and CSS.

Building the HTML body

As you can see in the following screenshot, we have an empty folder called `advanced-wp-html`, and we'll create a couple of files here. First, we'll create an `index.html` file, and then we'll create our style sheet, which will just be `style.css`.

Let's open both the files with Sublime editor. In the `index.html` file, add in our core html markup, as shown in the following code block:

```
<!DOCTYPE html>
<html>
<head>
    <title></title>
</head>
<body>

</body>
</html>
```

We'll update the code, as shown here:

```
<!DOCTYPE html>
<html>
<head>
    <title>Advanced WP Theme</title>
</head>
<body>
    <header>
        <div class="container">
            <h1>Advanced Wordpress Theme</h1>
        </div>
    </header>
</body>
</html>
```

Here, we have `Advanced WP Theme` as the title and added a link to our style sheet, and put an `href` attribute that's going to go to `style.css`. Then down in the body, we created our markup with the header. Since we're using HTML5 syntax, we used a `<header>` tag, and created a `<div>` with the `container` class. Inside the `container` class, we have a `<h1>` tag, which says `Advanced Wordpress Theme`; of course, when we actually create the WordPress theme, this will be dynamic and you'll be able to change it from within the admin area, but for now we'll just going to stick some static text in here.

Now, after the `<h1>` tag, we'll have another `div` class and we'll give this an `h_right` class for a header right. And this is where our search form is going to go, so for now we'll just put a `<form>` tag and an `<input>` tag as shown in the following code block. We'll give it a `placeholder`, and just say `Search...`:

```
<div class="h_right">
    <form>
        <input type="text" placeholder="Search...">
    </form>
</div>
```

Now, let's go underneath </header> and create our navigation, as shown in the following code block:

```
<nav class="nav main-nav">
   <div class="container">
      <ul>
      <li><a href="index.html">Home</a></li>
      <li><a href="about.html">About</a></li>
      <li><a href="#">Services</a></li>
      </ul>
   </div>
</nav>
```

As you can see, we have used a <nav> tag with nav class and added main-nav to it. Next we added <div> with class="container" just to move everything towards the center. Then, inside, we have placed <ul> with some <li> tags and some links. We have added Home, About, and Services. However, since we're not actually going to have a Services page, we will have an About page so that we have some perspective on using on an inner page. So, index page will be the blog post, About will be just a regular page.

Next, let's add the following code after the </nav> tag:

```
<div class="container content">
   <div class="main block">
      <article class="post">
         <p class="meta">Posted at 11:00 on May 9 by admin</p>
      </article>
   </div>
</div>
```

Here, we have added a div element, with a container class, and a content class. Then, inside, we have added another div element, with a class="main block". Here, block is a class that we can use all around the site, we can use it for widgets as well; it's just going to have some padding and also a border.

Now inside this div, we have our main post; so each post has an <article> tag with a post class. We have added a paragraph that has a meta class. This is where things such as the date of the posts and the author name will go. This might change a little bit as far as the format goes when we actually build the WordPress theme; for now we're just going to say Posted at 11:00 on May 9 by admin. So it'll look something like that.

We also need a title. For that, put an `<h2>` tag and say `Blog Post 1`, as shown in the following code:

```
<article class="post">
    <h2>Blog Post 1</h2>
    <p class="meta">Posted at 11:00 on May 9 by admin</p>
</article>
```

Now let's just add some content real quick. We will go to the `www.lipsum.com` and click on **Generate Lorem Ipsum**.

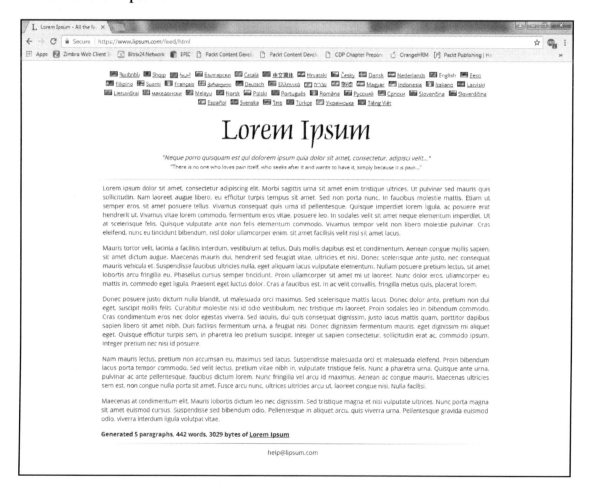

We will copy and paste some content and then we will add some paragraph tags. The next thing we need after that is a `Read More` button. We'll add a link; we'll give it a class of `button`, as shown in the following code block:

```
    <a class="button" href="#">Read More</a>
</article>
```

Then we'll copy the entire article post and paste it two more times. If we want to take a look at it, open the `index.html` file.

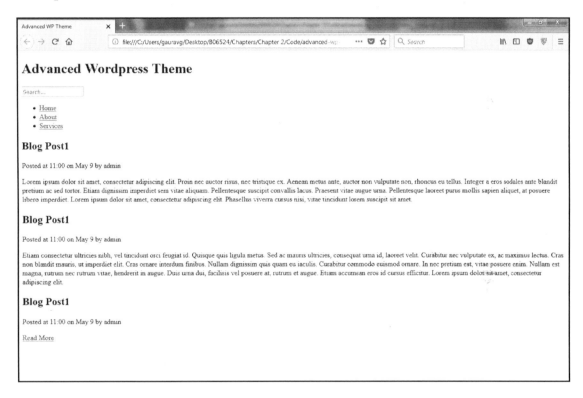

You can see in the preceding screenshot that it does not look pretty yet. So, now we'll add a footer. To do this, let's go to the last `<div>` tag and enter the following code:

```
<footer class="main-footer">
    <div class="container">
    <div class="f_left">
        <p>&amp;copy; 2017 - Advanced WP Theme</p>
    </div>
    <div class="f_right">
        <ul>
```

```
            <li><a href="index.html">Home</a></li>
            <li><a href="about.html">About</a></li>
            <li><a href="#">Services</a></li>
            </ul>
        </div>
        </div>
    </footer>
```

Here, we have added a `<footer>` tag with a `"main-footer"` class; we also have a container for it. In the container, we have a left side and a right side of the footer; so we have added `<div class="f_left">` and `f_right`. So, on the left-hand side, we will have a paragraph that will have a copyright, and then on the right-hand side, we will have another menu. For that, we have then copied the `<ul>` from above and pasted it. This is enough for the markup for the HTML. Now let's reload the file:

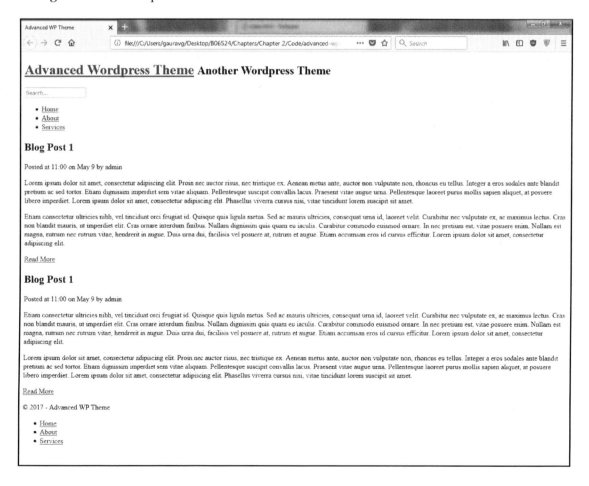

We have a footer down here; It looks pretty horrible, that's because we have no styling. Next, we will see how to add CSS.

Adding CSS

We will now see how adding CSS makes our page look a lot better. We have our `style.css` created; to it, let's add the body, as shown in the following code block:

```
body{
    font-family: Arial;
    color: #333;
    margin:0;
    padding:0;
}
```

Here, we have just added a `font-family` of `Arial`; the color of the text is going to be a really dark gray. We have set the body margin to `0` and the padding to `0`.

Let's start with some core styles for the unordered list. I want to just take off the margin and the padding, using the following code:

```
ul{
    margin:0;
    padding:0;
}
```

Now let's add the links or the `a` tags, as shown in the following code:

```
a{
    color:#009acd;
    text-decoration:none;
}
a:hover{
    color:#333;
}
.container{
    width:960px;
    margin:auto;
    overflow:auto;
}
header{
    background: #f4f4f4;
    padding:10px;
    border-bottom: 3px solid #009acd;
}
```

Here, we have added a light blue color, 009acd, and set text-decoration to none. We also require a hover color; in this case, the hover color will just be dark gray. Next, we have container, which brings everything to the middle. We have set a width of 960, and set margin to auto. The overflow is set to auto. We have header with a light gray background; we have set the padding of the header to 10px and border-bottom to 3px solid, and it's also of that same light blue color.

Now let's add header h1 with a margin and padding of 0:

```
header h1{
    margin:0;
    padding:0;
    color:#009acd;
    float:left;
}
```

As you can see, we have also added the color as light blue, and we want to float it to the left.

Then, we also want that <h1> to be a link. For this, we will go to the index.html file and wrap it in a tag, as shown in the following code block:

```
<header>
    <div class="container">
        <h1>
            <a href="index.html">Advanced Wordpress Theme</a>
        </h1>
```

Next, we will create header, h1 and a with the color of light blue. The text-decoration is set to none, as you can see in the following code block:

```
header h1 a{
    color:#009acd;
    text-decoration:none;
}
```

Now let's add a slogan or a tagline, because WordPress by default has an option for that. So right inside of the `<h1>` tag, we will put a slogan in a `<small>` tag, which will say `Another Wordpress Theme`:

```html
<h1>
    <a href="index.html">Advanced Wordpress Theme</a>
    <small>Another Wordpress Theme</small>
</h1>
```

Let's style that using the following code:

```css
header small{
    color:#666;
    margin-left:1px;
    font-size: 13px;
}
```

We have added `header small`, and given it a color of dark gray. We have set `margin-left` to 1px margin, and `font-size` to 13px.

Now for the right side of the header, add the following code:

```css
header .h_right{
    float:right;
}
```

We have `header .h_right` and we'll float that to the right.

Now, since it has an input, we'll style the input. Let's just make sure it's only for the text input. To do this, we will enter the following code:

```css
header .h_right input[type="text"]{
    width:250px;
    padding:5px;
    margin-top:5px;
}
```

Here, we have entered `type="text"` and set a width of 250px. We have also set a padding of 5px, and a margin-top of 5px.

Let's save it and take a look:

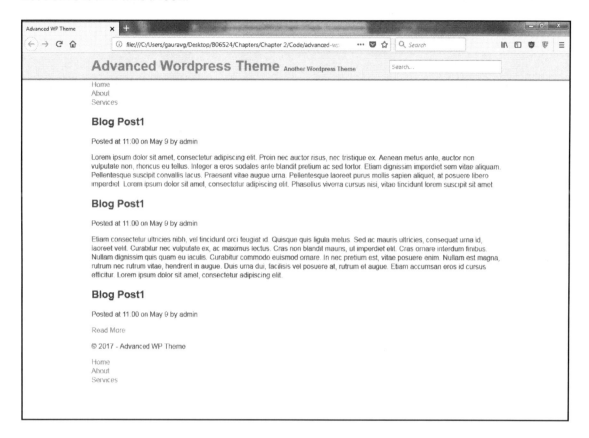

We can see our header.

Next, we'll work on the navigation. We want to have the main `nav` div for stuff like the height, background color, and similar customizations; however, we do want to have just a regular `nav` class to do the floats, so that our footer menu can have our list item floated, and stuff like that. So we will not put anything for that yet. We want to do `li` of the `nav` element. We'll make sure that we have that. You can see in the code we entered so far that we have the `nav` class and `main-nav`. Now, we'll float the list items to the left, and we'll enter `display:inline` and set a padding on the right of `15px`:

```
nav.nav li{
    float:left;
    display:inline;
    padding-right:15px;
}
```

Next, we'll add `nav.nav a`, and make sure that the text-decoration is set to `none`:

```
nav.nav a{
    text-decoration:none;
}
```

Now let's do `main-nav`:

```
nav.main-nav{
    height:45px;
    overflow:hidden;
    background:#333;
    color:#fff;
    padding-top:7px;
}
```

Here, we have set the height to `45px`, `overflow` is `hidden`, and we have set the background to dark gray. The color of the text will be white, and `padding-top` is set to `7px`.

Now let's add `main-nav li`:

```
nav.main-nav li{
    height:40px;
    line-height:40px;
}
```

We have set height to `40px`, and `line-height` to `40px`. Next, we'll add the a tag:

```
nav.main-nav a{
    color:#fff;
    text-decoration:none;
    padding:8px;
}
```

Here we set the color as white, `text-decoration` as none, and `padding` as 8px.

Now we need the hover state:

```
nav.main-nav a:hover{
    color:#009acd;
}
```

Here we have `nav.main-nava:hover`, and the hover `color` is set to light blue.

We'll save this, and look at our navigation:

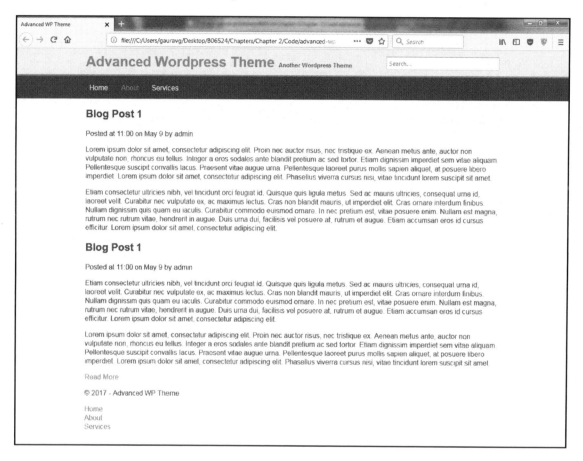

As you can see, the whole highlighted area has a class of content, we just want to push it down a little bit and set the line height of all the text:

```
.content{
    margin-top:30px;
    line-height:1.5em;
}
```

We have .content with margin-top set to 30px and line-height to 1.5em.

Now we will include a sidebar since we have not done that earlier. For this, let's open the index.html file and add the following code:

```
<div class="side">
```

```
<div class="block">
<h3>Sidebar Head</h3>
<p>Lorem ipsum dolor sit amet, consectetur adipiscing elit.
Nam vel diam hendrerit erat fermentum aliquet sed eget arcu.</p>
<a class="button">More</a>
</div>
</div>
```

We have put our sidebar right underneath the closing </div> tag. We have added a div class with a class of side. We have also added a <div> tag inside called block. Each element in the sidebar should have a class of block. Then we have an <h3> tag, which says Sidebar Head, and we have put a paragraph for which we have grabbed some text. Then, under this, we have placed a button, or a link that is formatted like a button. Now we can see our sidebar.

Let's go back to the style.css file. Here, we'll enter .main, which we'll float to the left, and we enter a width of 65% for it. Then, let's add a width of 30% for side, and float it to the right. Next, for the block style, we will set a border of light gray, which is 1px solid. We will also add some padding of 5px 15px 25px 15px and set the background to a really light gray and overflow to hidden. For h3 in the block, we will set border-bottom, which will be light gray, and solid of 1px; we'll also set a padding of 10px to the bottom:

```
.main{
    float:left;
 width:65%;
}

.side{
    width:30%;
    float:right;
}

.block{
    border:#ccc 1px solid;
    padding:5px 15px 25px 15px;
    background:#fcfcfc;
    overflow:hidden;
}

.block h3{
    border-bottom:#ccc solid 1px;
    padding-bottom:10px;
}
```

Let's take a look at this. You can see that now we have our main area and the sidebar:

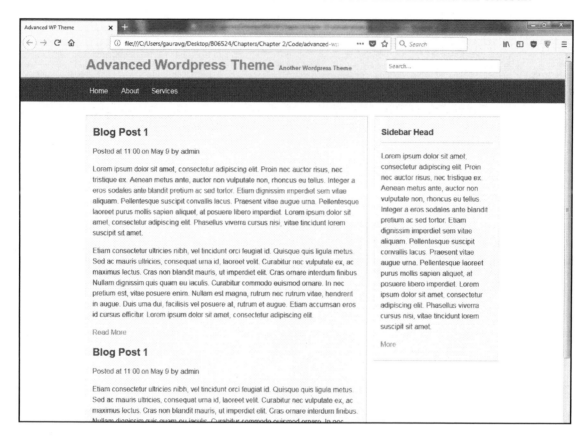

Next, let's add the article. We will place an `article` tag with a `post` class, and we will add `border-bottom`, `margin-bottom`, and `padding-bottom`, as shown here:

```
article.post{
    border-bottom: #ccc solid 1px;
    margin-bottom:10px;
    padding-bottom:20px;
}
```

Now let's style the meta area highlighted in the following image; we will give it a blue background:

To do this, let's enter the following code:

```
article.post .meta{
    background:#009acd;
    color:#fff;
    padding:7px;
}

.button{
    background:#009acd;
    color:#fff;
    padding:10px 15px;
    display:inline-block;
}
```

We have entered `article.post .meta` with a padding of `7px`. We also added the `button` class with the padding set to `10px 15px`. We also displayed it as an inline block. Let's take a look now:

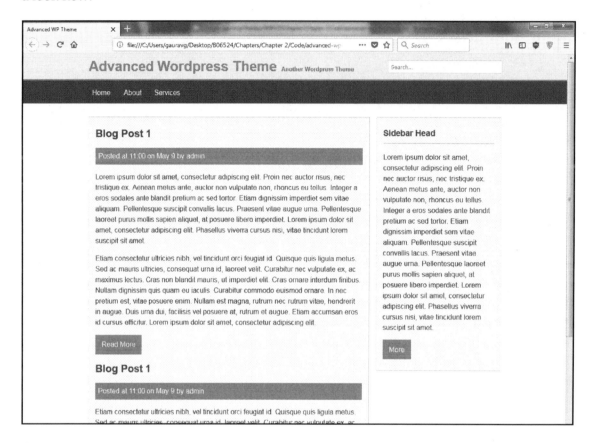

This looks pretty good.

Let's add the footer now. We will enter `footer`, give it the `.main-footer` class, and set a margin on the top of `40px`. We'll align everything to the center and give it a dark gray background. We'll set `color` as white, and height as `60px`, `padding-top:10px` and `overflow` as `auto`.

Next we will add the left- and right-hand side of the footer. To do this, we will enter `footer.main-footer .f_left` with a left float, and we'll do the same thing for the right-hand side, giving it a right float:

```
footer.main-footer{
    margin-top:40px;
    text-align:center;
    background:#333;
    color:#fff;
    height:60px;
    padding-top:10px;
    overflow:auto;
}

footer.main-footer .f_left{
    float:left;
}

footer.main-footer .f_right{
    float:right;
}
```

We will now move on to the menu. We'll enter `ul` with an inline display, and then we have `li`, as shown as follows:

```
footer.main-footer li{
    float:left;
    padding-right:10px;
    list-style:none;
}
```

For `li`, we have `float:left`, `padding-right` set as `10px`, and `list-style` set to `none`.

Lastly, we'll color the links white. Now, let's take a look:

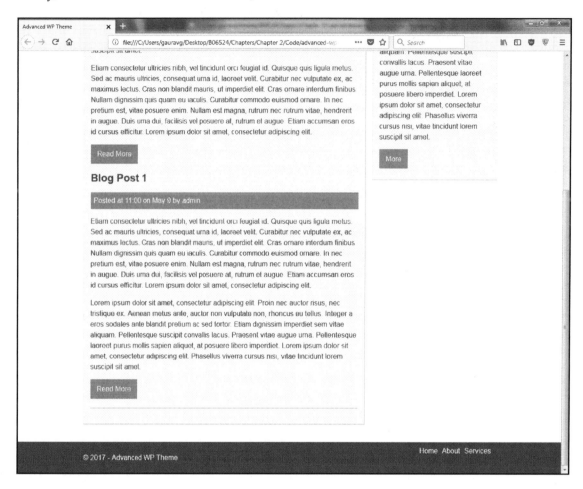

We'll just want to push footer down a little bit. To do this, enter the following code:

```
footer.main-footer .f_right{
    float:right;
    margin-top:15px;
}
```

Now, look at it:

This looks pretty good; it's a very simple design, we didn't want to go all out because the main point of this is to get you familiar with the syntax to create a WordPress theme, not so much about creating a great design. So now that we're done with HTML and CSS, we can move on to create our WordPress theme.

Creating a WordPress theme

Now we'll convert our HTML template into a WordPress theme. I have a fresh install of WordPress here with just the default **twentysixteen** theme. We will go to the WordPress folder, wp-content and then in the themes folder, we will create a new folder and name it advanced-wp.

Here we will create a style.css file and also an index.php file.

Now let's open the style sheet. Here we will put our declaration first, so that WordPress can see the theme. We will set Theme Name as Advanced WP and enter a value for Author. Next we will add Author URI, a description, and a version:

```
/*
    Theme Name: Advanced WP
    Author: Brad Traversy
    Author URI: http://eduonix.com
    Description: Advanced Wordpress Theme
    Version: 1.0
*/
```

Now we do have a screenshot as well in our project files, so we will add that.

Let's go to `C:`. Since I'm using AMPPS, I will go to my `www` folder and then to `wpthemes\content\themes`, and then to `advanced-wp`. We will go ahead and paste the image called `screenshot.png` here. If we go to the backend of WordPress, and we go to **Appearance** and then **Themes**, you can see that we have the **AdvancedWP** theme:

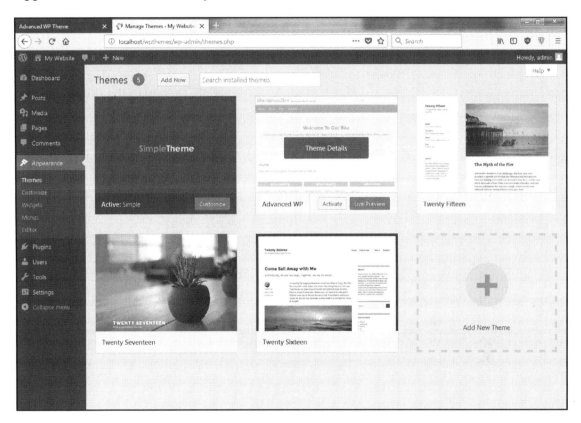

We will now go ahead and activate this. If we go to the frontend and reload, we just see a blank white page, as shown here:

Let's add styles here. Open the `style.css` file from the HTML template. We will copy all the code and paste it right in the style sheet.

We will save this, and then in the `index.php` file, we will copy everything from the `index.html` file and paste it in `index.php`:

Save it and reload the frontend. We'll see all the HTML and static HTML:

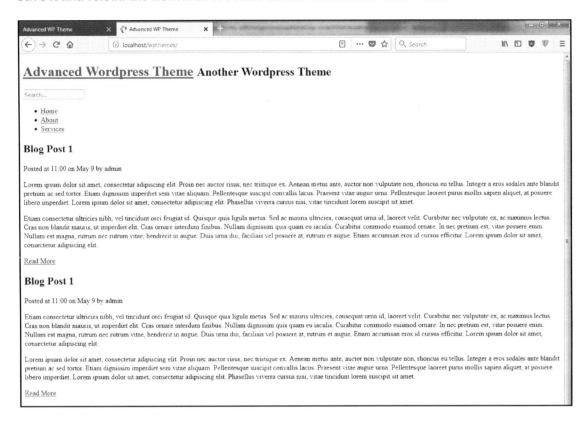

We cannot see the style sheet though, because we don't have it going to the right place. So let's update the code as follows. We will get rid of `style.css`. We will open up some `php` tags, and use `bloginfo`, and then we will just put `stylesheet_url`:

```
<head>
    <title>Advanced WP Theme</title>
    <link rel="stylesheet" href="<?php bloginfo('stylesheet_url'); ?>">
</head>
```

Let's save this and reload:

You can see that now the CSS is being read. All the stuff we're looking at here is just static content in the `index.php` file, it's not actually coming from WordPress yet. So let's do a few things here.

The best thing to do is to just start at the top and work our way down. Into the html tag, we will put the `language_attributes()` function. We will update the `<title>` tag with php `bloginfo`, and in it we will put `name`. We will also put the character set `<meta>` tag by adding `meta charset`. We can use the `bloginfo()` unction as shown and pass in `charset`. Next, we want enter the `wp_head()` function, hence we will add `<?php wp_head(); ?>`. Add a `viewport` function using the `<meta>` tag with the name `viewport`. We will set the `content` attribute to `width=device-width`. Then, we'll set `initial-scale` to `1.0`; this just helps with the responsiveness of the theme:

```
<!DOCTYPE html>
<html>
<head>
    <meta charset="<?php bloginfo('charset'); ?>">
    <meta name="viewport" content="width=device-width, initial-scale=1.0">
    <title><?php bloginfo('name'); ?></title>
    <link rel="stylesheet" href="<?php bloginfo('stylesheet_url'); ?>">
    <?php wp_head(); ?>
</head>
```

Now in the `<body>` tag, we want our `body_class()` function.

For the logo, or the heading, we will get rid of the static text and add php `bloginfo` with the name. Next, we will add the tagline to make that dynamic using `bloginfo`, and then we can pass in `'description'`:

```
<body <?php body_class(); ?>>
    <header>
        <div class="container">
            <h1>
                <a href="index.html">
                <?php bloginfo('name'); ?>
                </a>
                <small><?php bloginfo('description'); ?></small>
            </h1>
            <div class="h_right">
                <form>
                    <input type="text" name="s" placeholder="Search...">
                </form>
            </div>
        </div>
    </header>
```

Now the search form is pretty easy. We'll just take the `<form>` tag and add some stuff to it. We will update it with `method="get"` and then `action`, which is where it's submitted, and for this, we will enter `php` with the `esc_url()` function. We will then pass in `home _url` and then `/`. Then, in the input, we will added a `name` attribute and just set it to `s`:

```
<h1>
    <a href="index.html">
        <?php bloginfo('name'); ?>
    </a>
    <small><?php bloginfo('description'); ?></small>
</h1>
<div class="h_right">
    <form method="get" action="<?php esc_url(home_url('/')); ?>">
    <input type="text" name="s" placeholder="Search...">
    </form>
</div>
```

That's pretty much it. The rest will get taken care of by WordPress. Let's save this and look at it so far:

We have our logo, which is coming from WordPress, same thing with the tagline. We can't really test Search yet because we don't have any dynamic content down here. Now you'll see that we have the white space at the top; the reason for this is that we don't have the `wp_footer()` function yet, which will put the admin menu there. We'll add this next.

Let's go back and after the closing `</footer>` tag, add `wp_footer()`:

```
        </div>
    </footer>
    <?php wp_footer(); ?>
</body>
</html>
```

Let's save this and reload:

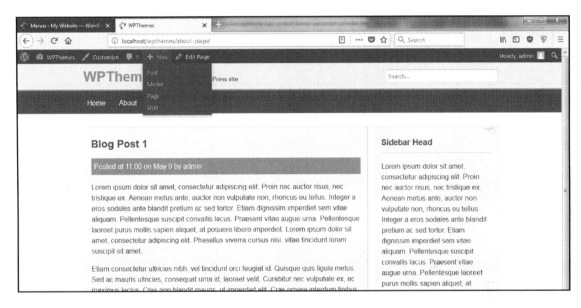

Now you can see that we have our admin bar.

Let's go back up, and take care of the menu. We'll go down to where we have our `nav` menu, and get rid of the whole `<ul>` tag and all the `<li>` tags. We'll first create a variable called `args`, and we'll set that to `array`, and the arguments can be passed into the `wp_nav_menu()` function. We'll just have one argument for now, which is going to be the location of the menu. So we will enter `theme_location` and we set it to `primary`. Next, we will enter `wp_nav_menu`, and pass in `args`:

```
<nav class="nav main-nav">
    <div class="container">
    <?php
        $args = array(
            'theme_location' => 'primary'
        );
    ?>
```

```
    <?php wp_nav_menu($args); ?>
    </div>
</nav>
```

If we go and look at it, we find that it is working here:

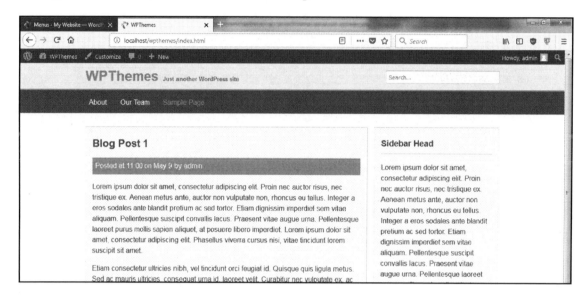

However, we want to specify in our functions file the different menu positions in our theme, and we have two. So let's go and create a new file. We'll save it as `functions.php`, and set a function for Theme Support.

We'll enter a function with `adv` as a prefix, and then `_theme_support`. All of our custom functions will have the `adv` prefix. Next, we'll register the `nav menus`. We will pass in an array and put our different positions; we have `primary`, which we will set to a readable name, so we enter `Primary Menu`, and then we will add another one in `footer`, and get this out of the way for now:

```php
<?php
    // Theme Support
    function adv_theme_support(){
        // Nav Menus
        register_nav_menus(array(
            'primary' => __('Primary Menu'),
            'footer' => __('Footer Menu')
        ));
    }
```

Now underneath the function we'll add `add_action` and `after_setup_theme`, and then the function we want to run is `adv_theme_support`:

```
add_action('after_setup_theme', 'adv_theme_support');
```

Let's save this and reload:

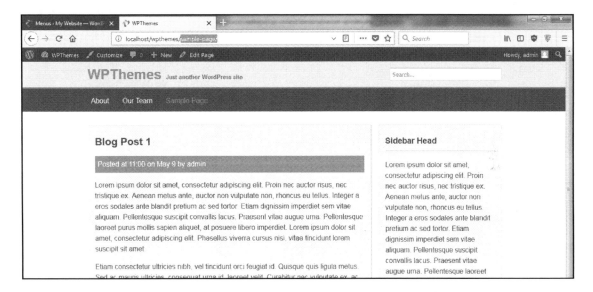

You can see that our menu is now here. If we click on it, you'll see the URL change, but you won't see any content change because this is all still just static HTML, but we do have our menu. Now, by default, every page that we have will show up here. Your pages might actually be different; you probably don't have **Our Team** because here I did a little bit of work with this WordPress site earlier, so your links may be a little different. Now if you look under **Appearance**, you'll see that we don't have a **Menus** option.

```
// Nav Menus
register_nav_menus(array(
    'primary' => __('Primary Menu'),
    'footer'  => __('Footer Menu')
));
```

Since we added `register_nav_menus` to the `functions` file, if we reload now, you will see a **Menus** link. Click on this, and you'll see that in Themes Locations we have **Primary** and **Footer** because we added them in the functions file.

Let's check the **Primary Menu**, and for menu name let's just enter Main Menu, and you can put whatever pages you'd like. We'll just leave one unchecked, we'll leave **Our Team** unchecked; and click on **Add to Menu**. Then, click on **Save Menu**:

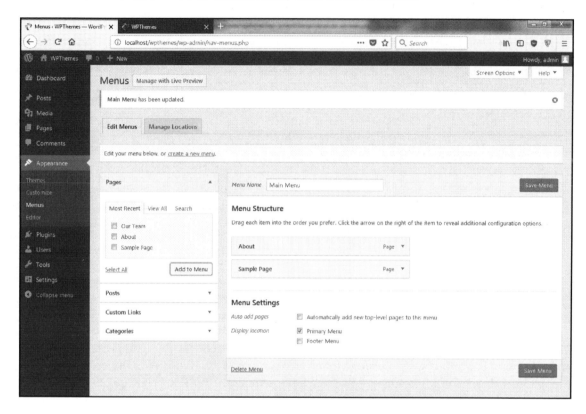

Now if we go to the frontend, you will see we only have **About** and **Sample Page**:

Now I will create a couple of pages, so that you have the same pages as I do. So we have an About page which just says **This is the about page**.

For Our Team page, we will choose the parent of About and we'll update it:

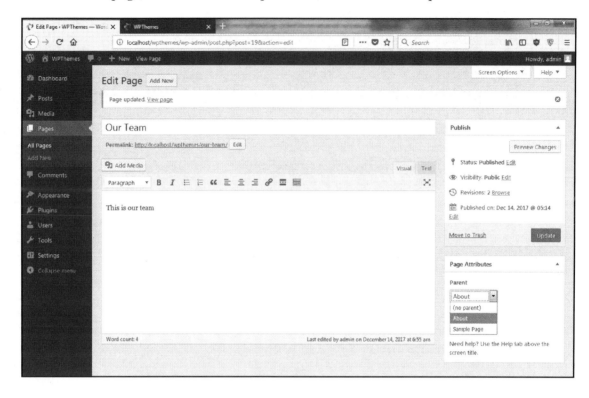

Now let's create a new page called FAQ. We will select the parent of **About**, and you'll see why we're doing this later on:

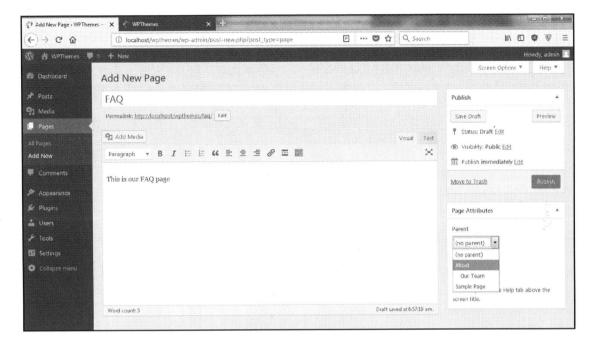

Then, we'll create another page called **Services**, and this will not have a parent. Next let's add **Services** to the menu as shown. We will not add **FAQ** or **Our Team** just yet. We will see how we can use submenus, but we'll do that later on:

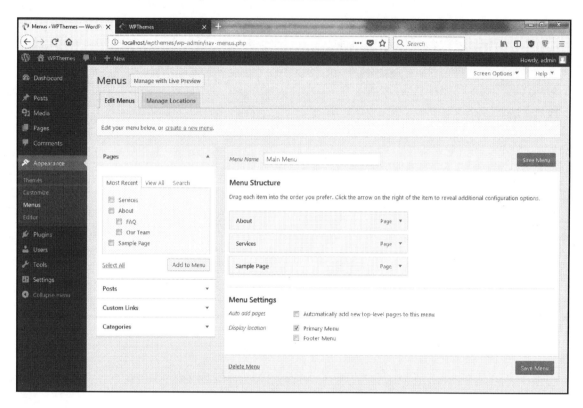

We'll save the settings, and then your menu should look like this:

We have the navigation bar, header, Search box, and all of our styles done. In the next section, we'll move on and start to create our main blog post loop.

Displaying blog post

We created the theme and added the header and navigation bar. All of this stuff on the page is now dynamic and integrated with WordPress, but this is all just static HTML.

Let's go back to our `index.php` page and go down to where we have the `container content` div, and we have different blog posts. We have three `article` tags with blog posts; we will delete two out of the three.

Then we will cut the paragraphs down and make it much shorter just so we can get it all in the page or in view. We want to write in this `main block` div, and we want to create our post loop.

First, we'll have to check for posts, and for that, we will enter `if(have_posts)`, and then we have to end it after the ending `</article>` tag. We will put an `else` statement as well. If there are no posts, then we will enter `php echo`, with the `wpautop()` function, where we can put the text that we want. In this case, we enter `'Sorry, no posts were found'`. Then, we will create our `while` loop, and then down under the `</article>` tag, we will end that `while` loop:

```
<div class="container content">
    <div class="main block">
        <?php if(have_posts()) : ?>
            <?php while(have_posts()) : the_post(); ?>
                <article class="post">
                <h2><?php the_title(); ?></h2>
                <p class="meta">Posted at 11:00 on May 9 by admin
                </p>
                <?php the_content(); ?>
                <a class="button" href="#">Read More</a>
                </article>
            <?php endwhile; ?>
        <?php else : ?>
            <?php echo wpautop('Sorry, no posts were found'); ?>
        <?php endif; ?>
    </div>
```

So it's going to loop through the posts and for every one it finds it's going to spit this out. Now to make it dynamic, we will use `php the_title()` and replace the paragraph with `php the_content()`, as shown in the preceding code block. We'll save this, and reload:

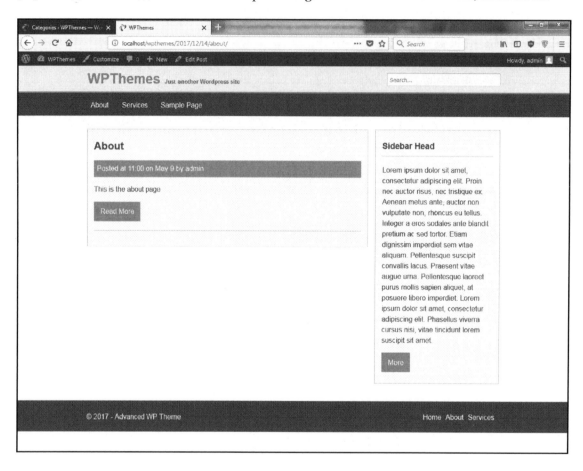

Now we're on the `About` page; let's go back to the `Home` page, which we don't have a link for. When we click on **WPThemes**, it should take us to the `Home` page, but if we click on it now, it takes us to `index.html`, so let's fix this.

We will update the `index.html` file with the following code:

```
<a href="<?php echo home_url('/'); ?>">
    <?php bloginfo('name'); ?>
```

Now if we reload and click on **WPThemes**, we will get this:

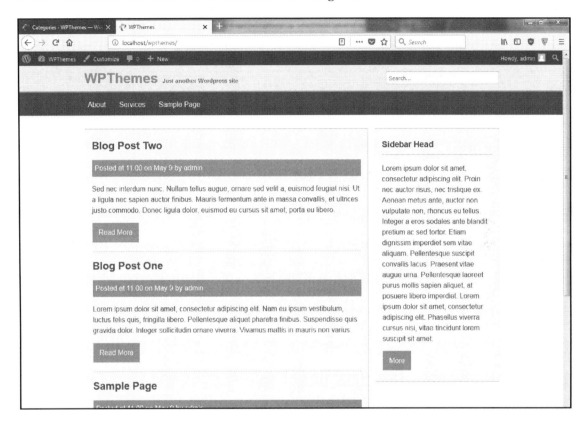

If we look at the posts, we get **Blog Post One** and **Blog Post Two**. Now you probably don't have these posts; you probably have a Hello World; if that's showing up, then that's fine. If you want to match your content to mine, just go ahead and create two posts, one as `Blog Post One`—I just have some sample content in it—and then `Blog Post Two` similarly:

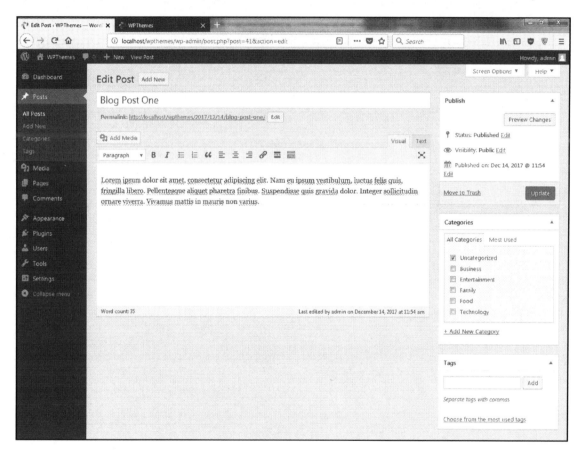

You can also create some categories, it doesn't really matter what they are. We're not really dealing with specific content, it's just for a sample content:

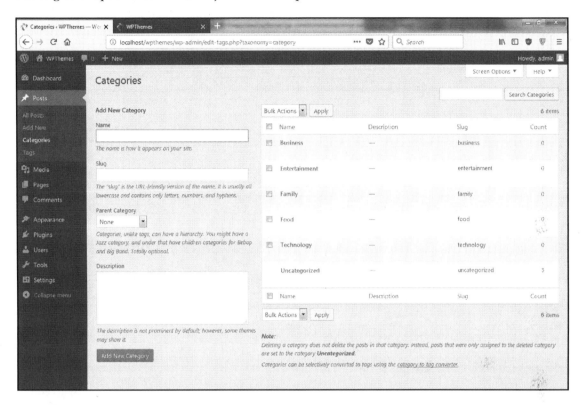

The meta info, as you can see, is still static, and so is the **Read More** button. When we click on this button, it doesn't do anything. So let's fix that next. Back in our post loop, where we have `<p class="meta">`, we will make the following changes to make it look dynamic:

```
<p class="meta">
Posted at
<?php the_time(); ?>
by
admin</p>
<?php the_content(); ?>
<a class="button" href="#">Read More</a>
```

Since we need to be more specific, for the date and time we use `the_time()`. If we just keep it like that, let's see what it gives us:

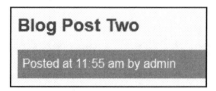

So it gives us just the time, **11:55 am**. I want the date as well, so we'll format this. However, we want to do this by just adding some parameters. We have added `F j, Y`, and then for time, we'll add `g:i a`:

```php
<?php the_time('F j, Y g:i a'); ?>
```

This pertains to the parameters of the `php date` function.

If you don't know how to format the time, you can go to `php.net` and just search for the `date` function, and that should give you all the formatting options.

Now if I reload, it gives the date, month, day, year, and also the time:

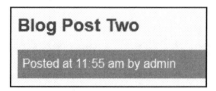

Now we also want the username of the user that created the post. To do this, we can just put in `<?php the_author(); ?>`, as shown in the following code block:

```php
<?php the_time('F j, Y g:i a'); ?>
by
<?php the_author(); ?></p>
<?php the_content(); ?>
```

If we reload now, you can see that we still get **admin** because that's the actual user's name. Now we want to be able to click on the author name and then have it bring us to all the posts archived from that user. This is pretty easy to do as well. We just want to put a link, as shown as follows. Inside the link, we enter php echo get_author_posts_url() and then pass get_the_author_meta() and ID:

```
<a href="<?php echo get_author_posts_url(
get_the_author_meta('ID')); ?>">
<?php the_author(); ?>
</a>
```

Let's save this, and then if we reload, you can see that it's now a link. We can't see it because of the color—we'll have to change the CSS—but if I click on it, it will take us to whatever the username is in the address bar, auth/author/ the username; it will show you all the posts from that user:

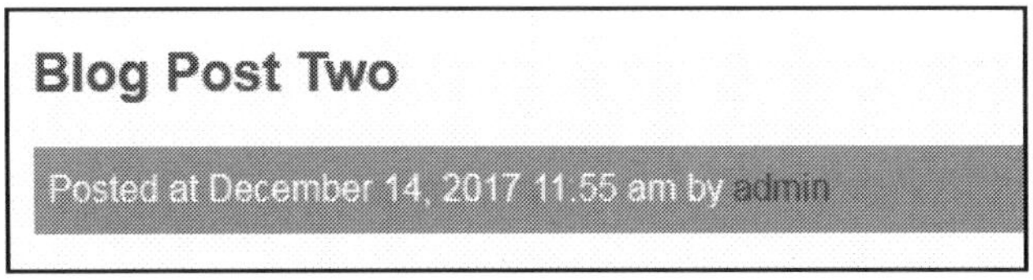

Blog Post Two

Posted at December 14, 2017 11.55 am by admin

Let's go into the CSS real quick and see where we have our meta class. We'll add article.post .meta a to it and set color to white, as shown here:

```
article.post .meta{
    background:#009acd;
    color:#fff;
    padding:7px;
}

article.post .meta a{
    color:#fff;
}
```

So now that's fixed.

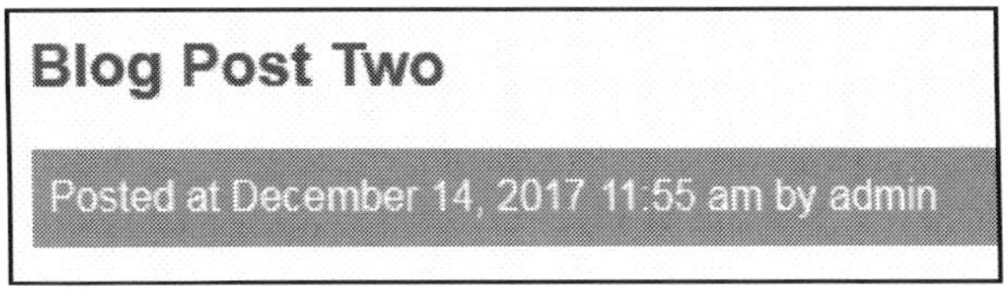

Blog Post Two

Posted at December 14, 2017 11:55 am by admin

Now we can also get the categories that the post is in. To do this, we'll go back to the `index.php` file and we will update the code, as shown in the following code block:

```
</a>
| Posted In
<?php
    $categories = get_the_category();
    $separator = ", ";
    $output = '';

    if($categories){
        foreach($categories as $category){
            $output .= '<a
href="'.get_category_link($category->term_id).'">'.
            $category->cat_name.'</a>'.$separator;
        }
    }

    echo trim($output, $separator);
?>
</p>
```

Right after the ending `</a>` tag of what we just did, of the author, we will put in a pipe | character, and then open up some php tags. Before the php tags, we'll enter `Posted In` and then we can place all the categories. To do this, we'll set a `categories` variable and set it to `get_the_category()`. Now this will give us an array of categories that this post is in. We can't just take the array and display it, so we have to loop through it. Before we do that, we'll create a variable called `separator` and separate that with a comma and a space. Then, we'll initialize a variable called `output` and set it to nothing for now. Next, we'll check for categories. To do this, we'll enter `if($categories)`, then we'll use a `foreach` loop with (`$categories as $category`). Next we'll append to that `output` variable, using `.=`. Now for each category to have a link as well, we'll use `href`. In order to do a little bit of concatenation here, we'll use dots and then add `get_category_link()`. We need to pass in a parameter, we'll take that `$category` variable and call `term_id`. Then we'll go back to our string right after the double quote, and we'll concatenate again, and enter `$category->cat_name`, closing it with the `</a>` tag. I know concatenation gets a little confusing, so we want a separator. Then, after the `if` statement, we'll use `echo` and wrap this in the `trim()` function to make it a little neater; we'll then enter `output`, and the second parameter will be `separator`.

Let's save this and see what we get. Now you can see that it says **Posted in Business**:

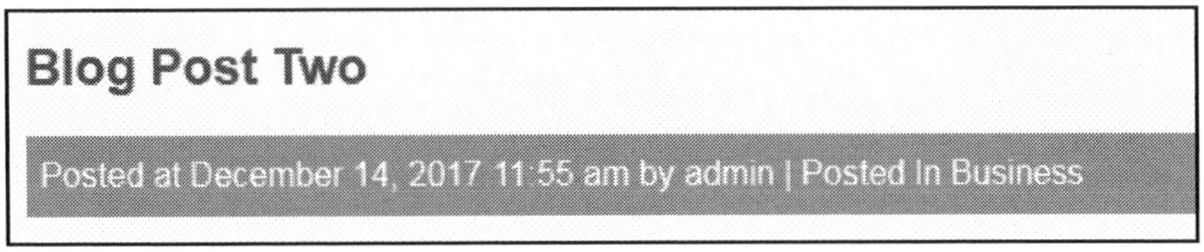

This one is **Posted In Uncategorized**:

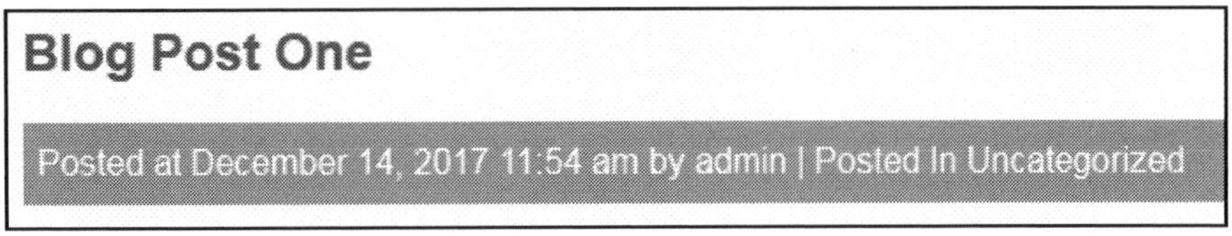

Now if I click on **Business**, it takes us to category/business, and you can see only this post is here; this is the only one in Business.

So this is working perfectly.

Now the last thing we want is the text to be shorter and the **Read More** button to work. So we'll go to where we put the content, and to make it shorter, we can just change it to the_excerpt();, as shown here:

```
</p>
<?php the_excerpt(); ?>
<a class="button" href="#">Read More</a>
```

If we look at it now, we have much shorter text:

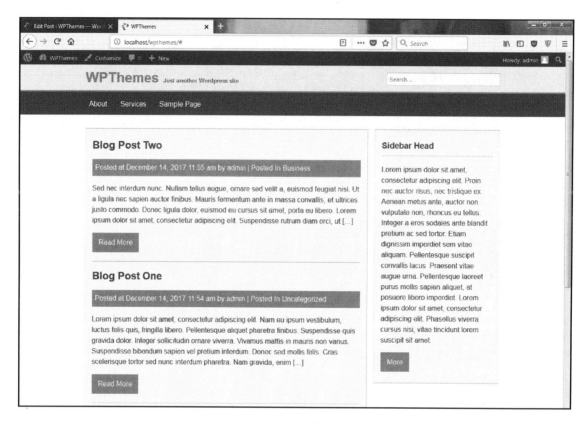

Now, by default I think it's 55 words, but we can change this:

Let's go to `functions.php` and add the `excerpt_length()` function. All we need to do here is to just return the number; let's say we want 25. Then we just need to create a filter, so we'll say `add_filter`; `add_action` means you're adding something, and `add_filter` means you're changing something. We want `excerpt_length`, so we will add `set_excerpt_length`, and we'll also use the `adv` prefix:

```
// Excerpt Length
function adv_set_excerpt_length(){
    return 25;
}
```

Let's save this and reload:

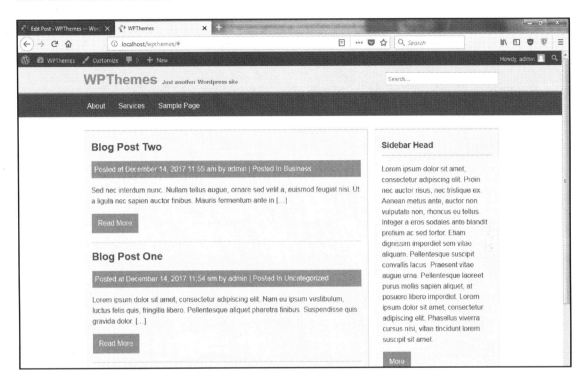

Now you can see that we get length of 25. Now, for the **Read More** to work, it is pretty easy. We'll go down to where we have the link and update the code as shown here:

```
</p>
<?php the_excerpt(); ?>

<a class="button" href="<?php the_permalink(); ?>">
Read More</a>
```

We'll reload and click on **Read More**. This brings us to that particular post:

Next we will see how to add a comment form and how we can add a featured image to our posts.

Creating a single post and adding an image

We will now see how to create a single post. If we click on **Read More** now, it takes us to the single post, but it's not what we want, we want to change this. Also, we want the ability to add a featured image to a post, also called a thumbnail. Let's start with the thumbnail. We'll first go to `functions.php` and we need to enable that support for our theme. For this, we'll go to the `adv_theme_support()` function and add a `Featured Image Support` comment. Next, we'll enter the `add_theme_support()` function and pass in `post-thumbnails`, as shown here:

```
// Theme Support
```

```
function adv_theme_support(){
    // Featured Image Support
    add_theme_support('post-thumbnails');
```

Let's save this, and if we go to, let's say `Blog Post One`, you'll see that we have the **Featured Image** block:

We will click on **Set featured image** and upload some files:

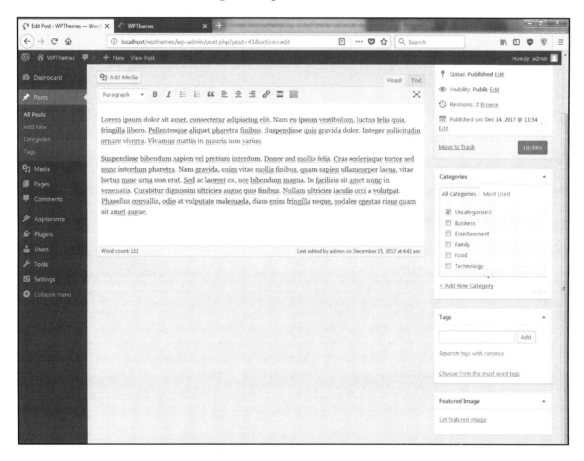

You should have a folder called `_images` with some images placed in it.

Let's choose the `phones.jpg` image and click on **Set featured image**, as shown in the following screenshot:

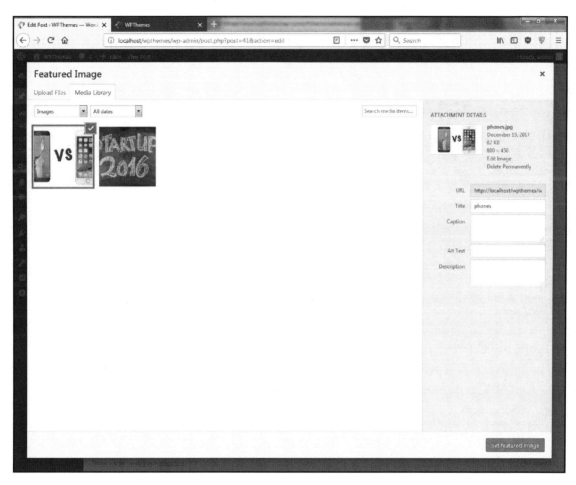

Next, we will set this to **Technology** for the category and click on **Update**:

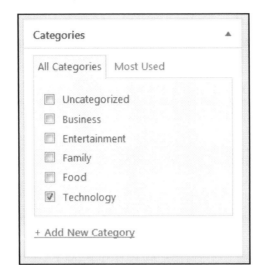

Now, let's go to `Blog Post Two` and click on **Set featured image**, and then on Upload, and then, grab the `surface.jpg` image. Now let's go ahead and click on **Update**.

If we go to the frontend and reload, you won't see the images; we actually have to add that to our theme.

So let's go to `index.php` and find out where you want to put the image. In this case, we will put it right above `the_excerpt()`, as shown in the following code block:

```
<?php if(has_post_thumbnail()) : ?>
   <div class="post-thumbnail">
      <?php the_post_thumbnail(); ?>
   </div>
<?php endif; ?>
<?php the_excerpt(); ?>
```

First, we will check for the image, and for that, we will add `<?php if(has_post_thumbnail()) : ?>`. Then we will create a `<div>` tag with a `post-thumbnail` class. We will then add `<?php the_post_thumbnail(); ?>`. Let's save this, go back, and reload.

Now you can see that we have the images. They're a little too big, so let's go to our CSS and edit the code. We'll go to where we have our article styles, and we'll add `article .post-thumbnail`. Then, we will set the image `width` to `100%`. Now it takes up 100% of the div, but the proportion is all out of whack. So we'll add `height` and set it to `auto`, as shown in the following code block:

```
article .post-thumbnail img{
    width:100%;
    height:auto;
}
```

Reload, and now you can see that they fit.

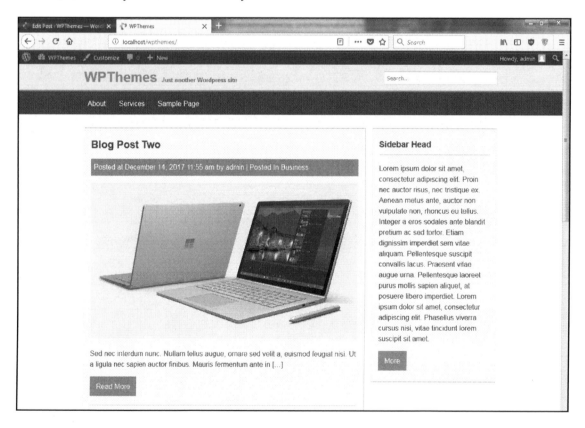

This looks good now!

Now we want to move on to the single post page. To do this, we'll set a new file and save it as `single.php`. We will just type in the word TEST. Now, if we go back to our single post and reload, you'll see that we get **TEST**, because this page has now overwritten the `index.php` page on the single post. You can also see that the main page still shows, it's just when we go to view a single post:

Let's copy everything that we have in the `index.php` file. We'll now split this up into a header and a footer file since we have not done that yet, and that's what you typically want to do with a WordPress theme, right? So we will create a new file and save it as `header.php`, and then, we'll create another one called `footer.php`.

In our `index.php` file, we'll figure out what we want to bring over to the header. So, we want the actual header and the navigation.

Let's start with `<nav>` and go up. We'll cut everything out and paste it in the header file.

Now, down at the bottom of `index.php`, we'll start selecting from the ending `</html>` tag up to where the `<footer>` starts. We'll cut that, and put it in our footer file, as shown here:

```
<footer class="main-footer">
    <div class="container">
        <div class="f_left">
            <p>&amp;copy; 2017 - Advanced WP Theme</p>
        </div>
        <div class="f_right">
            <ul>
```

```
                    <li><a href="index.html">Home</a></li>
                    <li><a href="about.html">About</a></li>
                    <li><a href="#">Services</a></li>
                </ul>
            </div>
        </div>
    </footer>
    <?php wp_footer(); ?>
</body>
</html>
```

Now if I save our `index.php` file as is, and we try to view it, you can see that it's all messed up:

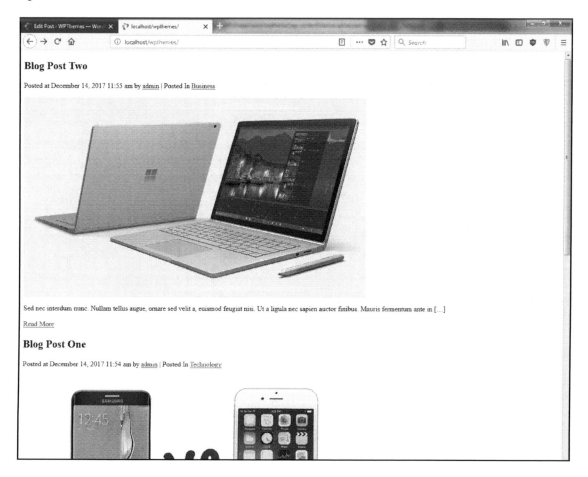

So at the top, we'll say `get_header()`:

```php
<?php get_header(); ?>
```

At the bottom, of course, we'll add `get_footer()`:

```php
<?php get_footer(); ?>
```

If we go back now, everything's back to normal:

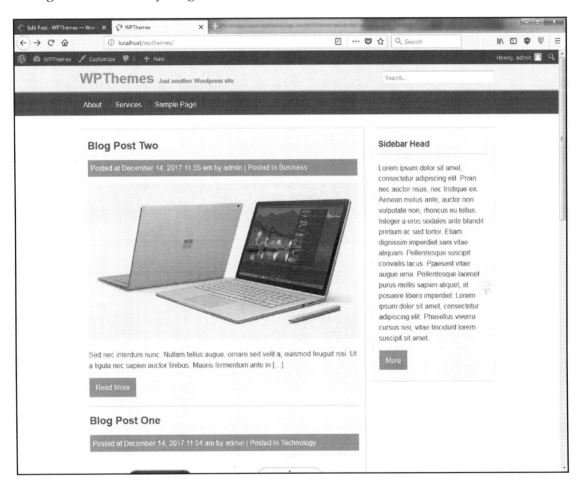

Now, we'll take everything from `index.php`, including `get_header()` and `get_footer()`, and we'll paste that into `single.php`.

We'll save this, and then if we go to the single post, we get what we had before:

Let's change a couple of things. One thing we want to change is that we want all the content to be shown. So we'll set `the_excerpt()` back to `the_content()`:

```
<?php endif; ?>
<?php the_content(); ?>
```

If we reload now, we get all the content.

Also, we don't want the **Read More** link, so we'll get rid of that:

```
<a class="button" href="<?php the_permalink(); ?>">Read More</a>
```

Now, reload, and you will see that the link is gone. So now we just have our single post.

Now the archive pages should work. If we click on **Business**, it'll show us all the Business posts; if we click on **admin**, it'll show us all the posts created by admin; similarly, **Search** should also work. If we search for Lorem, the two articles should show up.

Now all the things, such as search, the category, and user archive pages, can be actually customized; we can make them different from the main post style. This is what we'll do next.

Creating custom archive pages

Let's create custom archive pages. Now if we click on one of the categories, it'll take us to a category archive.

If we click on admin, the username, it will take us to the author archive. There are others as well. We can also have archives by dates, we can have them by tags, and so on. So let's go into our themes folder. We will create a new file and save that as archive.php and open that up.

Now if we go back and click on a category, you can see it's blank because it's looking at the archive.php page. We will copy what's in the index.php page and paste that in archive.php.

I want these pages to be much more simple. We don't need the meta, and we don't need the image; pretty much just the title and the date is all that we want. So let's go to where we have the <article> tag and get rid of the whole part.

We will replace this with a <div> tag and give it a archive-post class. We'll enter <h4>; then we'll insert a link, which will go to the_permalink(), and then we have the_title(). Next, we'll place a paragraph that says Posted On: <?php the_time, and we'll pass in the same formatting options as earlier:

```
<?php while(have_posts()) : the_post(); ?>
    <div class="archive-post">
    <h4>
    <a href="<?php the_permalink(); ?>">
        <?php the_title(); ?>
    </a>
```

```
    </h4>
    <p>Posted On: <?php the_time('F j, Y g:i a'); ?></p>
    </div>
<?php endwhile; ?>
```

Now let's take a look at this:

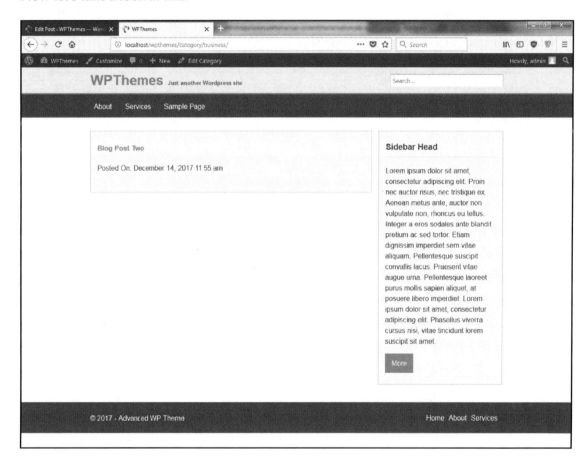

Let's update the style sheet real quick. We will add `.archive-post` with a border set on the bottom of light gray color, `1px solid`, and `padding-bottom:10px`. We'll also add `10px` on `margin-bottom`. Then for `h4` and the paragraph, we will remove the margin and padding:

```
.archive-post{
    border-bottom: #ccc 1px solid;
    padding-bottom:10px;
    margin-bottom:10px;
}

.archive-post h4, .archive-post p{
    margin:0;
    padding:0;
}
```

Now we will need to have a different heading depending on what type of archive it is. So let's go back to `archive.php` and add the following code right under the `main block` div:

```
<div class="main block">
    <h1 class="page-header">
        <?php
          if(is_category()){
            single_cat_title();
          } else if(is_author()){
            the_post();
            echo 'Archives By Authors: ' .get_the_author();
            rewind_posts();
          } else if(is_tag()){
            single_tag_title();
          } else if(is_day()){
            echo 'Archives By Day: ' .get_the_date();
          } else if(is_month()){
            echo 'Archives By Month: ' .get_the_date('F Y');
          } else if(is_year()){
            echo 'Archives By Year: ' .get_the_date('Y');
          } else {
            echo 'Archives';
          }
```

Here, we'll use some WordPress functions that are extremely helpful. We use `is_category()`, that'll happen if it's a category archive, and then we just use this `single_cat_title()` function, which can give us the category name. We then see if it is an author, and then, `echo 'Archives By Author: '`, the author's name, and `the_post()`. We also use `rewind_posts()`, and if it's a tag, we can actually give `tag_title()`; if it's by day, we can say `'Archives By Day: '` and then just say `get_the_date()`. We can also do the same for `Month`, and then for `Year`. If it's none of these, then it's just going to say `Archives`. Let's save this, and go back and reload:

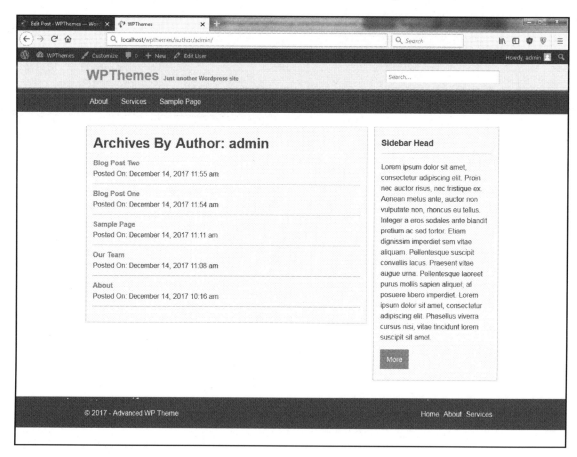

Now you can see that we get `Archives By Author: admin`. If we go back to a post and click on the category, it gives us the category name. So that's how that works. We want the same kind of view for the **Search**.

In order to search for something we'll create a new file and call it `search.php`.

We will copy what we have in `archive.php` and paste it in the `search.php` file. We will remove the ones which are not required and then we'll just say `Search Results`:

```php
<?php get_header(); ?>

<div class="container content">
    <div class="main block">
        <h1 class="page-header">
           Search Results
        </h1>

        <?php if(have_posts()) : ?>
        <?php while(have_posts()) : the_post(); ?>
            <div class="archive-post">
            <h4>
            <a href="<?php the_permalink(); ?>">
               <?php the_title(); ?>
            </a>
            </h4>
            <p>Posted On: <?php the_time('F j, Y g:i a'); ?></p>
            </div>
        <?php endwhile; ?>
        <?php else: ?>
            <?php echo wpautop('Sorry, no posts were found'); ?>
    <?php endif; ?>
</div>
```

Also, just to make sure **Search** is definitely working, let's put in the word `Hello` in `Blog Post Two`:

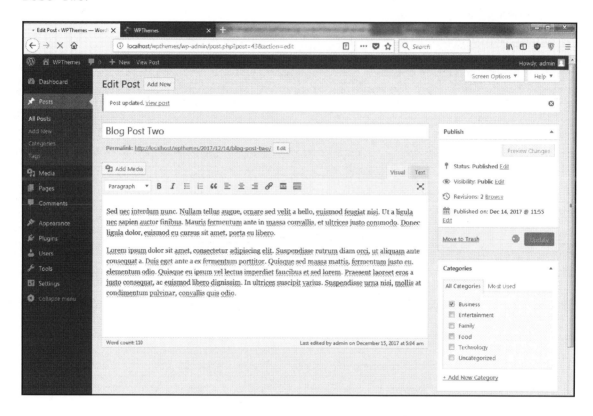

Now if we go back to the frontend and search for `Hello`, `Blog Post Two` comes up:

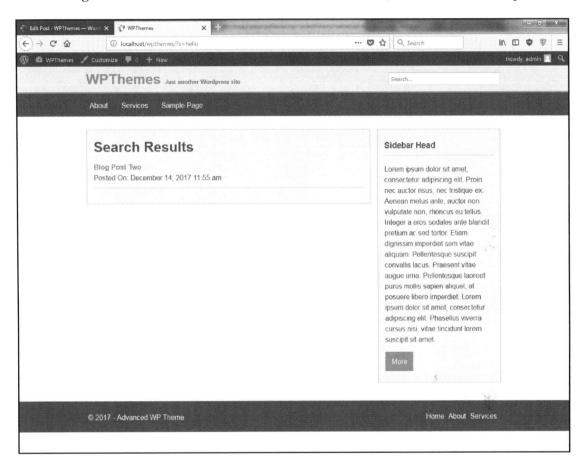

So this works!

Now we want a link to the **Home** page in the menu, so let's do that. To do this, let's go to **Menus**, and to **Custom Links**. For the URL, we will add `localhost/wpthemes`, and then for **Link Text** we'll just say `Home`. Click on the **Add to Menu** button, put that up here at the top, and save it.

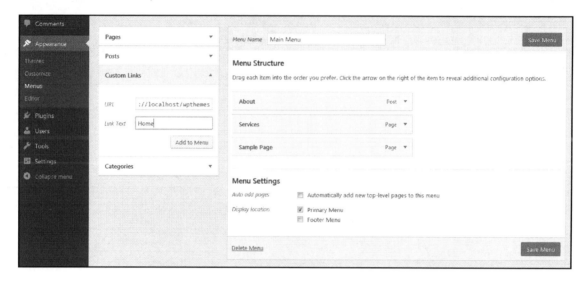

If we go back and reload, you can see a **Home** link.

Next, we will look at content types, and how to place things, such as galleries, a side content, and links.

Different post formats

Let's take a look at a few different things now. We'll look at post types or post formats. Right now, if we look at our theme, we have just basically one kind of post, and it's just a standard blog post. We can also have things, such as galleries, links, images, and quotes status updates, and we can format these different types of posts in different ways. We will now see how to do that, how to add these to our theme. Also, we'll look at a function called `get_ template_part()`, which allows us to stop repeating ourselves. For instance, if we look at our index page, we have `while (have_posts())`, and then we're just outputting our post. We observe the same thing in the archive, in `search.php`, and so on. So we want something that's going to stop us from repeating ourselves over and over. I know that each of these files have minor changes, but we can implement that inside of a specific content file. The best thing to do is to just jump in and show you.

Let's go to `index.php` and look at everything that is inside the `while` loop:

```php
<?php while(have_posts()) : the_post(); ?>
    <article class="post">
        <h2><?php the_title(); ?></h2>
        <p class="meta">
        Posted at
        <?php the_time('F j, Y g:i a'); ?>
        by
        <a href="<?php echo get_author_posts_url(
            get_the_author_meta('ID')); ?>">
        <?php the_author(); ?>
        </a> |
        Posted In
        <?php
            $categories = get_the_category();
            $separator = ", ";
            $output = '';
            if($categories){
                foreach($categories as $category){
                    $output .= '<a href="'.
                        get_category_link($category->
                        term_id).'">'.$category->cat_name.
                        '</a>'.$separator;
                }
            }
            echo trim($output, $separator);
        ?>
        </p>
        <?php if(has_post_thumbnail()) : ?>
            <div class="post-thumbnail">
                <?php the_post_thumbnail(); ?>
            </div>
        <?php endif; ?>
        <?php the_excerpt(); ?>
        <a class="button" href="<?php the_permalink();?>">
         Read More</a>
    </article>
<?php endwhile; ?>
```

We will grab everything that is in our `post` loop; basically, all that is in it from the `<article>` tag to the ending `</article>` tag. We'll cut this, paste it in a new file, and save it as `content.php`. We'll save this, go back to index, and in its place, we'll say `<?php` and then we'll use `get_template_part()`. Then we will pass in the name of the file which we just created, which is `content`. Let's save this and make sure that `content.php` is saved as well:

```php
<?php if(have_posts()) : ?>
    <?php while(have_posts()) : the_post(); ?>
        <?php get_template_part('content'); ?>
    <?php endwhile; ?>
```

Now if we reload, it looks the exact same, which is what we want.

Let's take a look at `archive.php`. You can see same content in the archive file. The idea is to get everything that's in the while loop, into that content file. So let's cut the highlighted part:

```php
<?php if(have_posts()) : ?>
    <?php while(have_posts()) : the_post(); ?>
        <div class="archive-post">
        <h4>
        <a href="<?php the_permalink(); ?>">
            <?php the_title(); ?>
        </a>
        </h4>
        <p>Posted On: <?php the_time('F j, Y g:i a'); ?></p>
        </div>
    <?php endwhile; ?>
<?php else : ?>
    <?php echo wpautop('Sorry, no posts were found'); ?>
<?php endif; ?>
```

Go to `content.php`. Now this is a little different than what we have for a regular blog post. So what we can do is we can use a condition and check to see whether we get an archive or a search result page. To do this, we'll say `<?php` with an `if` statement. We'll also use an `else` statement along with it:

```php
<?php if(is_search() || is_archive()) : ?>
    <div class="archive-post">
        <h4>
        <a href="<?php the_permalink(); ?>">
            <?php the_title(); ?>
        </a>
        </h4>
        <p>Posted On: <?php the_time('F j, Y g:i a'); ?></p>
    </div>
<?php else : ?>

<?php endif; ?>
```

For the `if` statement, we'll say `if(is _search())`. This means that if we're on a search results page, and if we search for something and this comes up, it's checking to see whether we're on this page. We can also check to see if it's on a category or an archive—not just category but any kind of archive. So let's say also `is_archive()`. If this is true then we want to just output what we just copied from the archive post page. Next, we will grab all the code in the `<article>` tag and paste that inside `else`, as shown here:

```php
<?php if(is_search() || is_archive()) : ?>
    <div class="archive-post">
        <h4>
        <a href="<?php the_permalink(); ?>">
            <?php the_title(); ?>
        </a>
        </h4>
        <p>Posted On: <?php the_time('F j, Y g:i a'); ?></p>
    </div>
<?php else : ?>
    <article class="post">
        <h2><?php the_title(); ?></h2>
        <p class="meta">
        Posted at
        <?php the_time('F j, Y g:i a'); ?>
        by
        <a href="<?php echo get_author_posts_url(
            get_the_author_meta('ID')); ?>">
        <?php the_author(); ?>
        </a> |
        Posted In
```

```php
<?php
    $catagories = get_the_catagory();
    $separator = ", ";
    $output = '';
    if($categories){
        foreach($catagories as $catagory){
            $output .= '<a href="'.
                get_category_link($category->
                term_id).'">'.$category->cat_name.
                '</a>'.$separator;
        }
    }
    echo trim($output, $separator);
?>
</p>
<?php if(has_post_thumbnail()) : ?>
    <div class="post-thumbnail">
        <?php the_post_thumbnail(); ?>
    </div>
<?php endif; ?>
<?php the_excerpt(); ?>
<a class="button" href="<?php the_permalink();?>">
 Read More</a>
</article>
<?php endif; ?>
```

Let's save this and then, in `archive.php`, we also want what we put in the `index.php` file. So we'll copy and paste that, as shown, and save it:

```php
<?php if(have_posts()) : ?>
    <?php while(have_posts()) : the_post(); ?>
        <?php get_template_part('content'); ?>
    <?php endwhile; ?>
```

Now if we reload the search page, it should look the exact same.

Just to make sure that it's coming from the content file, we'll just say TEST and then reload. Let's see it now:

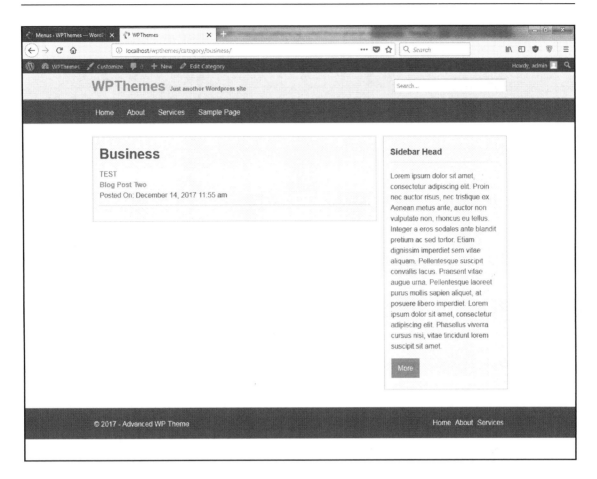

It's not giving us **TEST**. Oh, that's because we didn't put it in the search. We only put it in the archive, so let's test that first.

Now if we click on category name, you can see that we're getting **TEST**. Just like we did in the archive where we put this `get_template_part()`, we will copy and put that in the `search` page as well:

```php
<?php if(have_posts()) : ?>
    <?php while(have_posts()) : the_post(); ?>
        <?php get_template_part('content'); ?>
    <?php endwhile; ?>
<?php else : ?>
    <?php echo wpautop('Sorry, no posts were found'); ?>
<?php endif; ?>
```

This is the same exact code as we have seen earlier. We can just paste that in. Then, if we do a search, we now get **TEST**:

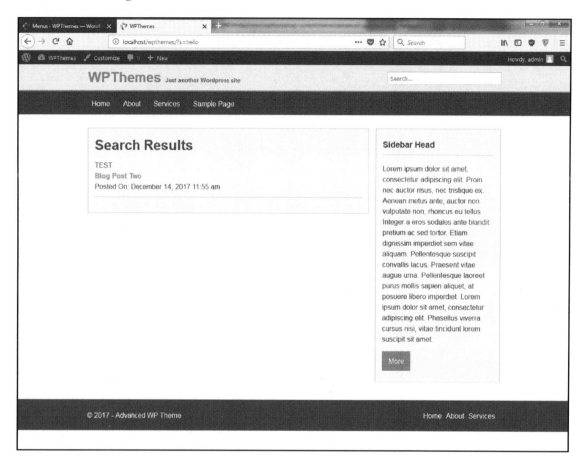

So we know that it's coming from `content` page in this conditional. We'll save this, and that's all set.

Now we can also implement our `content.php` file inside of the `single.php` file as well, because if we look at `single`, we have a lot of the same stuff that we had in the `index.php` file. We have an `<article>` tag. The only difference is that we're using the excerpt inside of the blog roll; also, we have the **Read More** link that's not in the `single.php` file. So we'll copy from the `<article>` tag to the ending `</article>` tag, paste that in `get _template_part()`, and save it. Now if we go to the `single` page, we lost that single page formatting. So we'll go into the `content.php` page and just add some conditionals where we want things to be different:

```php
<?php if(is_single()) : ?>
    <?php the_content(); ?>
<?php else : ?>
    <?php the_excerpt(); ?>
<?php endif; ?>
```

For instance, in `the_excerpt()`, we want to say `<?php if`. We can say `if(is_single)`; if it is single, then we want `the_content()`, if not, then we want `the_excerpt()`. So we'll paste the code in and then get rid of the old code. So let's go back to the single page, reload, and we see that now we have our content back.

We also want to get rid of the `Read More` link. So let's go down to where that is, and actually we don't even need to do another conditional. We can just grab it and paste it below `the_excerpt()`, as shown in the following code block:

```php
<?php else : ?>
    <?php the_excerpt(); ?>
    <a class="button" href="<?php the_permalink(); ?>">Read More</a>
<?php endif; ?>
</article>
```

So then the `Read More` won't show up on the single page anymore.

You can see how we've saved ourselves from repeating ourselves. Now, in `archive.php` inside the `while` loop, we just have this one line:

```php
<?php get_template_part('content'); ?>
```

We see the same thing with the other pages—search, `single` and `index`. Now we'll get into the post formats. So, let's add a gallery type.

First, let's go to our `functions.php` file. We need to enable these different formats that we want to use.

Right under `register_nav_menus()`, we can add `Post Format Support` and `add_theme_support()`. Also, we want to add `post-formats`. Then the second parameter will be an array of the types of formats we want. We will choose three; we'll take `aside`, `gallery` and `link`:

```
//Nav Menus
register_nav_menus(array(
    'primary' => __('Primary Menu'),
    'footer'  => __('Footer Menu')
));
//Post Format Support
add_theme_support('post-formats', array('aside', 'gallery', 'link'));
```

If we look at the documentation, the supported formats are as shown in the following screenshot:

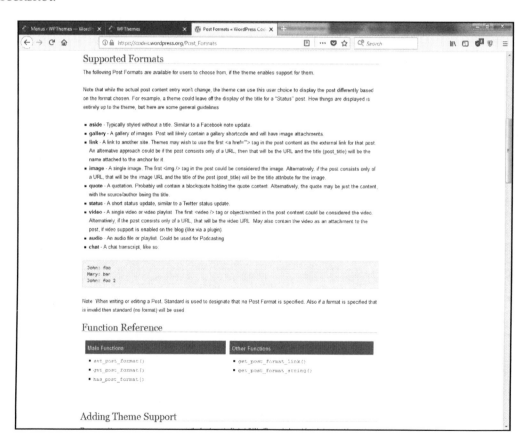

We're using **aside**, **gallery** and **link**, but we also have **image**, **quote**, **status**, **audio**, and **chat**. You might want to take a look at that. Let's save this, and since we put that in there, if we go to our **Posts** and say **Add New**, you'll now see that we have the **Format** box on the side, where we can choose what format we want for our post:

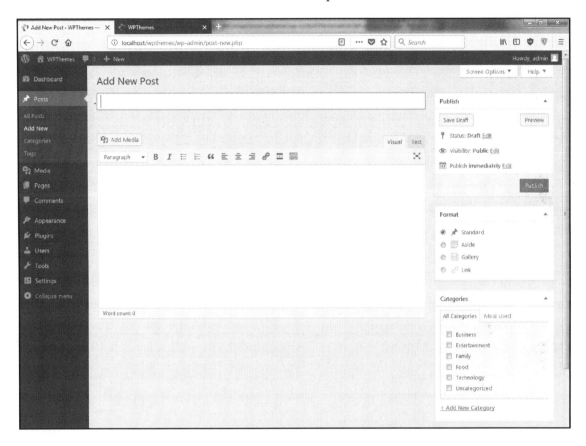

Now, as it is, it's not going to do anything different. So let's do something different.

We'll say `Sample Aside` and grab some content. We'll just take this content and paste it.

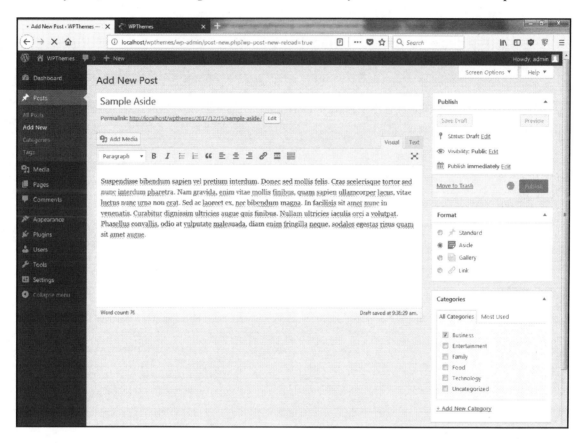

We'll choose **Aside** as a format, **Business** as a category, and click on **Publish.**

Now if we go to our frontend and reload, you can see that we have our **Aside**, but it's no different than these posts:

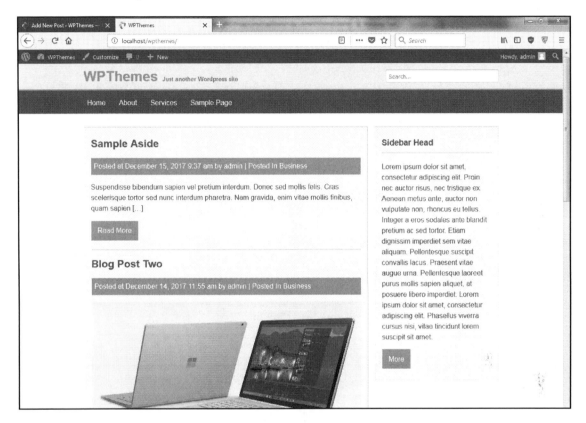

The point of this is to have this show up differently.

Now, the way we can do that is when we go to, let's say, `index.php`, where we put `get_template_part()`. We want to pass in a second parameter of `get_post_format()`, as shown in the following code block:

```php
<?php get_template_part('content', get_post_format()); ?>
```

This is a function and that's going to allow it to see what type of post format it is. We'll just replace all `get_template_part()` with the second parameter. We'll go to `archive.php` and paste `<?php get_template_part('content', get_post_format()); ?>`. Let's do the same for `search.php` and `single.php`.

Now, for each format, we'll create a content file. So let's say **New File** and save this as `content-aside.php`.

We'll also create `content-gallery.php` and, finally, `content-link.php`.

Now, with these different files, we can make our formats look differently. So let's start with the `content-aside.php` file. This is going to be very simple. It will have an `<article>` tag. We'll give it a `post` class and `post-aside`. We don't want to have any images or any of that stuff. We just want the actual content, the author, and the date. We will place it in a `<div>` tag with the `well` class, which is a bootstrap class, and then in there, we'll use a `<small>` tag and `the_author()`. You can kind of think of this as like a status update. Let's put the @ sign and then, `<?php the_ date(); ?>`. Then right under it, we'll put `the_content()`:

```
<article class="post post-aside">
    <div class="well">
    <small><?php the_author(); ?>@<?php the_date(); ?></small>
    <?php the_content(); ?>
    </div>
</article>
```

Now we'll save this. If we go back and reload, you can see that the post has changed because it's coming from this `content-aside` file:

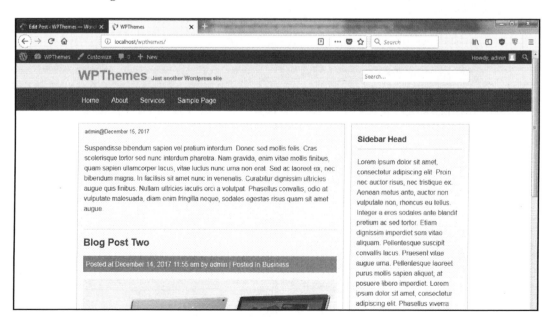

Now I want to make this look a little better. So we'll go into our style sheet. We'll go down to where we have the `article` stuff, and let's say `article.post-aside`. Actually, we don't want to do the core element. We want `small`, and we just want to make the text bold by adding `font-weight: bold`. We also want to format `well`. In addition, we will change the background from gray to a light blue by adding `#e0eefc`. We also want to add some padding:

```
article.post-aside small{
    font-weight: bold;
}

article.post-aside .well{
    background:#e0eefc;
    padding:10px;
}
```

Now you can see that it's formatted differently:

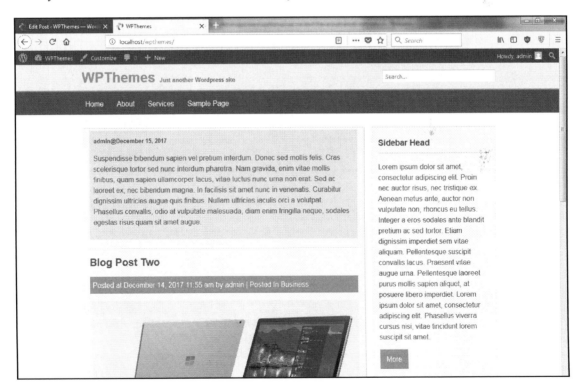

So this takes care of `aside`. Now let's do the link. For this, we'll go into `content-link.php`, copy what we have in `content-aside`, and update the code as shown in the following code block:

```
<article class="post post-link">
  <div class="well">
    <a href="<?php echo get_the_content(); ?>"><?php echo
    the_title();
    ?></a>
  </div>
</article>
```

We will add the link as shown and keep the `well` class, but this is going to be different!

Now if we go back into our posts, and click on **Add New** this time, we'll choose a **Link** as a format, and then, as a title, we'll add `Get awesome web dev courses at Eduonix`. Then, in the text area, we just want to put a link and that's it. We'll say **Publish** and go back and reload. Now you can see that we have a link that goes to `eduonix.com`:

We want to format this to make it appear a little better. So we'll go back to our style sheet and say `.post-link`:

```
article.post-link  .well{
    background: #f4f4f4;
    padding:10px;
}
```

Actually, we just want `well`. We'll say background, which will be just light gray, and then we'll enter `padding:10px`. So now we have a formatted link.

We have our regular post, we have the **aside** content or status updates, and we have links. So the last one we'll look at is the gallery. For this, let's go to `content-gallery.php`; this is actually going to be very simple. We'll say `<article class="post post-gallery">` and we enter the `<h2>` tag with `the_title()` and then, we just want `the_content()`; that's it:

```
<article class="post post-gallery">
<h2><?php the_title(); ?></h2>
<?php the_content(); ?>
</article>
```

Now we'll go to the **Add New** post. We will then go to **Add Media** and then to **Create Gallery**.

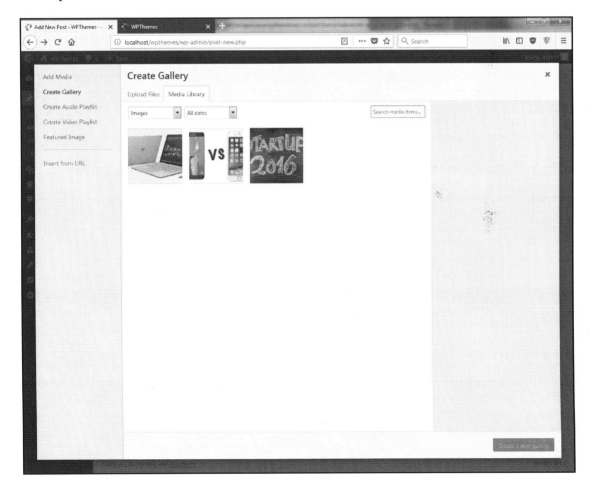

We have some images in here, but we want to upload some more, and you should have these in your files. We will upload a few images, as shown here:

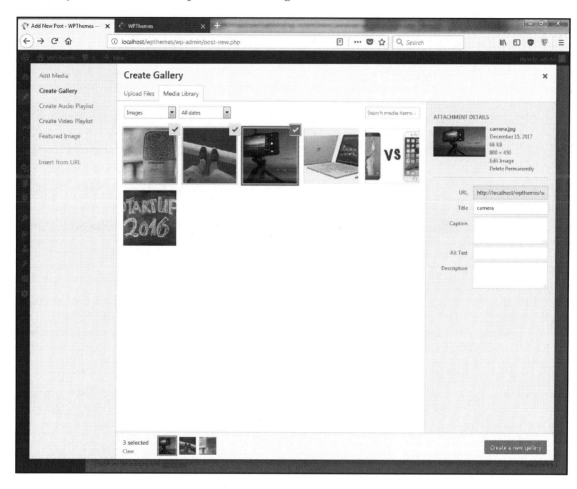

That's fine. We're just going to click on all of these images and then on **Create a new gallery**. Then you want to make sure that all of these are in there. To check them, click on **Insert Gallery** and make sure that **Gallery** is chosen inside the **Format** box:

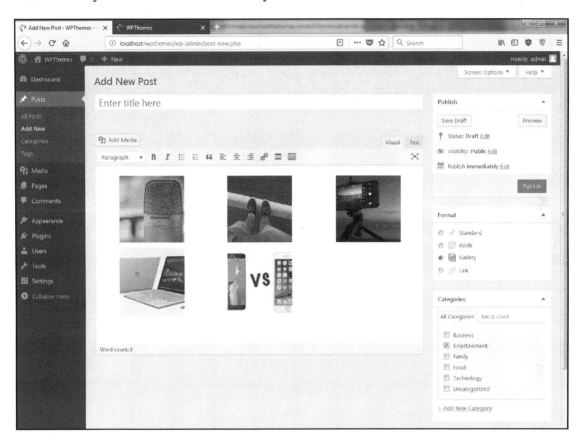

We'll choose **Entertainment** inside the **Category** box and click on **Publish**. Let's go back and reload, and there's our gallery:

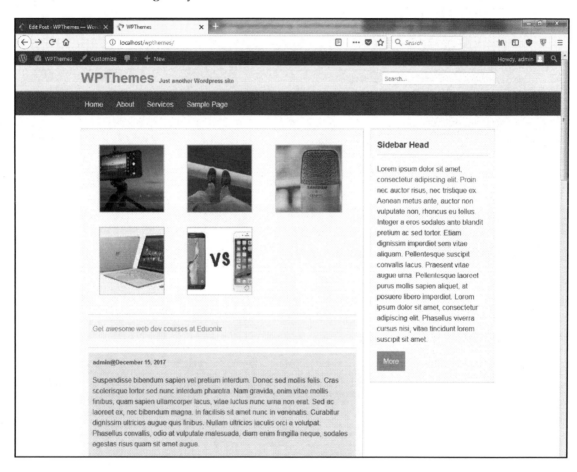

If we want to edit it, we can go back in, and you can choose the pencil icon to edit. Now, right now, they're linked to **Attachment Page**, but I want them to actually go to the media file. So you can see that when you click on them, it's just going to the image file:

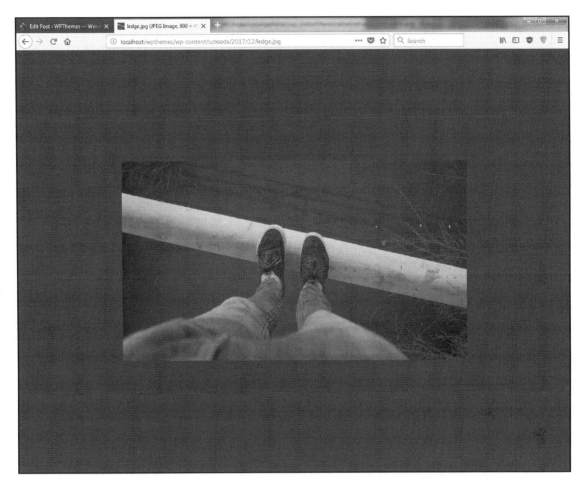

You can change this. You can have it go to a page or you can implement some kind of light box plugin, if you wanted to, as well, but we'll not get into that. Now, I want to go to my `style.css` file and just add some styles. We'll say `article.post-gallery` and we'll add a dark background. We'll set `color` as white. We'll also add some padding, say, `5px 10px` and then, `margin-top` will be `5px`:

```
article.post-gallery{
    background: #333;
    color:#fff;
    padding: 5px 10px;
    margin-top:5px;
}
```

Let's save this and reload.

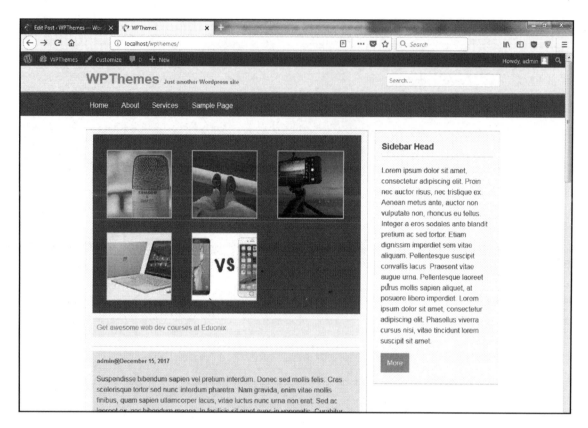

So, now we can post a gallery!

Pages, custom templates, and sub navigation

Now we'll move from the posts to pages. If we visit the **About** page, you can see that it's formatted just like a post, which is definitely not what we want.

We just want the pages to have the title, we don't want metadata, Read More, and stuff like that. So to change all that, we have to create a new file and save it as page.php.

Now if I go back to that page and reload, it's just a blank white page. It's looking to this file to parse it.

Just to start with, I'll grab what we have in the index page, paste it in page.php, and just change some stuff. We want the while loop, we'll not use get_template_part(), so we can get rid of that. We want an <article> tag, and let's give this a class of page. Let's also put in an <h2> tag. This is where the title will go, so we'll say <?php the_title(); ?>, and right under this, we'll put the_content():

```php
<?php get_header(); ?>

<div class="container content">
    <div class="main block">
        <?php if(have_posts()): ?>
            <?php while(have_posts()) : the_post(); ?>
                <article class="page">
                    <h2><?php the_title(); ?></h2>
                    <?php the_content(); ?>
                </article>
            <?php endwhile; ?>
        <?php else : ?>
            <?php echo wpautop('Sorry, no posts found.'); ?>
        <?php endif; ?>
    </div>

    <div class="side">
        <div class="block">
        <h3>Sidebar Head</h3>
        <p>Lorem ipsum dolor sit amet, consectetur adipiscing elit,
         sed do eiusmod tempor incididunt ut
         labore et dolore magna aliqua. Ut enim ad minim veniam, quis
         nostrud exercitation
         ullamco laboris nisi ut aliquip ex ea commodo consequat.</p>
        <a class="button">More</a>
        </div>
    </div>
</div>

<?php get_footer(); ?>
```

OK, really simple, save it, let's go to the **About** page, and now we have a very simple **About** page.

If we go to **Services**, we find that it uses the same format; even **Sample Page** uses the same format. Now I want to show you that we can actually create page templates for certain pages. For instance, let's take the **About** page. If I say **New File**, save it as `page-about.php`, and we'll say ABOUT and save and reload it, we get ABOUT:

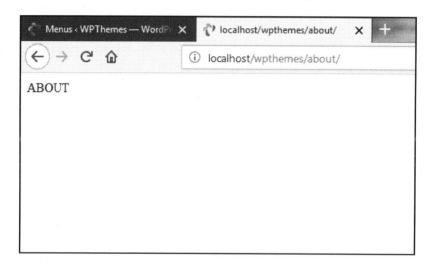

Now this isn't going to be on every page; you can see that **Services** shows up, **Sample Page**, it's only the **About** page. So it's using the slug that is up in the URL. We could just as well say page `services` and that would work. You would do this when you want something on the `About` page that you don't want anywhere else.

Now we'll just copy what's in `page.php`, put it in `page-about.php` and then go right above `the_content()`. There, we'll put a `<div>` tag with the `well` class, and we'll just put in `Company Phone`:

```
<article class="page">
<h2><?php the_title(); ?></h2>
<div class="well">Company Phone: 555-555-5555</div>
<?php the_content(); ?>
</article>
```

Now, go back to **About**, and you can see that we have the **Company Phone** there:

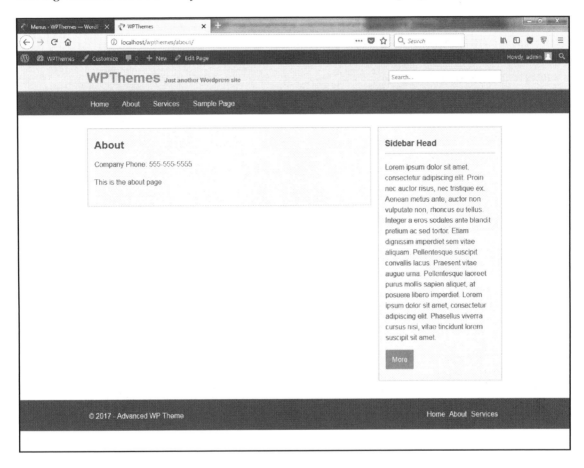

So, it's not on **Services**, it's not on **Sample Page** or any other pages. You can do this, but I think a better thing to do, when you want to have specific styles or content on certain pages, is to use a template. I'm going to get rid of the page-about file. I just wanted to show you that this is possible. So we got rid of that, and now we'll create a template. Let's create a new file and save it as company-template.php. We'll copy what we have in the page.php file, and paste it right in the company-template.php file.

Now at the top, we want to add a declaration or comment. Actually, this needs to be in the php tags. Next, we'll say Template Name and call this Company Layout. All we want to do here is to go right below the_title(), and put the phone number; however, I'll put it in a paragraph tag with a class of phone, and we'll put a 1-800-555-5555 number:

```php
<?php
/*
    Template Name: Company Layout
*/
?>
<?php get_header(); ?>

<div class="container content">
    <div class="main block">
        <?php if(have_posts()): ?>
            <?php while(have_posts()) : the_post(); ?>
                <article class="page">
                <h2><?php the_title(); ?></h2>
                <p class="phone">1-800-555-5555</p>
                <?php the_content(); ?>
                </article>
```

Now, save this. Let's quickly go into the style sheet and add a style for the phone class. This is probably something you would do, but it's just to give you an example to show you that you can have custom templates for certain pages. Let's give it a background, border, padding, and make the font bold:

```
.phone{
    background:#f4f4f4;
    border: 1px solid #ccc;
    padding:8px;
    font-weight: bold;
}
```

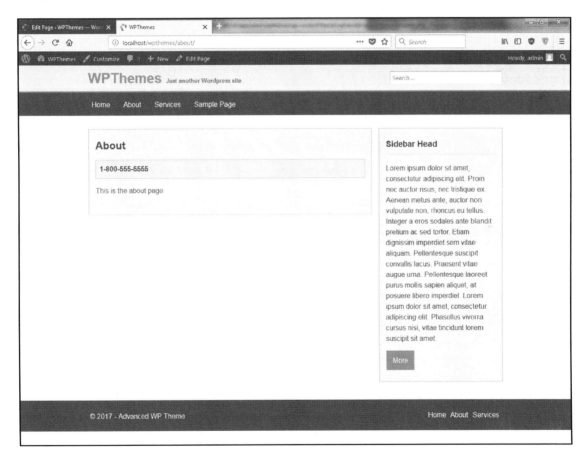

Now that we have that created, let's go into our pages, and go to **About**, and then, under **Template**, we can choose **Company Layout**. We'll update this, reload, and now you can see we have the phone number:

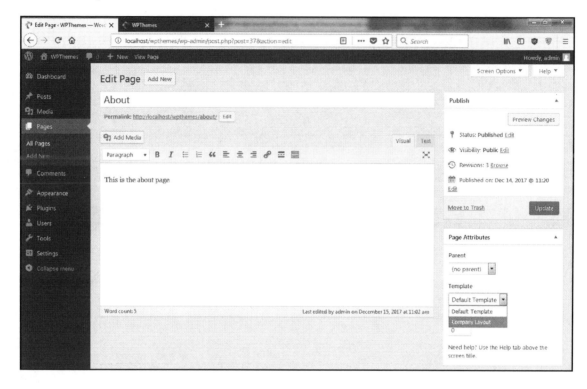

I actually want to put some text in front of it, though. We'll say `Call Us`:

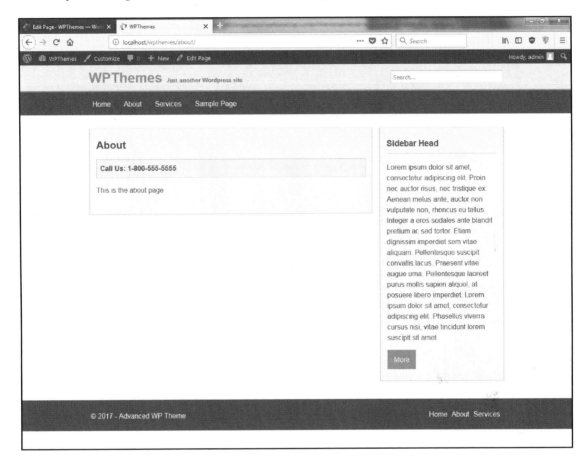

If we go to **Services**, you'll not see it because we didn't choose that template. However, I actually do want it for **Services**, so we'll simply go into the `Services` page and select **Company Layout**. Now, that should also have the phone number:

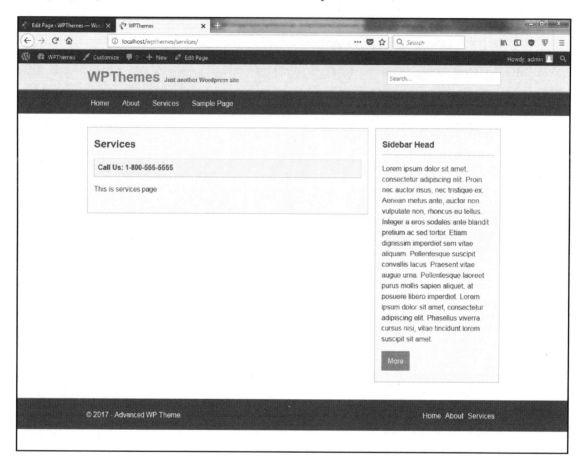

So the next thing that I want to show you is how we can create a submenu. What I mean by this is that if we have, let's say, the **About** page, the parent page, and in it we have child pages—I had put an **FAQ** page and an **Our Team** page under the **About** page. Now my goal is to have links on the **About** page for the child pages, and this is not just for the **About** page but any page that has a child. There are quite a few things that we have to do to accomplish this. Let's go to `page.php` and remove **Company Layout** from the **About** page. So, it shouldn't have the phone number anymore.

In `page.php`, let's go right under the `<article>` tag and say `<?php wp_list_pages();
?>`, as shown in the following code block:

```
<article class="page">
<?php wp_list_pages(); ?>
<h2><?php the_title(); ?></h2>
<p class="phone">1-800-555-5555</p>
<?php the_content(); ?>
</article>
```

Let's see what this does:

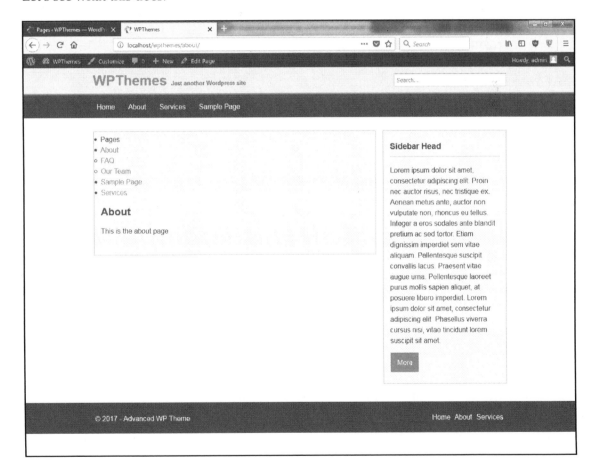

We can see that it's listing all of the pages that we have on our WordPress site, which obviously isn't what we want. Pay no attention to the style yet because we'll get to that after we get the functionality. We only want to get the About page and its child pages. So we'll go to the `page.php` file, and right above `wp_list_pages()` we'll say `<?php`. We'll create a variable called `args` and set that to an array. We'll then say `child_of`. Now there's no core function to get the parent, so we'll actually create a function called `get_top_parent()`. Then we also want to say `title_li` and set that to nothing. I'll explain that in a bit, but right now, we'll put our `args` variable right in `wp_list_pages()`:

```
<article class="page">
<?php
    $args = array(
        'child_of' => get_top_parent(),
        'title_li' => ''
    );
?>
<?php wp_list_pages($args); ?>
<h2><?php the_title(); ?></h2>
<p class="phone">1-800-555-5555</p>
<?php the_content(); ?>
</article>
```

If we go ahead and reload, we'll get an error, because there's no function called `get_top_parent()`. So let's go into `functions.php` and down at the bottom, create a function called `get_top_parent()`. We'll make the `post` object available to us by saying `global $post`. Then, we'll say `if($post->post_parent)`, and we'll create a variable called `$ancestors` and set it to `get_post_ancestors()`. We'll then pass in `$post->ID`. Now we'll say `return $ancestors` and we want the 0 index; then, under the `if` statement, say `return $post->ID`:

```
function get_top_parent(){
    global $post;
    if($post->post_parent){
        $ancestors = get_post_ancestors($post->ID);
        return $ancestors[0];
    }

    return $post->ID;
}
```

Now save this and reload:

Now you can see that we are only getting the child pages of the **About** page, which is **FAQ** and **Our Team**. Now we also want the **About** link to show up in here as well because we can go to **FAQ**, but we can't get back to **About** unless we use the main menu. So let's go back to page.php and inside the <article> tag, we'll create a <ul> tag. Above the <ul> tag, we'll create a <nav> tag and give it a class of both nav and sub-nav. Now under the <ul> tag, I'll put a <span> tag and give it a class of parent-link. Inside it, we'll place an <a> tag, which will go to <?php echo get_the_permalink(); ?>. We'll pass in the get_top_parent() function there. Then, for the link text we'll say <?php echo the_title(); ?>:

```
<nav class="nav sub-nav">
    <ul>
        <span class="parent-link"><a href="<?php echo
            get_the_permalink(get_top_parent()); ?>"><?php
            echo get_the_title(get_top_parent()); ?></a>
        </span>
        <?php
            $args = array(
                'child_of' => get_top_parent(),
                'title_li' => ''
            );
        ?>
        <?php wp_list_pages($args); ?>
    </ul>
</nav>
```

Let's save this and take a look:

Now we just have **About**. We can navigate using the menu here. However, if we go to **Sample Page** or any other page, it's going to still have this even though there's no child links. So, we'll create another short function in the `functions.php` file and call `page_is_parent`. Then, we'll say `global $post` and set `$pages` equal to `get_pages()`, and in here, we'll say `'child_of='` and concatenate the post ID. Next, we'll say `return` and then, we want the number of pages, so we'll `count($pages)`:

```
function page_is_parent(){
    global $post;

    $pages = get_pages('child_of='.$post->ID);
    return count($pages);
}
```

If the page count is more than zero, then we know that it's a parent. So let's go back to `page.php` and right above the `<nav>` tag, we'll put an `if` statement, which will end below the `<nav>` tag. We'll see if it's a parent `page_is_parent()`, or if there's any children `$post->post_parent is > 0`, then we'll do what follows:

```
<?php if(page_is_parent() || $post->post_parent > 0): ?>
<nav class="nav sub-nav">
  <ul>
    <span class="parent-link"><a href="<?php echo
        get_the_permalink(get_top_parent()); ?>"><?php
        echo get_the_title(get_top_parent()); ?></a>
    </span>
    <?php
        $args = array(
            'child_of' => get_top_parent(),
            'title_li' => ''
        );
    ?>
```

```
        <?php wp_list_pages($args); ?>
    </ul>
</nav>
<?php endif; ?>
```

Let's save that and then go back to **Sample Page**. We can see that menu is now gone, but if we go to **About** it's still there, because it has the child pages.

So everything is working correctly.

Now I just want to fix the display; I want it to move it and make it appear a little better. To do this, let's go to our style sheet and say .sub-nav. We'll then place some margin on the top, floating it to the right and setting it to 300px wide. Then we'll float ul to the right. Next, the parent link, which in this case is **About**; we'll float this to left and make it black, bold, and add a border to the right. Then, we'll make the parent link black, and we'll use current_page_item, because whatever page we're on, we want that to be bold:

```
.sub-nav{
  margin-top:10px;
  float:right;
  width:300px;
}

.sub-nav ul{
  float:right;
}

.sub-nav .parent-link{
  font-weight: bold;
  color:#000;
  float:left;
  margin-right:20px;
  padding-right:20px;
  border-right:1px solid #009acd;
}

.sub-nav .parent-link a{
  font-weight: bold;
  color:#000;
}

.sub-nav .current_page_item{
  font-weight: bold;
}
```

Let's save this and see what that looks like:

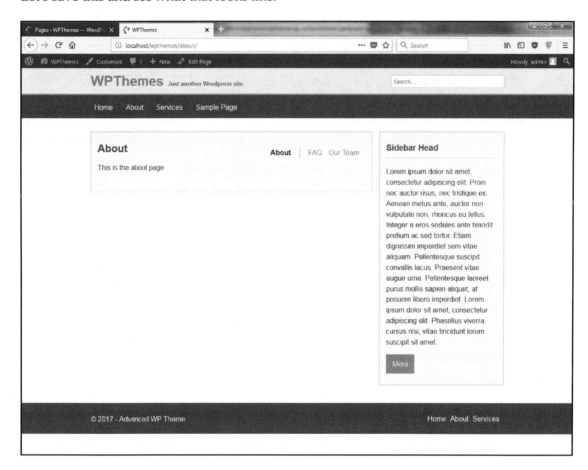

You can see that we have **About**, and if we go to **FAQ** that stays bold; if we go to **Our Team** even that's bold. This looks a lot better.

Next, we'll clear the float. To do this, we'll go to page.php, and under </nav> we'll add <div class="clr">. Then, we'll go to our style sheet and add .clr and say clear:both:

```
.clr{
    clear:both;
}
```

So now we see that it's above the title on the page:

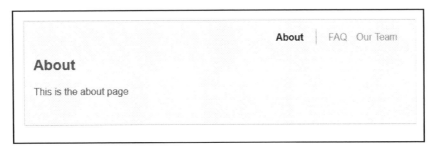

We did quite a bit in this section.

We set up our pages, and we saw how to create custom pages, custom templates, and also, how to create a sub navigation. In the next section, we'll get into widgets.

Working with Theme Widgets

In this section, we'll take a look at widgets.

Right now, we have a sidebar, but this is just static content in our php file. So we want this to come from the widget system. Also, we should be able to add multiple widgets in the sidebar. Now, on the blog page, and on any other page, this is going to be the only widget aside from a custom Home page that we'll create later on. However, we will add those positions in our functions file.

So, let's open up functions.php, and go right under the after_theme_setup action; this will be to set up widget locations. We'll create a function, call it init_widgets() and it will take an id; then, we'll say register_sidebar. Now, even though this is called register_sidebar, this is used with all widget positions, not just a sidebar. It takes in an array and it's going to take a name; this happens to be Sidebar, but it could be anything. Then, we'll also say before_widget and after_widget. Also, we'll say before_title and after_title of the widget:

```
add_action('after_setup_theme', 'adv_theme_support');

//Widget Locations
function init_widgets($id){
    register_sidebar(array(
        'name' => 'Sidebar',
        'id' => 'sidebar',
```

```
            'before_widget' => '',
            'after_widget' => '',
            'before_title' => '',
            'after_title' => ''
    ));
}
```

So, basically, these will be HTML tags that we want. If we say index.php and look at the sidebar, it has <div> with the class of block:

```
<div class="side">
    <div class="block">
    <h3>Sidebar Head</h3>
```

Now I don't want to add this div element in functions.php; so let's put it in index.php and <div class="block">. Let's also add a class called side-widget and, after widget, we'll close that </div> element. For the title, I'll put <h3>:

```
'before_widget' => '<div class="block side-widget">',
'after_widget'  => '</div>',
'before_title'  => '<h3>',
'after_title'   => '</h3>'
```

Let's save this and then go into index.php. We'll take out everything that's in this side div element and check to see whether there are any widgets in that position. To do this, we'll say if(is_active_sidebar) and then pass in the widget ID, which is sidebar. Then we'll say <?php dynamic_sidebar(); ?> and pass in the ID, sidebar:

```
<div class="side">
    <?php if(is_active_sidebar('sidebar')) : ?>
        <?php dynamic_sidebar('sidebar'); ?>
    <?php endif; ?>
</div>
```

If we look at the index page, nothing's there because we haven't added any widgets:

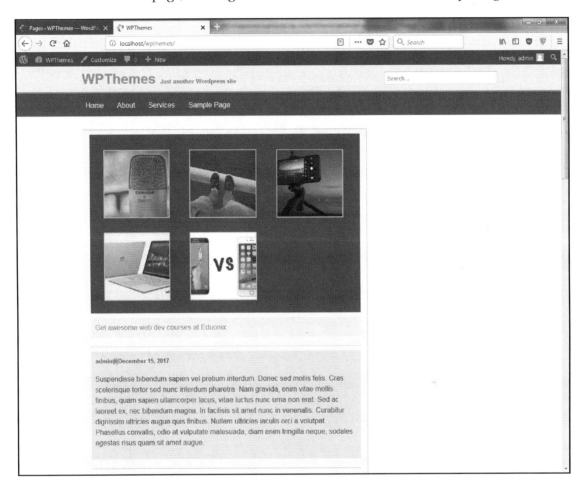

Now we'll need to replace all of the static sidebar code. Let's copy it; we'll start with `archive.php`. Then, we'll just paste that in. We'll go to `page.php`. Of course, you don't need to have a sidebar with all these pages: `search`, `single`, and `company-template`, but we're going to.

Now, we'll go to our backend and then to **Appearance**:

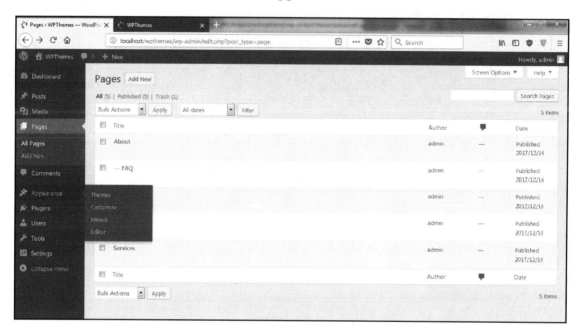

Now see how there's no widget. We need to initialize it, so back to `functions.php`, and then, right under `init_widgets()` we need to say `add_action()`. Now the hook we want to use is `widgets_init`, and then we just want to put the name of our function, which is `init_widgets`:

```
add_action('widgets_init', 'init_widgets');
```

Let's go back to our backend, reload, and now under **Appearance**, you should be able to go to **Widgets**:

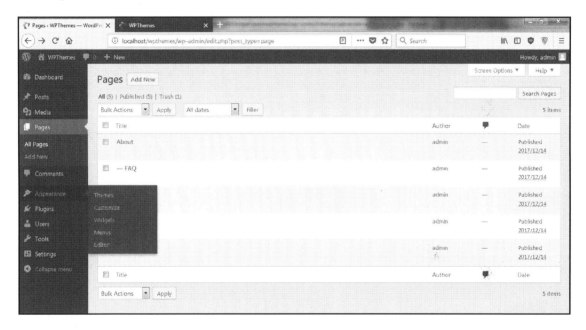

Now we'll add a custom **Text** widget, and let's just put title; we'll say `My Text Widget`. Then, I'll just paste a sentence or two in **Content**, and click on **Save**:

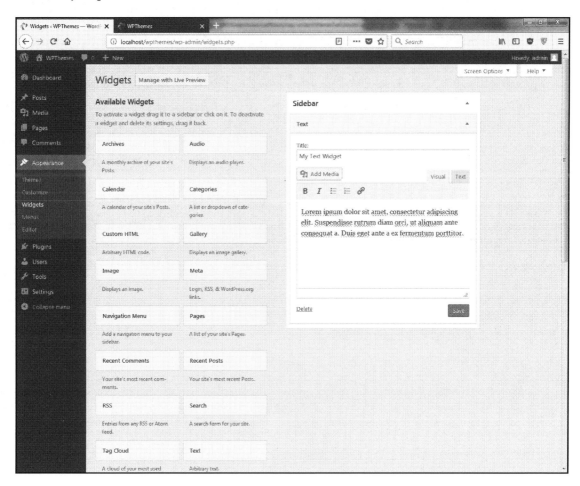

Now go back to our frontend and reload:

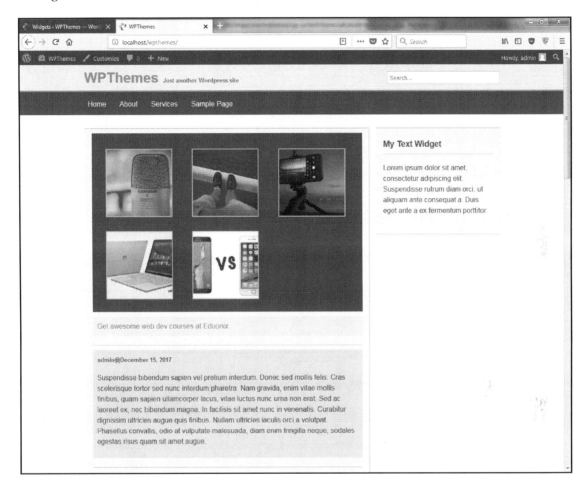

So this is coming from the **Text** widget.

Let's add a button in here as well, just for looks. Let's also put two line breaks. You can put whatever you like in a custom **Text** widget:

Now, another thing that we could do is to add some kind of dynamic widget, like, let's say, `Categories`.

Let's take that **Categories** widget, put it in **Sidebar**, and we'll save it. Let's go take a look:

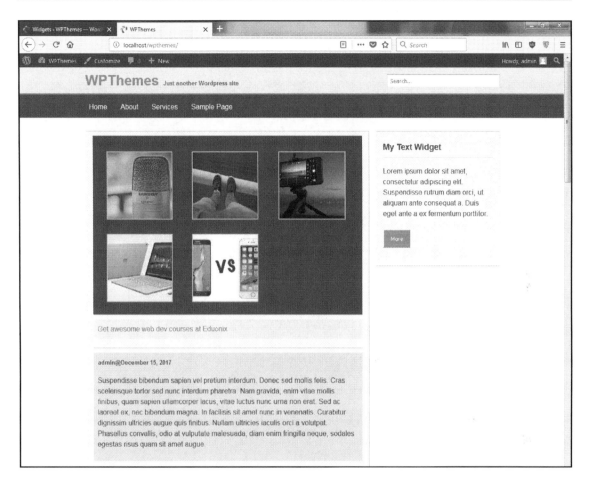

I want to make this look a little better, which we can do that with CSS. Let's go to the bottom and say .side-widget. I'll add margin-bottom: 20px, that will move it down a little. Then, to do the list items, we'll say list-style:none; we'll give it line-height of 2.1em, and for border-bottom, we'll do dotted, with the color gray:

```
.side-widget{
    margin-bottom: 20px;
}

.side-widget li{
    list-style: none;
    line-height: 2.1em;
    border-bottom: 1px dotted #ccc;
}
```

Save this.

Now, it looks a lot better:

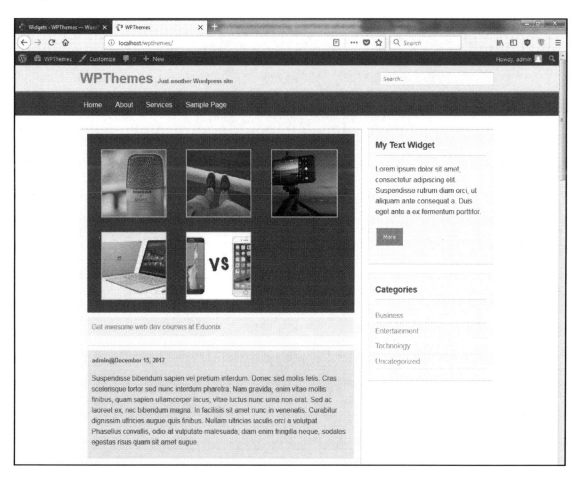

We can also put, let's say, `Recent Posts`, and change this to 3:

We actually didn't give a title for the gallery. So, let's just say `Photo Gallery`:

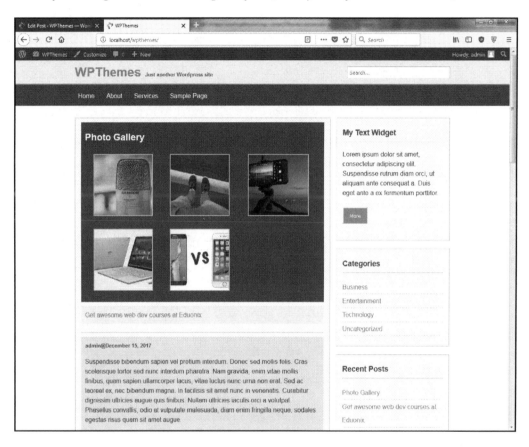

Now, I'll add the rest of the widgets into `functions.php`, or the rest of the widget positions, even though we'll not do it in this section. In the next section, we'll create a custom home page with those widgets.

We'll go right under `init_widgets()`, and copy and paste it four more times. So `Sidebar`, then we'll enter the `Showcase` area and change the class name. Then we'll have `Box 1`, `Box 2`, and `Box 3`. This will have a class of `box` and `box1`. I'll actually replace these two with `box` and `box1`. In next `register_sidebar` we'll change `name` to `Box 2`, and change `name` in final `register_sidebar` to `3`. Save it, and now if we were to go back into the widgets area, you can now see that we have those widgets. At least, we have the positions. If we put something in them now, nothing's going to happen because we don't have them in our template.

Custom home page

Now we'll create a custom home page and then add widgets to the positions that we added.

Let's create a new file and save this as `front-page.php`. If we reload the home page it goes completely blank because it's looking at `front-page.php` file. So I'll copy what we have in `page.php` and paste it in `front-page.php`.

Now let's reload:

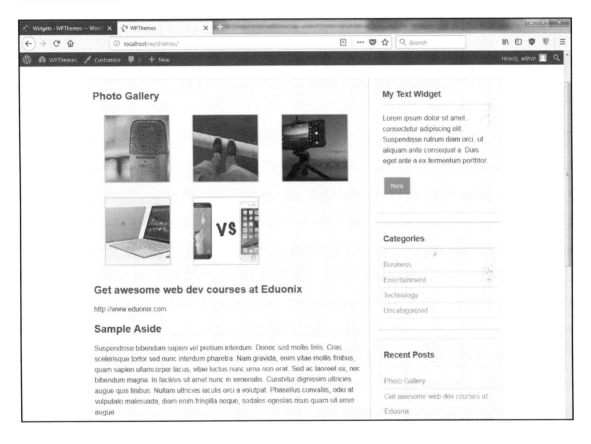

This doesn't look very good because we're showing the posts with just the page formatting. So let's go into pages, and create two new pages. We will call one Home; we'll just say This is the homepage, click on **Publish**, and similarly create a new one called Blog and **Publish**:

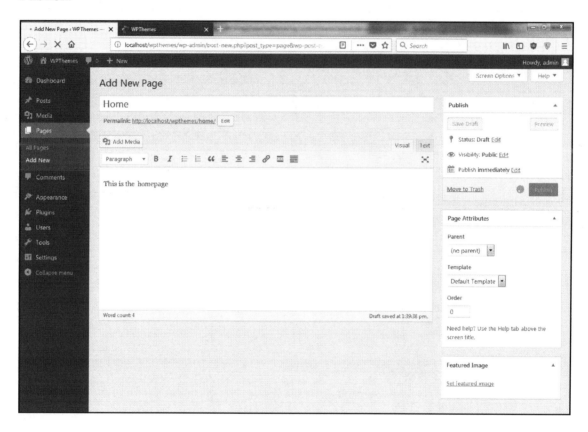

Now we'll go to **Settings** and then to **Reading**:

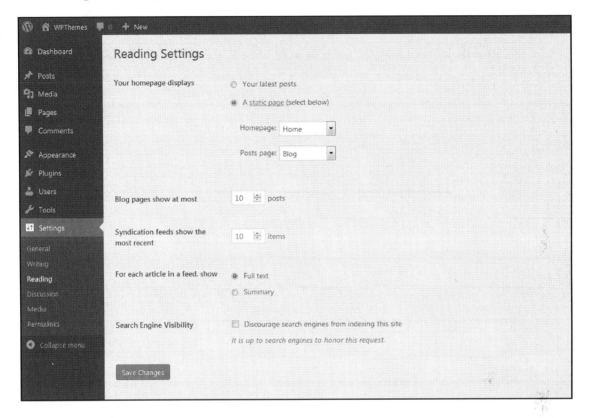

In **Your homepage displays**, we'll set **A static page**; for **Homepage**, we'll choose **Home**; for **Post page** we'll choose **Blog,** and then we'll save it.

Now we'll go to **Appearance** and then **Menus**:

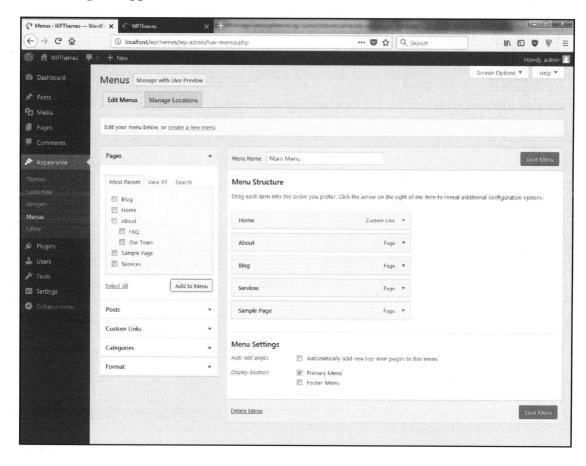

Let's go to tick **Blog** and click on **Add to Menu**. We'll put that right between **About** and **Services** and save it. Now if we go back and reload, we get the **Home** page, and if we click on **Blog**, that brings us to the blog:

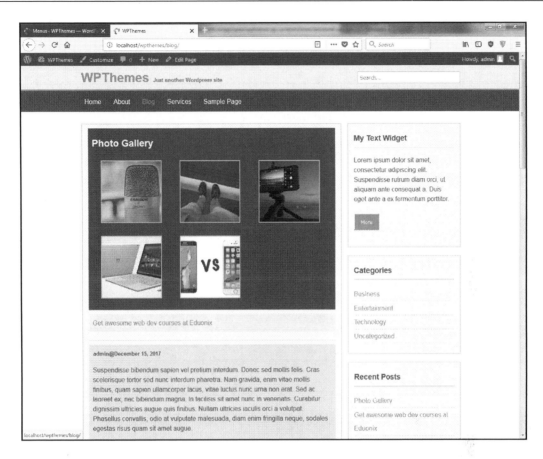

So, this is how we can handle that. Now we want to make this look a little different, I want to have a **Showcase** widget. Also, I want to get rid of the sidebar and have three boxes and three different widgets under this content. Let's go to `front-page.php` and get rid of the `main` class, highlighted in the following code block, because that's what limits this to this width:

```
<div class="container content">
    <div class="main block">
        <?php while(have_posts()) : the_post(); ?>
```

Then, we'll completely get rid of this `side` div element:

```
    </div>

    <div class="side">
        <?php if(is_active_sidebar('sidebar')) : ?>
            <?php dynamic_sidebar('sidebar'); ?>
```

```
        <?php endif; ?>
    </div>
</div>

<?php get_footer(); ?>
```

We'll look at it now; there's no more sidebar:

Let's do our **Showcase** widget, and see where it is going to go; right under `<div class="container content">`. I'll copy from `index.php` and grab the code shown in the following code block. We'll paste that in and then we just want to change the ID from `sidebar` to `showcase`; we'll do the same thing for `dynamic_sidebar()`. So, this takes care of the **Showcase** widget:

```
<?php if(is_active_sidebar('showcase')) : ?>
    <?php dynamic_sidebar('showcase'); ?>
<?php endif; ?>
```

Now we'll also want our three boxes, which we'll put down right above the last `div` element. So I'll paste this in three times. This one will be `box1`, `box2`, and `box3`. We'll save this:

```
<?php if(is_active_sidebar('box1')) : ?>
    <?php dynamic_sidebar('box1'); ?>
<?php endif; ?>
```

```php
<?php if(is_active_sidebar('box2')) : ?>
    <?php dynamic_sidebar('box2'); ?>
<?php endif; ?>

<?php if(is_active_sidebar('box2')) : ?>
    <?php dynamic_sidebar('box2'); ?>
<?php endif; ?>
</div>
```

Now let's go to the backend, to **Appearance**, and then **Widgets**:

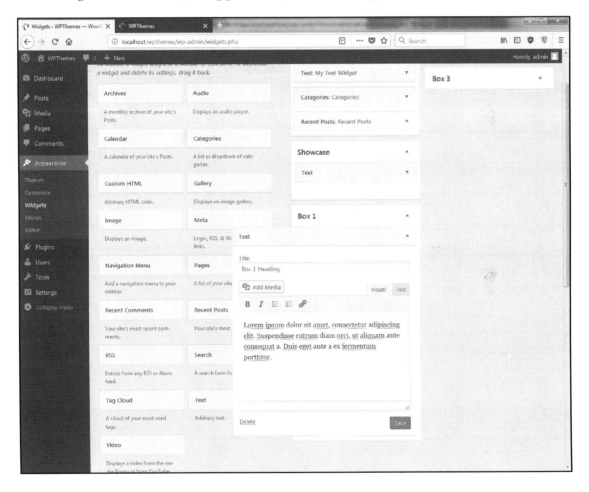

We'll grab **Text** and put that right in **Showcase**, and then we'll paste some code in the **Content** textbox; well, not some code, but just some HTML. We'll save this.

Now we'll grab another **Text**, put that in **Box 1**, and put a title in here, let's say `Box 1 Heading`. Then I'll just paste some sample text in there. Let's do the same thing for **Box 2** and for **Box 3**.

Let's do something different. We'll grab the **Recent Posts** widget and put that in there, and set that **Title** to `Latest News`:

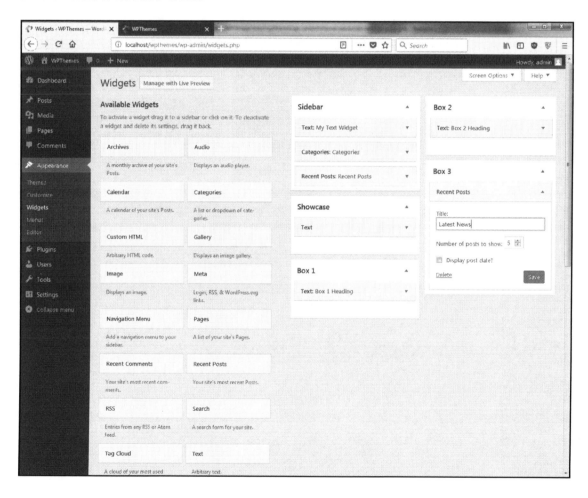

We'll save this, go to the frontend, and reload. Now we have our widgets.

They don't look too good, we need to style them. So let's go to `style.css`. We'll paste in the styling for showcase first. We'll give it a background, padding of 40px, and `margin-bottom`, and align everything to the center. Let's do the same thing for h1:

```
.showcase{
    background:#e0eefc;
    padding:40px;
    margin-bottom:30px;
    text-align: center;
}

.showcase h1{
    text-align: center;
}
```

Now for the `box` class, we set it to `32%` width, `float:left;` then for h3, we center it, add a background and some padding:

```
.box{
    width:32%;
    float:left;
    padding:0 6px;
}

.box h3{
    text-align: center;
    background:#009acd;
    padding:5px;
    color:#fff;
}
```

Let's save this and reload:

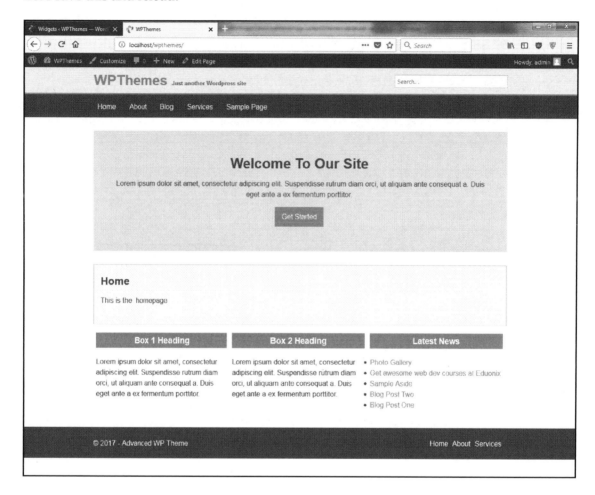

There's our **Home** page. You can see that we have **Latest News**; we can click on there and go to the different posts. There's Gallery and Blog Posts, and just to make this look a little better, I'll go to where we put `side-widget li` and add `.box li`:

```
.side-widget li, .box li{
    list-style: none;
    line-height: 2.1em;
    border-bottom: 1px dotted #ccc;
}
```

Now that looks better. So let's actually set the number of posts to be seen to 3.

This isn't the best looking style, but the point of this whole project isn't the design or style, or to create something beautiful, it's to get you familiar with the functionality of creating a WordPress theme.

We'll have one more section and that's going to be for the comments, because right now in our blog, if we go to a regular post there's no comment functionality.

Comment Functionality

In this section, we'll add the custom comment functionality.

Let's open up `single.php` and go right under `endif`. We'll say `<?php comments_template(); ?>`:

```
        <?php endif; ?>

        <?php comments_template(); ?>
    </div>
```

Let's save this and reload. We have our comment section now:

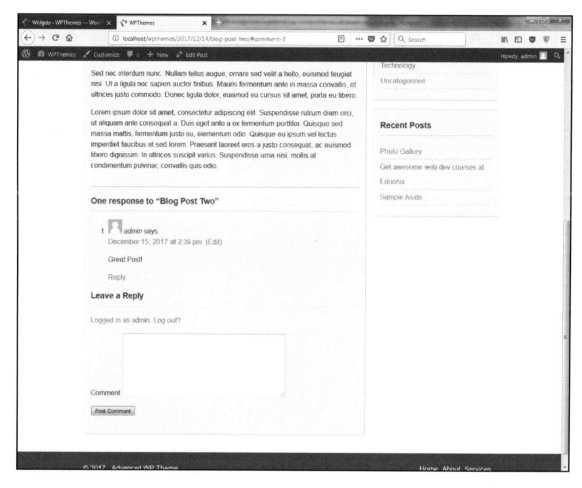

Let's say `Great Post`, click on **Post Comment**, and it works!

Now this will work as far as functionality goes, but it doesn't look too good, so I want to show you how we can customize this.

We'll create a new page, or a new file, and we'll call this `comments.php`. If we go back now and reload you'll see there's nothing here, it's reading from this file; if we say `Test` and reload, we get **Test**:

So it's up to us to customize how we want this to work.

There's actually some helpful code in the documentation at `https://codex.wordpress.org/Function_Reference/wp_list_comments` for our `wp_list_comments`, and this is what we want.

In the `comments.php` file enter the following code:

```php
<?php $args = array(
        'walker'            => null,
        'max_depth'         => '',
        'style'             => 'ul',
        'callback'          => null,
```

```
              'end-callback'        => null,
              'type'                => 'all',
              'reply_text'          => 'Reply',
              'page'                => '',
              'per_page'            => '',
              'avatar_size'         => 32,
              'reverse_top_level'   => null,
              'reverse_children'    => '',
              'format'              => 'html5', // or 'xhtml' if no 'HTML5' theme
                                               // support
              'short_ping'          => false,  // @since 3.6
              'echo'                => true    // boolean, default is true
    ); ?>

    <?php wp_list_comments($args, $comments); ?>
```

Let's first of all put an `<h2>` tag and say `Comments`.

We can create an arguments array. I'll grab that. Obviously, we don't need most of this stuff, but it's not going to hurt us to keep it in there; you'll see a lot of this is set to null, just in case you wanted to change anything later on. I'll change `avatar_size` to `80`, make it a little bigger. The rest we can leave. These arguments will now get plugged into the `wp_list_comments()` function. Next, we'll pass in `args` and `comments`. So, that takes care of the comments. Now we need the form so that can also take some arguments.

From the bottom I'll grab this code, paste that in; it just needs a `php` tag. We'll set another argument array, `comments_args`; actually let's call this `form_args`, and then change `comments_args` to `form_args`. Let's set the label of the submit button, what you want in the `title_reply` field, comment after, `comment_notes_after`, and then the `comment_field` itself; in this case, they give you a paragraph with the class of `comment-form-comment` as the label. I don't think we really want to change anything here. For the text area, we'll add in a couple of attributes; we'll set `cols` to `45` and `rows` to `8`:

```
    <?php
    $form_args = array(
          // change the title of send button
          'label_submit'=>'Send',
          // change the title of the reply section
          'title_reply'=>'Write a Reply or Comment',
          // remove "Text or HTML to be displayed after the set of comment
          // fields"
          'comment_notes_after' => '',
          // redefine your own textarea (the comment body)
          'comment_field' => '<p class="comment-form-comment">
          <label for="comment">' . _x( 'Comment', 'noun' ) . '</label>
```

```
        <br /><textarea id="comment" name="comment" cols="45" rows="8"
aria-required="true">
        </textarea></p>',
); ?>

comment_form($form_args);
```

We'll save it and reload. This is good:

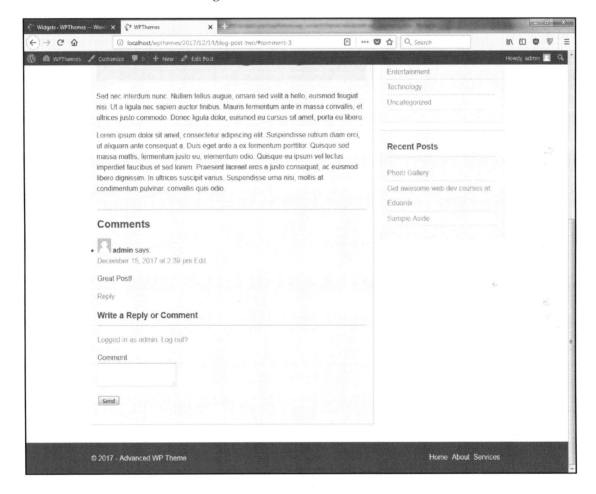

The rest of it we'll do in CSS.

We'll now go to `style.css`. Let's go down to the bottom and paste this code in; this is going to be `comment-body`, we'll give it a `border`, `margin`, and `padding`. We also want the meta which is this area here, the avatar, and then the date and all that stuff; let's paste that in:

```
.comment-body{
  border:#ccc 1px solid;
  margin-bottom:10px;
  padding:20px 10px;
}
```

We'll add a dark background, some padding, and for the image, I'll float it to the left, add the time and some margin to that. Next, we'll format reply-link to make it look like a button, and then the form itself:

```
.comment-meta{
  background:#333;
  color:#fff;
  padding:10px;
  overflow:auto;
}

.comment-meta img{
  float:left;
  margin-right:10px;
}

.comment-meta time{
  margin-left:12px;
}
```

For the form input and the text area, we'll just set width to `100%`, and we'll add some padding, border, and stuff like that:

```
.comment-reply-link{
  background:#009acd;
  color:#fff;
  display:inline-block;
  padding:10px 15px;
}

.comment-form input,.comment-form textarea{
  width:100%;
  padding:3px;
  border:#ccc 1px solid;
  margin-bottom:20px;
}
```

```
.comment-form input{
    height:30px;
}
```

Let's save this and reload, we can see that it looks a lot better:

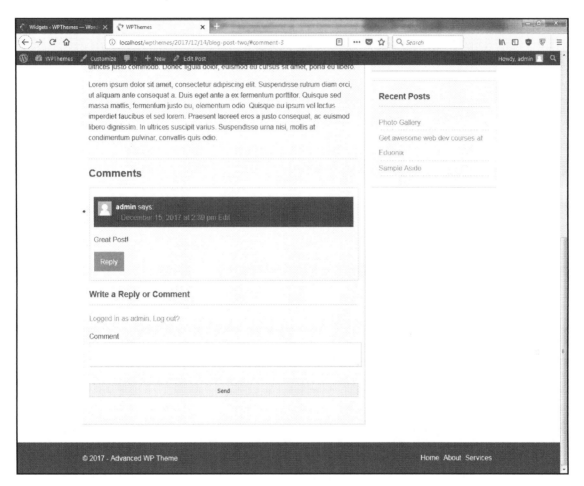

Let's type something here. If we're logged out, then we also have the **Name**, **Email**, and **Website** fields:

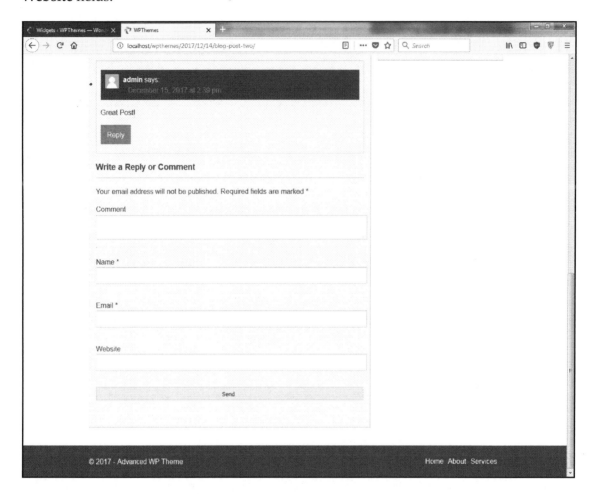

I think that looks pretty good. It looks a lot better than the default. Let's say `This is a great article` and click on **Send**:

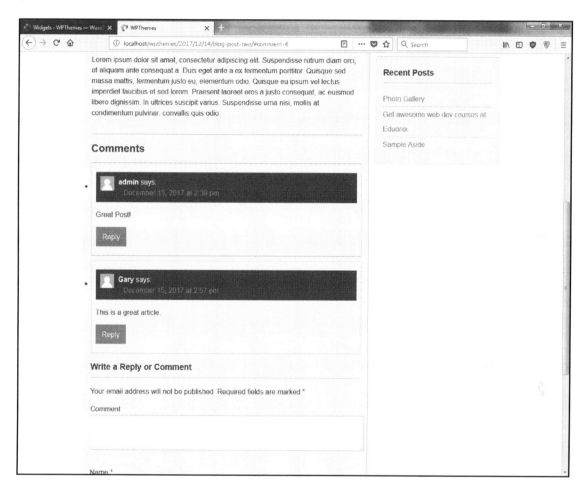

Since we weren't logged in, it just says it's awaiting moderation, and that's good; it's working great!

Summary

Great! So that was pretty much it. The purpose of this project wasn't to build a beautiful theme, it was to really get you familiar with the different files that we need to create the syntax, the different functions, and things like that.

We saw different post formats and created design using HTML and CSS. We created a WordPress theme by learning how to display blog posts, single posts, custom archive pages, and different post formats. We also saw how to add an image to the post and dealt with pages, custom templates, and sub navigation. We also worked around theme widgets, custom homepages, and the comment functionality.

So, hopefully you enjoyed this chapter.

In our next chapter, we will build a WordPress theme for the photo gallery.

3
Building a WordPress Theme for Photo Gallery

In this chapter, we'll build a WordPress theme for a photo gallery. We'll use just the core WordPress post system, and we'll not need any kind of third-party photo gallery. The following image is what it's going to look like; it's called *PhotoGenik*. This is the theme we are going to work on:

As shown in the preceding screenshot, you can see on the home page we have some images. If we hover over them we get a nice effect, and if we click on one it brings us to the single image page where it has a little animation that comes in. It also gives us the title, description, and then we have some meta info as shown in the following screenshot:

On the left-hand side at the top in the preceding screenshot, we have the core categories module. When we click on that, and you can see it only shows the pictures from that category, and they have a nice fade-in effect. We also have the **Search** bar on the right-hand side at the top. In the search box we can just type in, let's say one of the titles of the images, and search; that particular image will come up.

For this project, we are going to be using the W3.CSS framework (`https://www.w3schools.com/w3css/default.asp`), which is pretty similar to Bootstrap. It's really easy to work with, and it provides a lot of nice-looking elements that you can see on the W3.CSS page. The animations that we have is actually coming from this framework, and there are some JavaScript widgets that we'll get into.

In the backend (refer to the following screenshot), if we look at our **Posts**, you can see we have each photo has its own post:

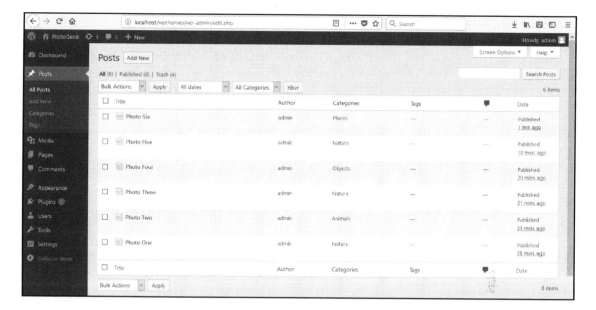

If we click on the post, we'll find what we're using is the featured image:

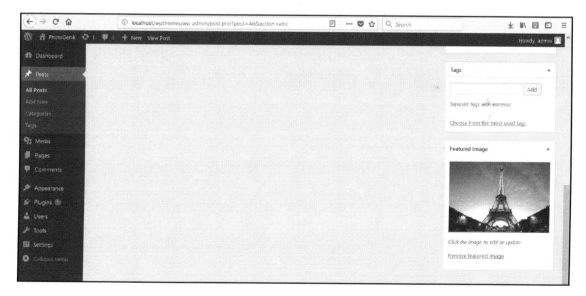

So all we have to do is upload a feature image, give it a title, description, and choose the **Gallery** format, and it'll show up:

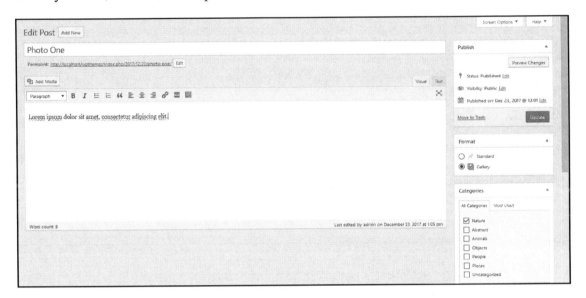

In our case, we'll have a custom gallery post format, and you can also use the standard format for just regular posts as well.

That's what we'll be doing. Let's go ahead and get started.

Creating the layout of the home page in HTML and CSS

Now before we get into building a photo gallery theme for WordPress, we'll create the layout in HTML. As explained in the introduction, we'll use the W3.CSS framework to create this layout. For this, first we'll create a new folder and call it `photogenik_html`:

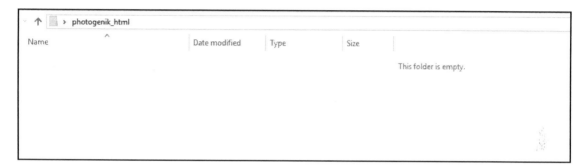

Next, inside the folder, we'll create a couple of files and folders. We'll create the `index.html`, `style.css`, and `single.html` files and also have a folder called `images`:

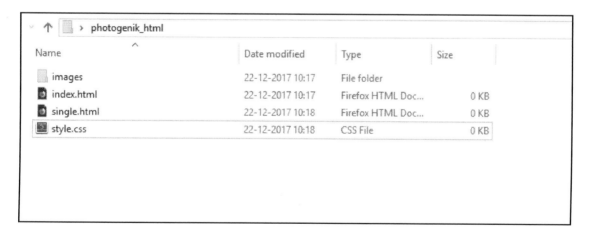

The `single.html` file is going to represent the single image. Once we click on one of the images in the gallery, it'll take us into this folder.

Creating the HTML layout

Now, let's open up the `index.html` file with Sublime Text, or of course, whichever editor you'd like, and we'll get a base HTML structure in the editor:

```
<!DOCTYPE html>
<html>
<head>
  <title></title>
</head>
<body>
</body>
</html>
```

Now, in this HTML layout first, we'll add `PhotoGenik` in the title:

```
<!DOCTYPE html>
<html>
<head>
  <title>PhotoGenik</title>
</head>
<body>
</body>
</html>
```

Since we're using the W3.CSS framework, we have to include the stylesheet. So we're just going to use the CDN here. For this, we'll add the following style sheet link next to the title in the HTML layout:

```
<link rel="stylesheet" href="http://www.w3schools.com/lib/w3.css">
```

We also want to include our own CSS file as shown here:

```
<link rel="stylesheet" href="style.css">
```

So that's `style.css`. Now that's all we need in the head.

Creating the header

The next thing we want to do is to create the header. To create this, follow these steps:

1. First, we'll use the HTML5 `<header>` tag as shown here:

   ```
   <!DOCTYPE html>
   <html>
   ```

```
<head>
  <title>PhotoGenik</title>
  <link rel="stylesheet"
        href="http://www.w3schools.com/lib/w3.css">
  <link rel="stylesheet" href="style.css">
</head>
<body>
  <header>

  </header>
</body>
</html>
```

 Some of this HTML layout might change once we are actually building the WordPress theme, just to adapt to the WordPress conventions.

2. Next, we'll give this header a class. If we take a look at the documentation page (`https://www.w3schools.com/w3css/default.asp`) for the framework and go to **W3.CSS Containers**, it should have headers class as shown here:

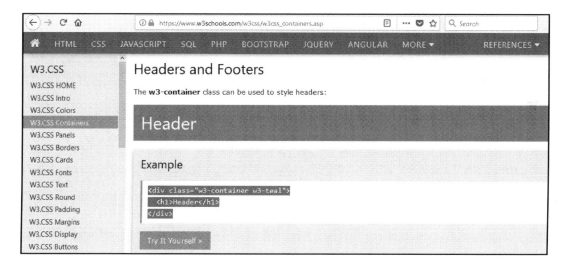

3. Now to make the header a class, copy the header class syntax from the containers documentation page (`https://www.w3schools.com/w3css/w3css_containers.asp`) and paste it in our HTML header as shown here:

```
<body>
  <header class="w3-container w3-teal">
    <h1>Heading</h1>
  </header>
</body>
```

4. Let's make sure that everything is actually working so far. For this, we'll open the `index.html` file with Chrome, and as shown in the following screenshot, we'll find our `Heading`:

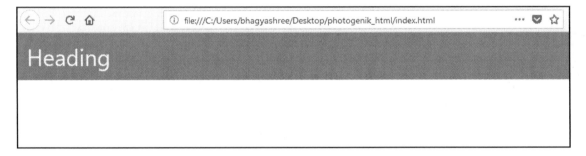

So we have our heading. In the next subsection, we will use the grid system.

Adding the title and search box

If you've used Bootstrap, Foundation, or any one of those CSS HTML frameworks, then you know what the grid system is. Basically, the **grid system** gives us 12 columns across, and we can set certain divs or certain elements to span across a certain amount of columns.

If we go to our documentation page and then go to **W3.CSS Grid** (`https://www.w3schools.com/w3css/w3css_grid.asp`), you'll see the syntax we'd need as shown in the following screenshot:

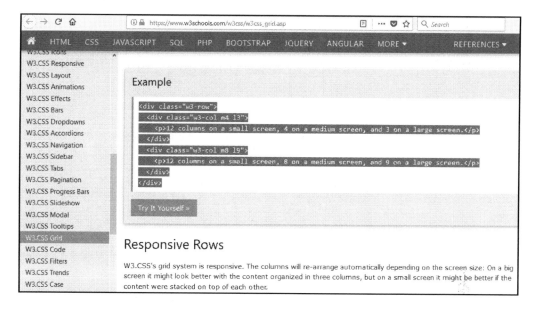

Copy the example row shown in the preceding screenshot, and paste this right in the header as shown here:

```
<body>
    <header class="w3-container w3-teal">
        <div class="w3-row">
            <div class="w3-col m4 l3">
                <p>12 columns on a small screen, 4  on a medium screen,
                and 3 on a large screen.</p>
            </div>
            <div class="w3-col m8 l9">
                <p>12 columns on a small screen, 8  on a medium screen,
                and 9 on a large screen.</p>
            </div>
        </div>
    </header>
</body>
```

Firstly, for the first w3-col class, we'll change l3 to l9 (this is for **large 9**). We use l9 for large screens and m4 for medium screens. However, here we'll just keep the same for both—9 columns. The second w3-col class will have m3 and l3 as shown in the following code:

```
<body>
    <header class="w3-container w3-teal">
        <div class="w3-row">
```

```
        <div class="w3-col m9 l9">
            <p>12 columns on a small screen, 4  on a medium screen,
            and 3 on a large screen.</p>
        </div>
        <div class="w3-col m3 l3">
            <p>12 columns on a small screen, 8  on a medium screen,
            and 9 on a large screen.</p>
        </div>
    </div>
  </header>
</body>
```

Next, we can get rid of the paragraphs inside of the w3-col classes as shown here:

```
<header class="w3-container w3-teal">
  <div class="w3-row">
    <div class="w3-col m9 l9">
    </div>
    <div class="w3-col m3 l3">
    </div>
  </div>
</header>
```

Inside the first w3-col class, we are going to add the heading, so this will be <h1> and say PhotoGenik, and put a <span> tag around the word Photo because we'll make that a different color:

```
<div class="w3-col m9 l9">
  <h1><span>Photo</span>Genik</h1>
</div>
```

Then inside of the second w3-col class, we'll have our input, and that's going to have its own class of w3-input. We'll give it a type of text and then give it a placeholder—Search...:

```
<div class="w3-col m3 l3">
  <input class="w3-input" type="text"
  placeholder="Search...">
</div>
```

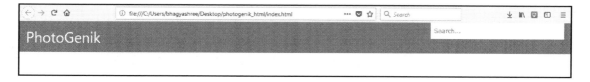

Shifting the search box

Now, I want to bring the search box down. For this, we'll go to our `style.css` file. In the `style.css` file, we'll add `header input` with `margin-top` of value 15px:

```
header input{
  margin-top:15px;
}
```

Now, reload our WordPress page and you can see our header as shown here:

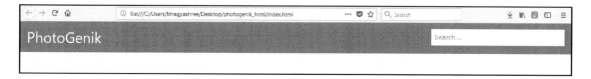

Adding the sidebar and main area

Next we want the sidebar and main area, so we'll use the grid for that as well. First, we'll look into the sidebar and then get into the main area.

Adding the sidebar

In the `index.html` file, copy the `w3-col` classes and put that down under the header as shown here:

```
    </header>
      <div class="w3-row">
        <div class="w3-col m9 l9">
          <h1><span>Photo</span>Genik</h1>
        </div>
        <div class="w3-col m3 l3">
          <input class="w3-input" type="text"
```

```
          placeholder="Search...">
        </div>
      </div>
    </header>
  </body>
</html>
```

Because we want the sidebar on the left, we'll switch the columns, and then we can just get rid of the content inside as shown here:

```
</header>
  <div class="w3-row">
    <div class="w3-col m3 l3">
    </div>
    <div class="w3-col m9 l9">
    </div>
  </div>
</body>
</html>
```

For the three columns (the first `w3-col` class in the preceding code), we'll add a list of categories. So let's add `<ul>` and give it a class of `w3-ul`:

```
<div class="w3-col m3 l3">
  <ul class="w3-ul">
  </ul>
</div>
```

Then inside `<ul>`, we'll have the `<li>` tags with links. The first one will say `Nature` and these are just going to be categories. Similarly, we'll add `Animals`, `Objects`, `People`, and `Abstract` as shown here:

```
<ul class="w3-ul">
  <li><a href="#">Nature</a></li>
  <li><a href="#">Animals</a></li>
  <li><a href="#">Objects</a></li>
  <li><a href="#">People</a></li>
  <li><a href="#">Abstract</a></li>
</ul>
```

Let's save this, take a look at the page, and we can see our categories:

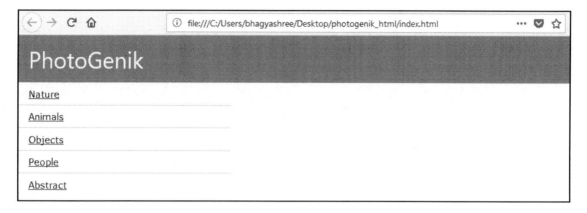

Changing the color of the background and text of the sidebar

Now we want the background to be black and the text to be white, so let's go to our stylesheet and just add some core styles there. The first thing we'll add is body, and we'll give it a background of black and a color of white:

```
body{
   background: #000;
   color: #fff;
}
```

Then for the links I want to take the underline away, so we'll add text-decoration: none. For the list items (li), we don't want to have any bullets so we'll add list-style: none. For the input, we want the text to be in a dark color, so let's add color: #333 as shown here:

```
a{
   text-decoration: none;
}
li{
   list-style: none;
}
input{
   color: #333;
}
```

Let's save this, and we can see the changes as follows:

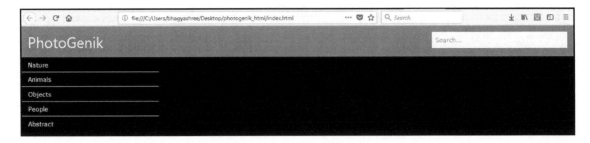

Adding the main area

For the main area, we'll put another grid inside of the present grid. We'll add three images in a row. In the index.html file, we'll copy the w3-row class with the columns and paste this inside of the second w3-col class in the header:

```
<div class="w3-col m9 l9">
  <div class="w3-row">
    <div class="w3-col m9 l9">
      <h1><span>Photo</span>Genik</h1>
    </div>
    <div class="w3-col m3 l3">
      <input class="w3-input" type="text"
      placeholder="Search...">
    </div>
  </div>
</div>
```

Next, we'll get rid of the <h1> and <input> content. Then we'll change both of the columns to m4 and l4 as shown here:

```
<div class="w3-col m9 l9">
  <div class="w3-row">
    <div class="w3-col m4 l4">
    </div>
    <div class="w3-col m4 l4">
    </div>
  </div>
</div>
```

We'll need one more column, so I'm going to copy one of the `w3-col` classes and paste that in as shown here:

```
<div class="w3-col m9 l9">
  <div class="w3-row">
    <div class="w3-col m4 l4">
    </div>
    <div class="w3-col m4 l4">
    </div>
    <div class="w3-col m4 l4">
    </div>
  </div>
</div>
```

Adding images to the column

Now, we have three columns, so we need an image inside there and then also text underneath the images. Now as far as the images go, you should have those in your project files. So, I have added some black and white images and they're named `1.jpg` through `6.jpg` as shown here:

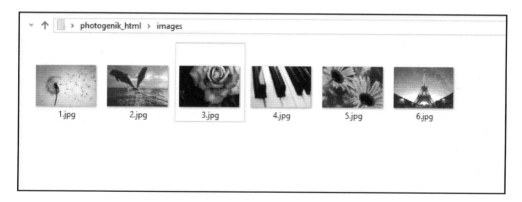

Let's go back to our code editor and add the `<image>` tag. We'll point to each one, so add `src` and then that's going to go to `images/1.jpg`. We'll also have a paragraph underneath with some sample text as shown here:

```
<div class="w3-row">
  <div class="w3-col m4 l4">
    <img src="images/1.jpg">
    <p>Lorem ipsum dolor sit amet,
    consectetur adipiscing elit.</p>
  </div>
```

We'll need to do this for all of our columns as shown here:

```
<div class="w3-row">
  <div class="w3-col m4 l4">
    <img src="images/1.jpg">
    <p>Lorem ipsum dolor sit amet,
    consectetur adipiscing elit.</p>
  </div>
  <div class="w3-col m4 l4">
    <img src="images/2.jpg">
    <p>Lorem ipsum dolor sit amet,
    consectetur adipiscing elit.</p>
  </div>
  <div class="w3-col m4 l4">
    <img src="images/3.jpg">
    <p>Lorem ipsum dolor sit amet,
    consectetur adipiscing elit.</p>
  </div>
</div>
```

We'll save it, reload our page, and can see the images as follows:

Now we need to set the width of these images to a 100% of their container because as shown in the preceding screenshot, they're busting out of their container. So in the `style.css` sheet, we'll add the image and set `width` to `100%`:

```
img{
  width:100%;
}
```

If we go and reload our page, we'll see the following:

These are all fit nice and neat. In order for us to get more images, we have to put in some more rows. In the `index.html` file, copy the three divs we have defined and just put that right underneath the previously added `<img>` tags. We'll then change the image source filenames to `4.jpg`, `5.jpg`, and `6.jpg`. We also want to center the text underneath the images as well. So in each `<div>` tag, we'll also going to add a class of `pic`, so that each picture div has its own class as shown here:

```
<div class="w3-col m4 l4 pic">
  <img src="images/4.jpg">
  <p>Lorem ipsum dolor sit amet,
  consectetur adipiscing elit.</p>
</div>
<div class="w3-col m4 l4 pic">
  <img src="images/5.jpg">
  <p>Lorem ipsum dolor sit amet,
  consectetur adipiscing elit.</p>
</div>
<div class="w3-col m4 l4 pic">
  <img src="images/6.jpg">
  <p>Lorem ipsum dolor sit amet,
  consectetur adipiscing elit.</p>
</div>
```

Now, in the `style.css`, we'll add `.pic` and `text-align: center`, as shown in this code, so that the text below the images look aligned:

```
.pic{
  text-align: center;
}
```

If we now go and reload our page, we can see in the following screenshot that we have six images and our text is aligned:

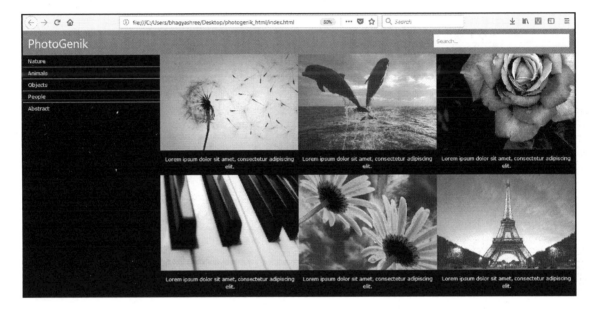

Adding a footer in the main area

Now down at the bottom of the page, we want a simple footer. To add this, in the `index.html` file, we'll go after the last div, add `<footer>`, and then add a paragraph. We'll add `PhotoGenik` and a copyright symbol 2017 as shown here:

```
<footer>
  <p>PhotoGenik &copy; 2017</p>
</footer>
</body>
```

Let's save this. In the stylesheet, add `footer` with the `text-align`, `margin-top`, and `border-top` properties set to appropriate values, as shown in the following code:

```
footer{
   text-align: center;
   margin-top: 40px;
   border-top: #333 solid 1px;
}
```

Save and reload the page, and now we have our footer as shown in the following screenshot:

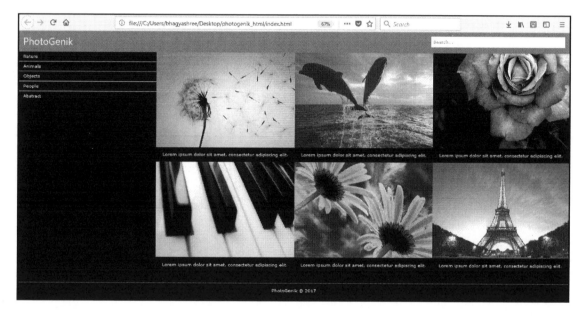

In the next section, we'll implement animation and also create our `single.html` page.

Implementing the animation and single.html page

In this section, we want to implement the animation, which is going to be very simple. We're using the W3.CSS framework that has built-in animation.

Let's take a look at the W3.CSS animation page (`https://www.w3schools.com/w3css/w3css_animate.asp`) as shown in the following screenshot. We can see the different types of animations:

- **Top**
- **Bottom**
- **Left**
- **Right**
- **Fade In**
- **Zoom**
- **Spin**

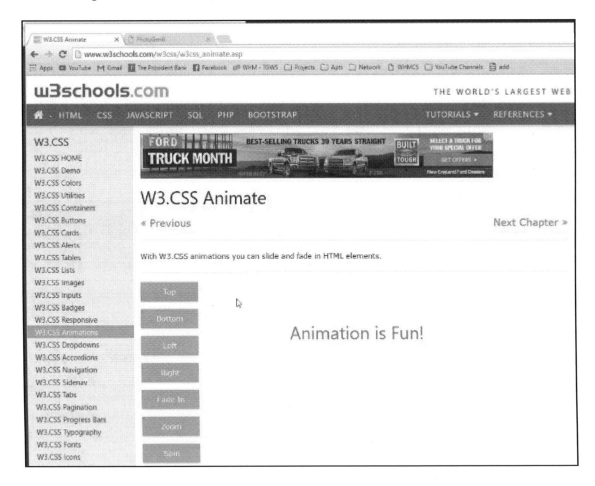

Implementing the Fade In animation

Now using the different type of animations, we want to change the theme of our WordPress home page. First, we want to fade in the photos on the home page. For this, we will need the fade in class shown in the following screenshot:

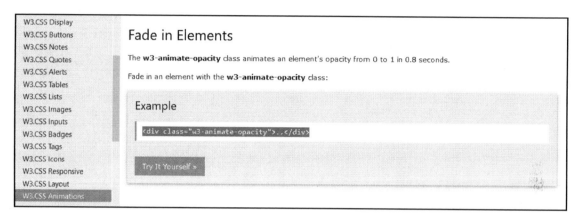

Let's copy `class="w3-animate-opacity"` and go to the `index.html` page, and on each `<image>` tag paste this in as shown here:

```
<div class="w3-col m9 19">
  <div class="w3-row">
    <div class="w3-col m4 14 pic">
      <img src="images/1.jpg" class="w3-animate-opacity">
      <p>Lorem ipsum dolor sit amet, consectetur adipiscing elit.</p>
    </div>
```

Let's refresh the home page, and you will see that the images just fade in.

Creating animation on the single page

Now, we will use an animation on the `single.html` page. Open the `single.html` file with the Sublime Text editor.

Next, we will link each of the images on the home page to the `single.html` page. We'll just link the first one here. In the `index.html` page, put the `<a>` tag that will go to `single.html` as shown in the following code:

```
<div class="w3-col m9 l9">
  <div class="w3-row">
    <div class="w3-col m4 l4 pic">
      <a href="single.html">
        <img src="images/1.jpg" class="w3-animate-opacity">
      </a>
    </div>
```

You could put this tag for the rest of the images if you want, but it doesn't really matter. This is just the HTML; this isn't the actual theme.

Refresh the home page and click on the first image. This will take us to the `single.html` page. We will now copy the code that's in `index.html` and put it in the `single.html` page.

Next, we will empty up the 9-column div, everything else is going to stay the same. After removing the 9-column div, our code will look like this in the `single.html` page:

```
<div class="w3-col m3 l3">
  <ul class="w3-ul">
    <li><a href="#">Nature</a></li>
    <li><a href="#">Animals</a></li>
    <li><a href="#">Objects</a></li>
    <li><a href="#">People</a></li>
    <li><a href="#">Abstract</a></li>
  </ul>
</div>
<div class="w3-col m9 l9">

</div>
</div>

<footer>
  <p>PhotoGenik &copy; 2017</p>
```

```
    </footer>
  </body>
</html>
```

Adding a single image for animation

Now, in the 9-column div in the `single.html` page, we will put our single image. For this, first we will put an `<article>` tag and give it a class of `post`. Then add a paragraph with the class of `meta`, as shown here:

```
<div class="w3-col m9 l9">
  <article class="post">
    <p class="meta">
    </p>
  </article>
</div>
```

Next, add `Posted at 2:00pm on 03-29-2017 by Brad` in the `meta` class:

```
<p class="meta">
Posted at 2:00pm on 03-29-2017 by Brad
</p>
```

After this, put `<hr />` and then the actual image by adding `src="images/1.jpg"`. As we want this image to animate, we will give it a class of `w3-animate-right`, as shown here:

```
<div class="w3-col m9 l9">
  <article class="post">
    <p class="meta">
      Posted at 2:00pm on 03-29-2017 by Brad
    </p>
    <hr/>

    <img src="images/1.jpg" class="w3-animate-right">
  </article>
</div>
```

Then under this image, we will add another row, w3-row, and a column, w3-col, with 12; this column is where we will put the Back button. Then we'll add a column with 110 as shown here:

```
<div class="w3-row">
  <div class="w3-col 12">

  </div>
  <div class="w3-col 110">
  </div>
</div>
```

Now in column 12, let's put a line break <br /> and then add a link that will go back to the index.html page. We will give the link the w3-btn and w3-red classes to format it as a button as shown here:

```
<div class="w3-row">
  <div class="w3-col 12">
    <br />
    <a href="index.html" class="w3-btn w3-
red">Back</a>https://epic.packtpub.com/index.php?module=KReports&offset=1&s
tamp=1490607763044301800&return_module=KReports&action=DetailView&record=1d
5f883c-a9a3-ee7f-1d3c-5887f8190664
  </div>
```

Then in column 110, we'll add Photo Title and also the description. In the description, just paste a sample text in as shown here:

```
<div class="w3-col 110">
  <h1>Photo Title</h1>
  <p>Lorem ipsum dolor sit amet, consectetur adipiscing elit.</p>
</div>
```

Let's save this code and go back to `single.html` in the browser. We can see the image comes in from the right-hand side:

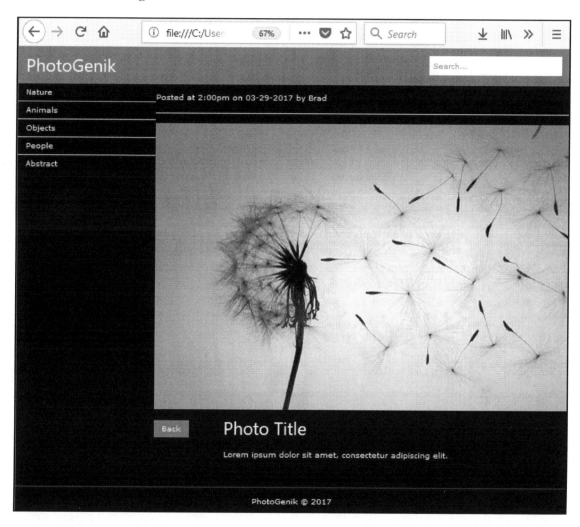

Now, as shown in the preceding screenshot, we can find that the columns are too close. You can see they're up against each other. So, we will add some padding to the `post` class that we specified for the `<article>` element. For this, add `padding:20px` in the `style.css` file:

```
.post{
  padding:20px;
}
```

Also, we will add the class of `pic` to that main image as shown here:

```
<img src="images/1.jpg" class="pic w3-animate-right">
```

Now you can see that the photo actually fits in there, and we're not right up against the side column:

So we have the title, description, and the **Back** button on the main image. In the next section, we're ready to start creating our WordPress theme.

Adding the theme header and footer

In the previous section, we went ahead and finished up the HTML template. We're now ready to convert that template into a WordPress theme. Here we have a fresh installation of WordPress:

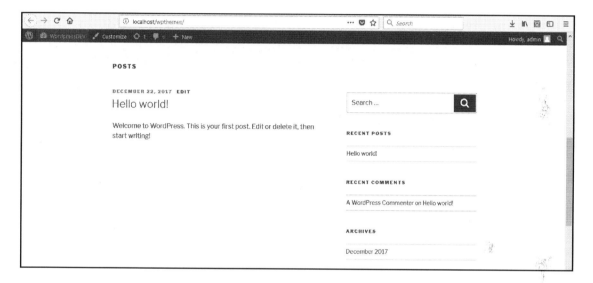

We'll use this as our starting point. In the editor, open the `wpthemes` folder as shown in the following screenshot:

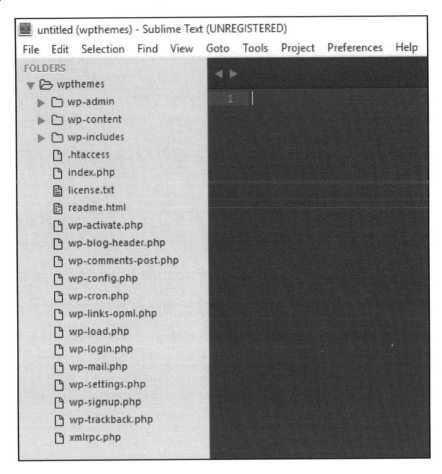

Creating a theme inside the wpthemes folder

We'll start with creating a theme inside the `themes` folder, which is inside the `wp-content` folder, called `photogenik`:

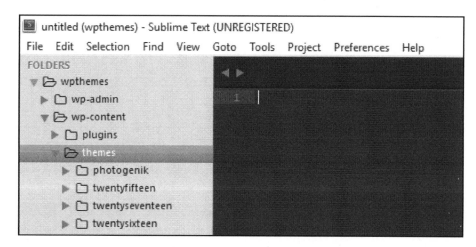

Adding a theme

The first thing we will create in the `photogenik` folder is a `style.css` file. This is where we will put all of our theme data. In the `style.css` file, we will put a comment and format it like this:

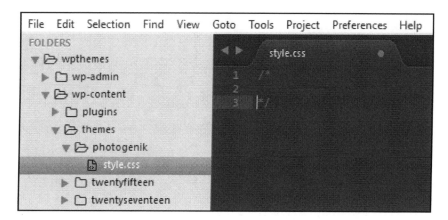

Add a few details in this comment. These are:

- `Theme Name:` This will be `PhotoGenik`
- `Author:` You can put your own name here
- `Author URI:` You can put whatever you want here. Here we will put `http://eduonix.com`
- `Description:` For the description we'll add `Photo gallery theme`
- `Version:` This will be `1.0.0`

```
/*
    Theme Name: PhotoGenik
    Author: Brad Traversy
    Author URI: http://eduonix.com
    Description: Photo gallery theme
    Version: 1.0.0
*/
```

After this create an `index.php` file. Save this and we will now be able to see it inside our admin area. Let's now reload and go to **Appearance** | **Themes** as shown in the following screenshot. You can see we have the theme **PhotoGenik**:

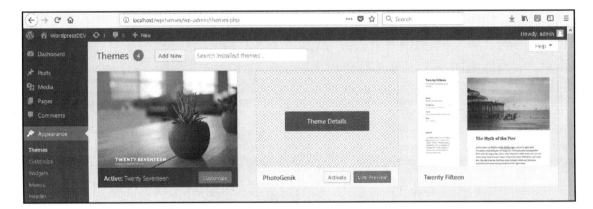

Next, we will upload a screenshot for the theme. For this, go to the `xampp` folder or wherever your WordPress installation is.

Here, we'll go to `wpthemes\wp-content\themes\photogenik` and paste it. When you want to use a screenshot, it should be named as `screenshot.png`. Reload the **Themes** page, and you will see a little screenshot as shown here:

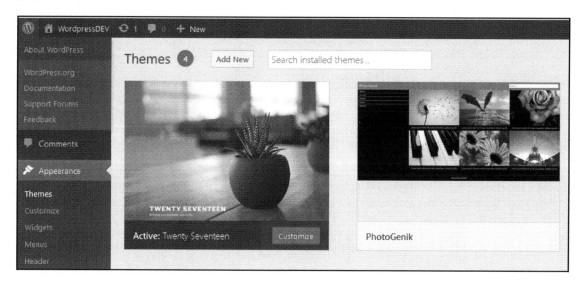

Activating the theme

Now, let's activate this theme by pressing the **Activate** button on the theme. If we go to the frontend page and reload it, we're obviously not going to get anything there.

The first thing to do in this case is to put in the style, the CSS. We will open the stylesheet (`style.css`) from our HTML template, copy its code, and then put it right under the comment we have added earlier:

```
/*
    Theme Name: PhotoGenik
    Author: Brad Traversy
    Author URI: http://eduonix.com
    Description: Photo gallery theme
    Version: 1.0.0
*/

body{
```

```css
    background: #000;
    color: #fff;
}
a{
    text-decoration: none;
}
li{
    list-style: none;
}
input{
    color: #333;
}
img{
    width:100%;
}
.post{
    padding:20px;
}
.pic{
    text-align: center;
}
header input{
    margin-top:15px;
}
footer{
    text-align: center;
    margin-top: 40px;
    border-top: #333 solid 1px;
}
```

If we go to the frontend page and reload it, it's still not going to make any change in our frontend page because we have nothing in our `index.php` file.

Open the `index.php` file, paste everything that we have in our `index.html` file, and save it. After this, if we go and reload the frontend page, it will show us the static HTML:

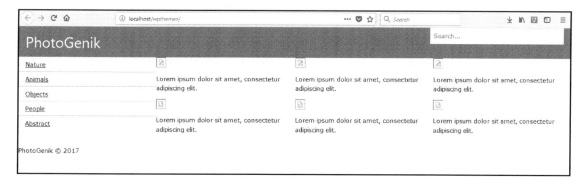

Now, none of this static HTML is coming from WordPress. We will slowly convert it from static markup to WordPress.

Converting static markup to WordPress

Let's go to the top of the index.php page, and the first thing will do is include the correct style sheets in the code:

```
<!DOCTYPE html>
<html>
<head>
  <title>PhotoGenik</title>
  <link rel="stylesheet"
        href="http://www.w3schools.com/lib/w3.css">
  <link rel="stylesheet" href="style.css">
</head>
<body>
```

We will take out the style.css from the href link in the preceding code and replace it with php bloginfo();. In the parentheses, we'll add stylesheet_url as shown here:

```
<head>
  <title>PhotoGenik</title>
  <link rel="stylesheet" href="http://www.w3schools.com/lib/w3.css">
  <link rel="stylesheet" href="<?php bloginfo('stylesheet_url'); ?>">
</head>
```

Save this, go to the frontend page, and reload it. You will now see the stylesheet is included as shown in the following screenshot:

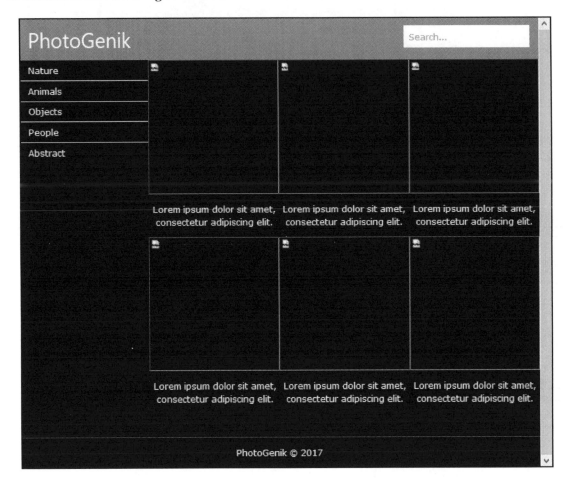

You might not see the images because the path is wrong. We'll look into that in a later section.

Adding the wp_head function

Now another thing we want to put in the head is the `wp_head` function. Here, we can add any head content that we need, for example an extra style sheet for a WordPress plugin. So we will add `<?php wp_head(); ?>` as shown here:

```
<link rel="stylesheet" href="<?php bloginfo('stylesheet_url'); ?>">
<?php wp_head(); ?>
</head>
```

We also want the character set. In the head, we will add `<meta charset="<?php bloginfo(); ?>">`. Then inside the parentheses, we'll add `charset` as shown here:

```
<title>PhotoGenik</title>
<meta charset="<?php bloginfo('charset'); ?>">
```

Now, we will make `<h1>` inside the header dynamic. We'll add `<?php bloginfo(''); ?>` and pass in `name` as shown here:

```
<body>
  <header class="w3-container w3-teal">
    <div class="w3-row">
      <div class="w3-col m9 l9">
      <h1><?php bloginfo('name'); ?></h1>
      </div>
```

Let's save that and see what that gives us by reloading the frontend page:

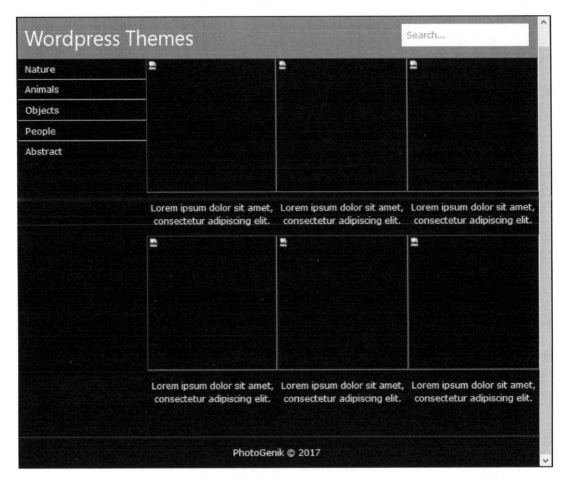

As shown in the preceding screenshot, our code is going to give us whatever the site name is; in our case, it is **WordPress Themes**, which we can change inside the admin area.

Adding the body_class function

For the body, we'll include the `body_class` function:

```
<body <?php body_class(); ?>>
```

For now, we will leave the main content as it is.

Adding the footer

We will add `<?php bloginfo('name'); ?>` to the footer, as we did in `<h1>`. This will give whatever the name of the blog is; in our case, it is `WordPress Themes`:

```
<footer>
  <p><?php bloginfo('name'); ?> &copy; 2017</p>
</footer>
```

Splitting the header and footer

Now, we will split our `index.php` file into a header and footer file. Inside the `photogenik` folder, we will create two new files called `header.php` and `footer.php`.

Let's figure out what we need to put in the `header.php` file. We will add the following code from our `index.php` file into the `header.php` file:

```
<!DOCTYPE html>
<html>
<head>
  <title>PhotoGenik</title>
  <meta charset="<?php bloginfor('charset'); ?>">
  <link rel="stylesheet"
  href="http://www.w3schools.com/lib/w3.css">
  <link rel="stylesheet" href="<?php bloginfo('stylesheet_url'); ?>">
  <?php wp_head(); ?>
</head>
<body <?php body_class(); ?>>
  <header class="w3-container w3-teal">
    <div class="w3-row">
      <div class="w3-col m9 l9">
        <h1><?php bloginfo('name'); ?></h1>
      </div>
      <div class="w3-col m3 l3">
        <input class="w3-input" type="text" placeholder="Search...">
      </div>
    </div>
  </header>
  <div class="w3-row">
    <div class="w3-col m3 l3">
      <ul class="w3-ul">
        <li><a href="#">Nature</a></li>
        <li><a href="#">Animals</a></li>
        <li><a href="#">Objects</a></li>
        <li><a href="#">People</a></li>
```

```
      <li><a href="#">Abstract</a></li>
    </ul>
  </div>
  <div class="w3-col m9 l9">
    <div class="w3-row">
```

For the footer, we will cut the following code from `index.php`, put that in `footer.php`, and save it:

```
      </div>
    </div>
  </div>
  <footer>
    <p><?php bloginfo('name'); ?> &copy; 2017</p>
  </footer>
<body>
</html
```

After splitting the header and footer code, the remaining code inside the `index.php` file will look like this:

```
<div class="w3-col m4 l4 pic">
  <a href="single.html">
    <img src="images/1.jpg" class="w3-animate-opacity">
  </a>
  <p>Lorem ipsum dolor sit amet,
  consectetur adipiscing elit.</p>
</div>
<div class="w3-col m4 l4 pic">
  <img src="images/2.jpg" class="w3-animate-opacity">
  <p>Lorem ipsum dolor sit amet,
  consectetur adipiscing elit.</p>
</div>
<div class="w3-col m4 l4 pic">
  <img src="images/3.jpg" class="w3-animate-opacity">
  <p>Lorem ipsum dolor sit amet,
  consectetur adipiscing elit.</p>
</div>
<div class="w3-col m4 l4 pic">
  <img src="images/4.jpg" class="w3-animate-opacity">
  <p>Lorem ipsum dolor sit amet,
  consectetur adipiscing elit.</p>
</div>
<div class="w3-col m4 l4 pic">
  <img src="images/5.jpg" class="w3-animate-opacity">
  <p>Lorem ipsum dolor sit amet,
  consectetur adipiscing elit.</p>
```

```
</div>
<div class="w3-col m4 l4 pic">
 <img src="images/6.jpg" class="w3-animate-opacity">
 <p>Lorem ipsum dolor sit amet,
 consectetur adipiscing elit.</p>
</div>
```

If we reload now, you can see as shown in the following screenshot that all we're getting is the index.php file:

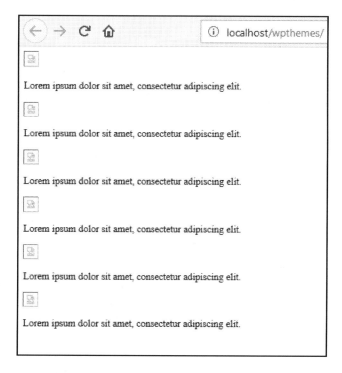

We need to include the header and footer in the index.php file, so let's do that next. For header, we need to add <?php get_header(); ?> at the top of the code as shown here:

```
<?php get_header(); ?>

<div class="w3-col m4 l4 pic">
  <a href="single.html">
    <img src="images/1.jpg" class="w3-animate-opacity">
  </a>
  <p>Lorem ipsum dolor sit amet,
  consectetur adipiscing elit.</p>
</div>
```

Then we will do the same thing for the footer. We will add `<?php get_footer(); ?>` at the end of the code as shown here:

```
<div class="w3-col m4 l4 pic">
 <img src="images/6.jpg" class="w3-animate-opacity">
  <p>Lorem ipsum dolor sit amet, consectetur adipiscing elit.</p>
</div>

<?php get_footer(); ?>
```

If we go back and reload our frontend page, you can see that it's back to normal:

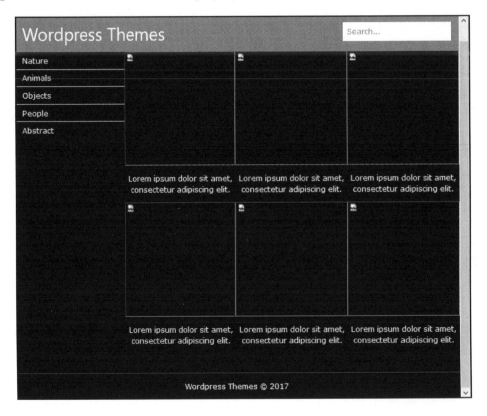

Changing the site name

To change the name of the site, in the backend page, we'll go to the **Settings** section and select **General**:

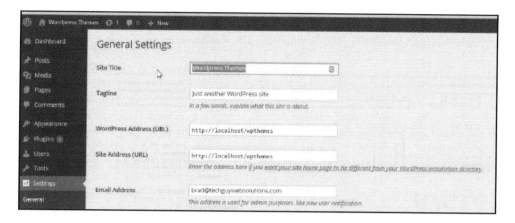

Here, we'll change **Site Title** from `Wordpress Themes` to `PhotoGenik` and save the changes. When we reload the frontend page, and the changes should reflect as follows:

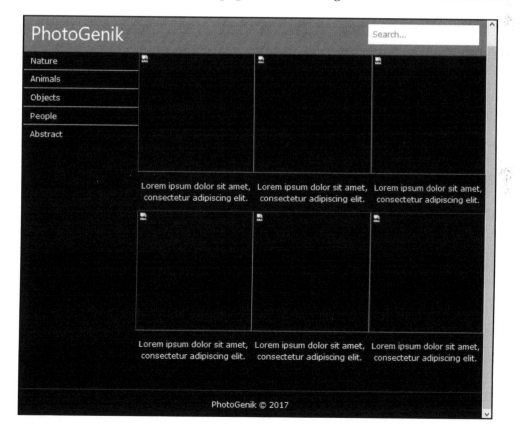

In the next section, we will look at the content in the posts because that's what we want the post to be showing in the index. Okay, so we'll get to that next.

The post loop

In the previous section, we created the header and footer files and included them in the `index.php` file. In this section, we will work on the main post area. So far, we have a bunch of static HTML which we need to change. We will have two types of posts:

- **Regular post**: This will be a standard blog post with a title and paragraph
- **Gallery post**: This will have the image with the description underneath

We will add support for content or post formats. So what we need to do is create a `functions.php` file inside our `photogenik` theme.

Adding the theme support function

We will create a function to set up certain support for our theme. For instance, to be able to use the featured image or thumbnails. In `function.php`, we'll add a comment `Theme Support` and declare the `theme_setup` function as shown here:

```php
<?php
// Theme Support
function theme_setup(){
}
```

Now, when we go to a post as shown in the following screenshot, we don't have a **Featured Image** box below the **Tags** section. That's what we will add inside the function:

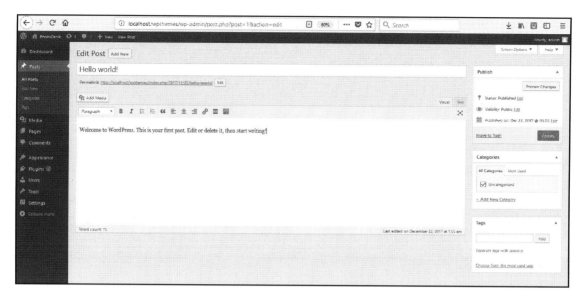

To set up the featured image support, we'll add `add_theme_support` inside the `theme_setup` function. Then, inside the parentheses, we will add `post-thumbnails` as shown here:

```php
<?php
// Theme Support
function theme_setup(){
  // Featured Image Support
  add_theme_support('post-thumbnails');
}
```

For the thumbnail size, we will put the max image size because we'll use CSS to shrink the images down. Next, to the `theme_setup` function we'll add `set_post_thumbnail_size` with size 900 x 600, as shown here:

```php
<?php
// Theme Support
function theme_setup(){
  // Featured Image Support
  add_theme_support('post-thumbnails');
  set_post_thumbnail_size(900, 600);
}
```

Next, we will add our gallery post format support. We will use the same add_theme_support function we used earlier, except we will replace post-thumbnails with post-formats. Then for the second parameter, we will put in an array of the formats we want to include. All we want besides the standard format is the gallery format, so we will put in gallery as shown here:

```php
<?php
// Theme Support
function theme_setup(){
  // Featured Image Support
  add_theme_support('post-thumbnails');
  set_post_thumbnail_size(900, 600);
  // Post Format Support
  add_theme_support('post-formats', array('gallery'));
}
```

Passing the function into action

Now that we have the theme_setup function, we need to pass this function into an action. So let's add add_action and the action will be after_setup_theme. The second parameter will be the function we want to run, which is theme_setup as shown here:

```php
function theme_setup(){
  // Featured Image Support
  add_theme_support('post-thumbnails');

  set_post_thumbnail_size(900, 600);

  // Post Format Support
  add_theme_support('post-formats', array('gallery'));
}

add_action('after_setup_theme', 'theme_setup');
```

Now, let's save this code and reload the backend page. As shown in the following screenshot, you will now see that we have the **Featured Image** section under the **Tags** section, and we also have support for the gallery format:

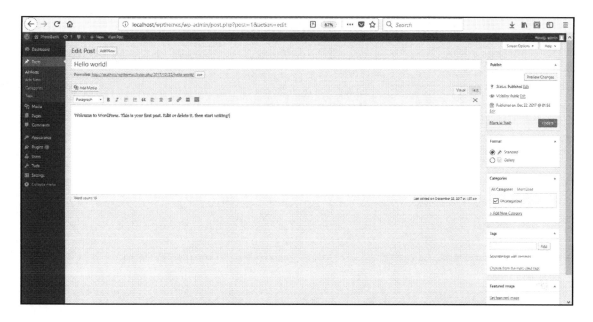

Now since we have both standard and gallery formats, we need to create the two different files for the content. In the `photogenik` folder create one file for content, as `content.php`, and another for gallery, as `content-gallery.php`.

Before we actually work on these files, we will simplify our `index.php` file.

Working on index.php for the content post

To simplify the `index.php` file, open the file in the editor and get rid of all the code present in it except the `<?php get_header(); ?>` and `<?php get_footer(); ?>` lines. This is how our `index.php` will look like:

```
<?php get_header(); ?>

<?php get_footer(); ?>
```

We will then check for posts and if there are posts, loop through them and spit out the correct content file. Now, we will add `<?php if(have_posts()) : ?>` and then we'll use the shorthand syntax as shown here:

```
<?php get_header(); ?>
<?php if(have_posts()) : ?>
<?php endif; ?>
```

Adding the while loop for the post

If there are posts then we want to loop through them. We can use a `while` loop to do that. So, inside the `if` statement, we'll add `<?php while(have_posts()) : the_post(); ?>`. Then end the `while` loop by adding `<?php endwhile; ?>` as shown here:

```
<?php if(have_posts()) : ?>
  <?php while(have_posts()) : the_post(); ?>

  <?php endwhile; ?>
<?php endif; ?>
```

While it has post, we want to spit out the content file, whether it's `content.php` or `content-gallery.php` that pertains to whatever format we choose in the post. So, we'll add `<?php get_template_part(); ?>` inside the `while` loop. Next, pass in `content` and for the second parameter, pass `get_post_format()`. This will determine whether the post is a gallery or just a standard post. Here is how our code will look like:

```
<?php if(have_posts()) : ?>
  <?php while(have_posts()) : the_post(); ?>
    <?php get_template_part('content', get_post_format()); ?>
  <?php endwhile; ?>
<?php endif; ?>
```

Adding an else statement

Next, we will add an `else` statement to the `if` statement we have defined, which will come into the picture if there are no posts. If there are no posts, we will echo a message saying `Sorry, there are no posts`:

```
<?php if(have_posts()) : ?>
  <?php while(have_posts()) : the_post(); ?>
    <?php get_template_part('content', get_post_format()); ?>
  <?php endwhile; ?>
<?php else : ?>
  <?php echo wpautop('Sorry, there are no posts'); ?>
<?php endif; ?>
```

Now let's save the `index.php` file. For the content files, we'll add STANDARD CONTENT in the `content.php` file as shown here:

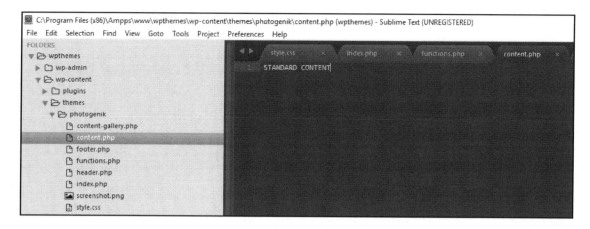

And add PHOTO in the `content-gallery.php` file, as shown here:

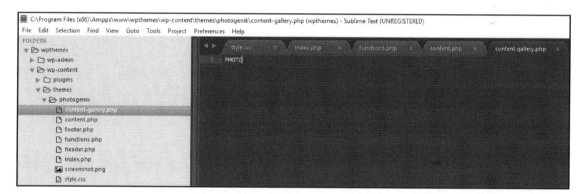

If we go to the frontend page and reload it, we get **STANDARD CONTENT** because if we look at our posts, we just have one post, Hello world!:

Now add another post named `Test`, choose the **Gallery** format for this post, and publish it:

Reload the frontend page, and you can now see that we get **PHOTO STANDARD CONTENT**:

So that's our two posts. They're on the same line but this is actually two different posts. We now know that our code is working. In the next section, we'll work on both of the photo and standard content files so that we can output the posts correctly.

Displaying the post content

In this section, we'll work on the content pages, both the regular post content and also the gallery.

Adding a regular post content

For adding a regular post, we'll start with the `content.php` file in the editor. We'll add title, metadata, thumbnail, and lastly, the main content to the post. To start with, we will create an `article` tag and give it a class of `post`:

```
<article class="post">
</article>
```

Adding a title to the regular post content

Next, we need the title. We will put the title inside of an `<h2></h2>` tag. We can get the title by adding `<?php echo the_title(); ?>`:

```
<article class="post">
<h2><?php echo the_title(); ?></h2>
</article>
```

Just to check, reload the main page and you can see with the regular content posts we actually get the title:

Adding metadata

Next, we will add the metadata. Let's put that in a paragraph with a class called `meta` as shown here:

```
<p class="meta">

</p>
```

In the `meta` class, we will add `Posted at` and then get the date and time. To get the date and time, we will add `<?php the_time(); ?>` and `<?php the_data(); ?>` respectively:

```
<p class="meta">
Posted at <?php the_time(); ?> on
<?php the_date(); ?> by
</p>
```

Next, we want to add the user's name, and we will put that in a link. For this, we will add `<a href=""> </a>`, add the php tag, and echo out `get_author_posts_url()` as shown here:

```
<p class="meta">
Posted at <?php the_time(); ?> on
<?php the_date(); ?> by
<a href="<?php echo get_author_posts_url(); ?>"></a>
</p>
```

Now, we need to put the ID for the author, which we can add with `get_the_author_meta()` and pass in `ID`. This will get us the author's ID. Then for the actual text, we will add `<?php the_author(); ?>`, as shown here:

```
<a href="<?php echo get_author_posts_url(get_the_author_meta('ID'))
?>"><?php the_author(); ?></a>
```

If we check it out, we'll see the page as shown in the following screenshot:

This shows **Posted at 1:55 am on December 22, 2017 by admin.**

Checking the thumbnail in content post

Next, what we'll do is check to see if there's a thumbnail or a featured image. For this, we'll add an `if` statement:

```
<?php if() : ?>
</article>
```

In the `if` statement, add `has_post_thumbnail()` and let's end the `if` statement as shown here:

```
<?php if(has_post_thumbnail()) : ?>
<?php endif; ?>
</article>
```

If there's a thumbnail, we'll create `<div>` and give it a class of `post-thumbnail`. In `<div>` we'll add `<?php the_post_thumbnail(); ?>` as shown here:

```
<?php if(has_post_thumbnail()) : ?>
  <div class="post-thumbnail">
    <?php the_post_thumbnail(); ?>
  </div>
<?php endif; ?>
```

Now, under the `if` block add a `<br />` tag, and then we will need the main content which is really easy; we can just add `<?php the_content(); ?>` as shown here:

```
<br/>

<?php the_content(); ?>
</article>
```

Let's save this and reload the home page, and you can see that we have the title, metadata, and content of that post as shown in the following screenshot:

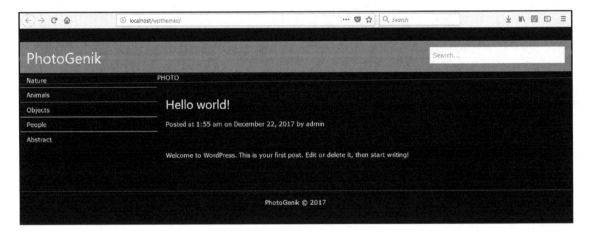

Adding a gallery post

For the gallery post, the code is going to be a little different. We will start with the `content-gallery.php` page.

Let's just take a look at our `index.html` page that we created in the earlier section. Similar to the `index.html` page, we will add a 4-column `<div>` in the `content-gallery.php` page. We will give `<div>` a class of `w3-col m4 l4 pic` as shown here:

```
<div class="w3-col m4 l4 pic">

</div>
```

Checking the thumbnail in the gallery post

As we want to check for the thumbnail, as we did in the previous section, we will use the same code in the `content-gallery.php` page:

```
<div class="w3-col m4 l4 pic">
  <?php if(has_post_thumbnail()) : ?>
    <div class="post-thumbnail">
      <?php the_post_thumbnail(); ?>
    </div>
  <?php endif; ?>
</div>
```

This is going to be a little different than the regular content post. We will remove the `<?php the_post_thumbnail(); ?>` line. After removing it, the code should look like the following:

```
<div class="w3-col m4 l4 pic">
  <?php if(has_post_thumbnail()) : ?>
    <div class="post-thumbnail">
    </div>
  <?php endif; ?>
</div>
```

 Thumbnail or featured images mean the same thing.

Creating an array of attributes

We want to do a little extra in the `content-gallery.php` file. We will add a class to the images so that we can do the animation and stuff like that. For this, we will create an array of attributes. In the div, let's add the following code:

```
<div class="post-thumbnail">
  <?php
    $attr = array(
    );
  ?>
</div>
```

Next, in the array, we will put in `class` and we want that to be `w3-animate-opacity` class. Then, we also want a hover effect for which we can use `w3-hover-opacity`:

```
<div class="post-thumbnail">
  <?php
    $attr = array(
       'class' => 'w3-animate-opacity w3-hover-opacity'
     );
  ?>
</div>
```

Now, each image is going to have a link around it. So, after the array of attribute, we will add `<a href="php echo the_permalink()"></a>`:

```
<a href="<?php echo the_permalink(); ?>">
</a>
</div>
```

This link will take us to the single post. Then to show the thumbnail we will add `<?php echo get_the_post_thumbnail(); ?>` in the anchor tag as shown here:

```
<a href="<?php echo the_permalink(); ?>">
  <?php echo get_the_post_thumbnail(); ?>
</a>
```

In the `get_the_post_thumbnail()` function, we will pass in ID, the size which will be `large`, and then the attributes as shown here:

```
<a href="<?php echo the_permalink(); ?>">
  <?php echo get_the_post_thumbnail($id, 'large', $attr); ?>
</a>
```

Next, underneath the `endif` statement, we will put the content:

```
<?php endif; ?>
<?php the_content(); ?>
</div>
```

Now save the code and reload the home page. We will not see anything because we didn't actually add any content to that photo post:

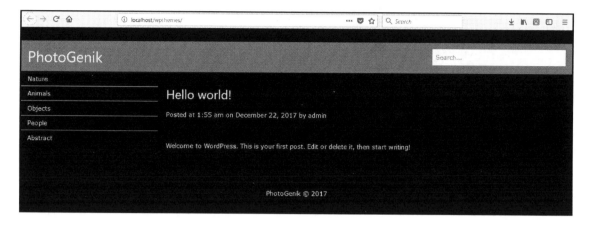

Adding a new post

Before adding a new post, delete the post we created in the previous sections. As shown in the following screenshot, go to the **Posts** section in our WordPress page, select both the posts, and move them to trash:

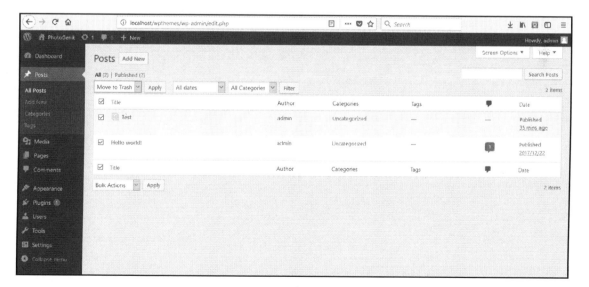

Now, we will create a new post. For this, we want to make sure to add a few sections. These are:

- **Title section**: First, we'll add a title. Let's call it `Photo One`.
- **Description section**: Add a small paragraph or some sample content which will be the description:

- **Format**: Make sure to choose **Gallery** as our post format:

- **Categories:** We will create a few categories. We'll add `Nature`, `Objects`, `People`, `Places`, and `Abstract` categories. After creating the categories, choose `Nature`:

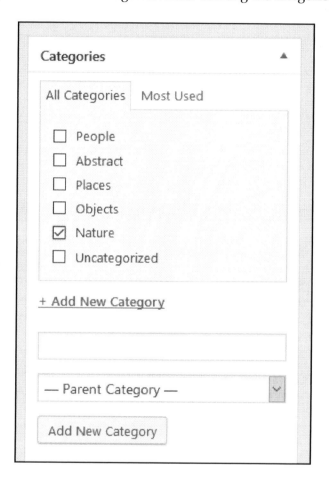

- **Featured Image**: To add a featured image, follow these steps:

1. When we click on the **Set featured image**, it'll lead us to the following page:

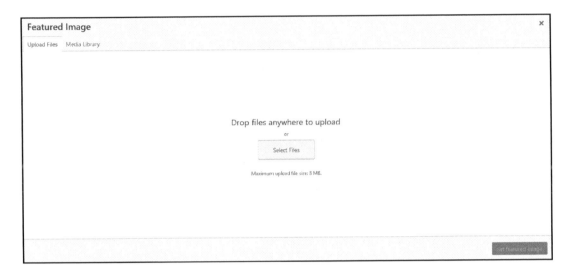

2. To upload a file, we'll click on the **Select Files** button.
3. We will go to our `photogenik_html` folder, then the `images` folder, and choose the first image:

4. We can give the image a title, `Photo One`, and add a caption and description as shown in the following screenshot:

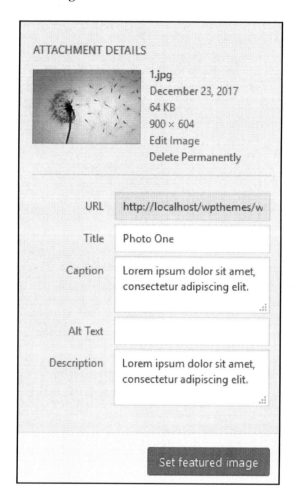

5. Then we'll click on the **Set featured image** button.

6. Now, hit the **Publish** button and take a look at the frontend. It should look like this:

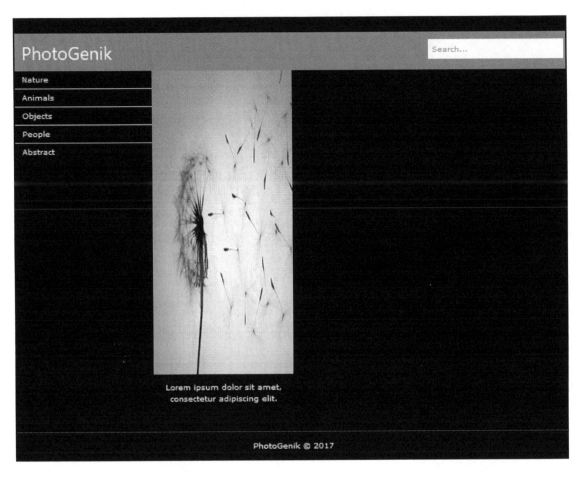

So there's our image, it fades in, but the proportion is incorrect.

Adding proper proportions to the image

To fix the proportions of the image, we'll go to our `style.css` page and go down to pic. In our case, we want the actual image, so we will add `.pic img` and set the `width` to `100%` and make that important. Then we will set `height` to `100%` as shown here:

```
.pic{
    text-align: center;
```

```
}
.pic img{
  width:100% !important;
  height:100% !important;
}
```

Reload the home page, and this time we should see something like this:

Now, that looks good! Similarly, we will upload the rest of the images we have in the `photogenik_html\images` folder:

We can see that we have our six photos at the backend in the **Posts** area as shown in the following screenshot:

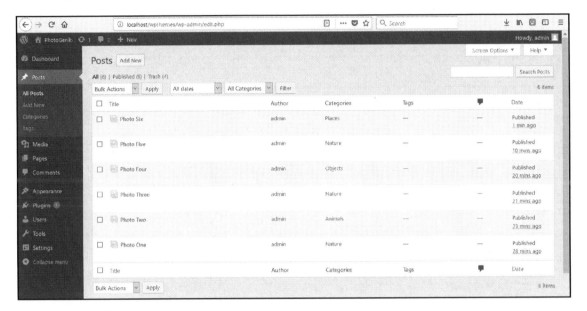

So we now have that functionality down. In the next section, we'll work on the categories, and we want it to be a WordPress widget.

Adding the category widget and search option

In this section, we will work on the categories widget shown on the left-hand side of the following screenshot. Right now, we just have a static HTML unordered list:

Adding a function to use the category widget

In order to use widgets, first we have to include the initialization code in our
`functions.php` file:

```php
<?php
// Theme Support
function theme_setup(){
  // Featured Image Support
  add_theme_support('post-thumbnails');
  set_post_thumbnail_size(900, 600);

  // Post Format Support
  add_theme_support('post-formats', array('gallery'));
}

add_action('after_setup_theme', 'theme_setup');
```

Specifying the widget locations

In the `function.php` file, underneath the `add_action` function, we will specify the locations. For this, we will add a function called `init_widgets`, pass in `&id`, and then add `register_sidebar` as shown here:

```
// Widget Locations
function init_widgets($id){
  register_sidebar();
}
```

The `register_sidebar` function is used for creating any kind of widget position. Even though it says sidebar, it doesn't have to be in the sidebar; in our case, it is but it doesn't have to be.

Next, we will pass in an array to the `register_sidebar` function. Add a name, `Sidebar`, and an ID, `sidebar`, as shown here:

```
  register_sidebar(array(
    'name' => 'Sidebar',
    'id' => 'sidebar'
  ));
}
```

Then we will declare the action using `add_action`. The hook we will use is `widgets_init` and put in the function we just created, which is `init_widgets`, as shown here:

```
add_action('widgets_init', 'init_widgets');
```

Next, we will register the widgets.

Registering the widgets

Let's now register the widgets. We will only have the sidebar in this particular template. Add a function, `custom_register_widgets`, and call `register_widget` as shown here:

```
// Register Widgets
function custom_register_widgets(){
  register_widget('');
}
```

Here, we will use the categories widget, but we will create a custom version of it and put it in our template in our `themes` folder. So in the `register_widget` parentheses, we'll add `WP_Widget_Categories_Custom` as shown here:

```
// Register Widgets
function custom_register_widgets(){
  register_widget('WP_Widget_Categories_Custom')};
}
```

Then we will add the action using `add_action`, pass in `widgets_init` as we want this to run, and then add the `custom_register_widgets` function as shown here:

```
add_action('widgets_init', 'custom_register_widgets');
```

Next, we will style our widgets.

Styling our category widgets

In this section we will style our widgets. In our `photogenik` theme folder, we will create a new folder called `widgets`. Inside the `widgets` folder, we will create a new file named `class-wp-widget-categories.php`.

Now we will go into the core `widgets` folder, which is present in the `wp-includes` folder. Open the categories widget file called `class-wp-widget-categories.php` and copy-paste its code into the file that we have created:

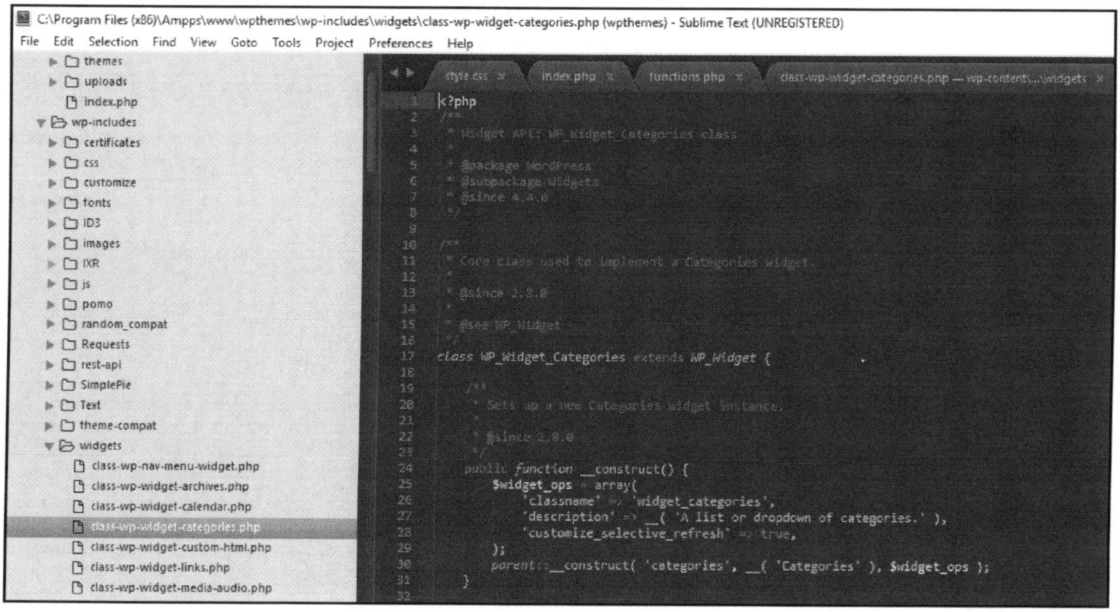

Now, in the code shown in the preceding screenshot, we will change the class name. Remember in our `functions.php` file, we called this class `WP_Widget_Categories_Custom`, so that's what we want here in the `class-wp-widget-categories.php` file:

```
class WP_Widget_Categories_Custom extends WP_Widget {
```

Now in order to use this we have to include the `class-wp-widget-categories.php` file in our `functions.php` file. We are including this file to style the widget as shown in the following screenshot:

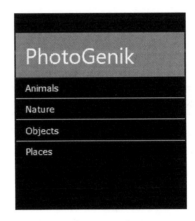

In `functions.php`, we will add `require_once` and then we'll add `widgets/class-wp-widget-categories.php` as shown here:

```php
<?php

require_once('widgets/class-wp-widget-categories.php');

//Theme Support
function theme_setup(){
  // Featured Image Support
  add_theme_support('post-thumbnails');
  set_post_thumbnail_size(900, 600);

  // Post Format Support
  add_theme_support('post-formats', array('gallery'));
}

add_action('after_setup_theme', 'theme_setup');
```

Let's save this and then go into our admin area. Now you will be able to go to the **Appearance** section and then will see a **Widgets** item as shown here:

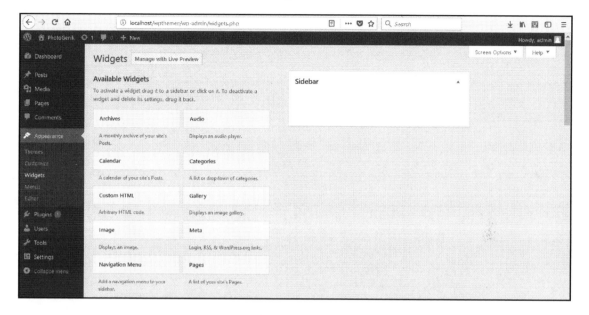

OK, and you can see we have our sidebar. We'll drag and drop **Categories** over **Sidebar** and click on **Save**:

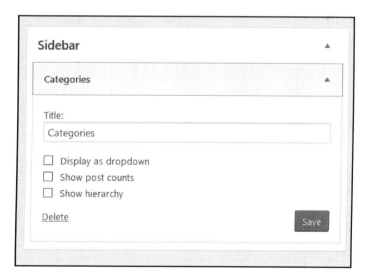

Adding the widget to the code

Now, go into `header.php` where we have the unordered list:

```
<div class="w3-row">
  <div class="w3-col m3 l3">
  <ul class="w3-ul">
    <li><a href="#">Nature</a></li>
    <li><a href="#">Animals</a></li>
    <li><a href="#">Objects</a></li>
    <li><a href="#">People</a></li>
    <li><a href="#">Abstract</a></li>
  </ul>
</div>
<div class="w3-col m9 l9">
  <div class="w3-row">
```

We will just get rid of this list and replace it with the following highlighted code:

```
<div class="w3-row">
  <div class="w3-col m3 l3">
    <?php if(is_active_sidebar('sidebar')) : ?>
      <?php dynamic_sidebar('sidebar'); ?>
    <?php endif; ?>
</div>
<div class="w3-col m9 l9">
  <div class="w3-row">
```

This is how we add a widget to our code. The first thing we do is check whether `sidebar` is active by using the `is_active_sidebar` Boolean function. If it is active, then we will call `dynamic_sidebar` and pass in the `sidebar` position. This could be anything you wanted it to be, but in our case we named it `sidebar`. Let's reload the home page, and there we go, there's the **Categories** widget:

If we click on one of the categories, it will show us the images that are in that particular category.

You can see in the preceding screenshot that the appearance of the widget did change. That's why we need to put it in our own file here to edit because you never want to edit any other core widget files.

Removing the title

Ensure that it's actually reading it from the current file. Let's add some changes. We will get rid of the title. For that, we will comment out the highlighted code shown here:

```
$title = apply_filters('widget_title', empty($
    instance['title']) ? _('Categories') : $
    instance['title'], $instance, $this->id_base);

$c = ! empty( $instance['count'] ) ? '1' : '0';
$h = ! empty( $instance['hierarchical'] ) ? '1':'0';
$d = ! empty( $instance['dropdown'] ) ? '1' : '0';

echo $args['before_widget'];
if($title) {
  // echo $args['before_title'] . $title . $args['after_title'];
}
```

Now reload the frontend, and you will see that the **Categories** title is gone:

Adding the class

Next, we will add our class. So we need to find where `ul` starts:

```
<ul>
<?php
  $cat_args['title_li'] = '';
  /**
    * Filter the arguments for the Categories widget.
    *
    * @since 2.8.0
    *
    * @param array $cat_args An array of Categories widget options.
    */
  wp_list_categories( apply_filters(
    ' widget_categories_args', $cat_args));
```

In this line, we will add `class="w3-ul"`:

```
<ul class="w3-ul">
```

Now, reload the frontend page, and now it looks like it did before as shown in the following screenshot:

Adding a link at the top of the widgets

Next, we will add a link at the top of the widgets in our WordPress page. That link is named All Photos so we can go back to just seeing all the photos.

We will go right under that `<ul>` and let's put an `<li>` tag. Then add the `href` link and specify the name of the folder (whatever your folder is called); in our case, this is `wpthemes`. Then we will name the link as All Photos as shown here:

```
<ul class="w3-ul">
<li><a href="/wpthemes">All Photos</a></li>
```

Reload the page and now we have an **All Photos** link at the top of the widgets as shown in the following screenshot:

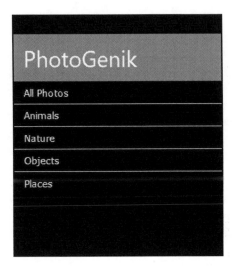

Changing the top margin of the page

One other thing we want to take care of is the top margin above the title of the post, as shown in the following screenshot. The reason it is like this is because it's making room for the admin bar which isn't showing right now:

In order for the admin bar to show, we have to call `wp_footer` inside of our `footer.php` file. So let's go there and add `<?php wp_footer(); ?>`:

```
</div>
    </div>
    </div>
    <footer>
      <p><?php bloginfo('name'); ?> &copy; 2017</p>
    </footer>
    <?php wp_footer(); ?>
</body>
</html>
```

Reload the frontend page and now you can see we have our admin bar, and of course, this only shows two people that are logged in as an admin:

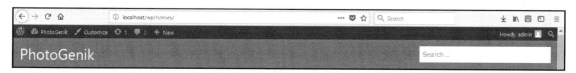

Making the search bar functional

Lastly, we will make the search bar functional. Right now if we put something in the `Search...` box here and press *Enter*, it's not doing anything. We know the search bar should be in the `header.php` file, so let's open it:

```
.<?php wp_head(); ?>
</head>
<body <?php body_class(); ?>>
  <header class="w3-container w3-teal">
    <div class="w3-row">
      <div class="w3-col m9 l9">
        <h1><?php bloginfo('name'); ?></h1>
      </div>
      <div class="w3-col m3 l3">
        <input class="w3-input" type="text"
        placeholder="Search...">
      </div>
    </div>
  </header>
```

In the preceding code, right now we have a simple `<input>` tag. We will turn this input into a form, so put the `<form>` tags around it:

```
<form>
  <input class="w3-input" type="text" placeholder="Search...">
</form>
```

Next, we will put in a `get` method in the `<form>` tag. Then specify an action by adding `action="<?php echo esc_url(); ?>"`. Inside the `esc_url` parentheses we will add the `home_url` function and pass in a parameter of `/`. Also, we should give this input a name of `s` for search as shown in this code:

```
<form method="get" action="<?php echo esc_url(home_url('/')); ?>">
  <input name="s" class="w3-input" type="text"
  placeholder="Search...">
</form>
```

Reload the frontend page and search for `photo two`:

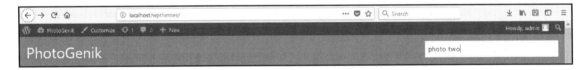

If we hit *Enter*, we can see it's giving us `2.jpg` as shown here:

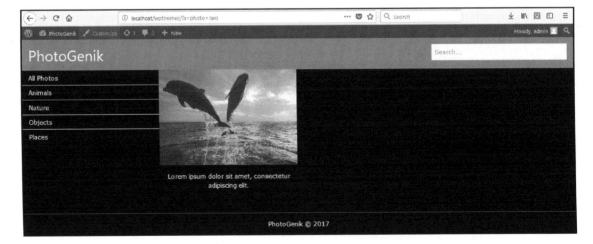

Similarly, we can search the remaining photos. In the next section, we will work on the single page.

Working on the single post theme

Next, we want to do now is the single page that's what we have left of this theme. When we click on one of the images, it takes us to the correct place as shown here, but it doesn't look too good:

We want this image to look like the single HTML page that we created. For this, we need to follow the steps discussed in the following subsections.

Creating a single HTML page

First, in our `photogenik` theme folder we will create a new file named `single.php`:

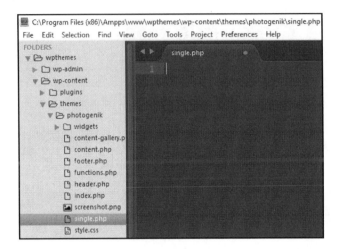

Next, we will go into the `index.php` file and copy and paste its code it in the `single.php` file as shown here:

```php
<?php get_header(); ?>

<?php if(have_posts()) : ?>
  <?php while(have_posts()) : the_post(); ?>
    <?php get_template_part('content', get_post_format()); ?>
  <?php endwhile; ?>

<?php else : ?>
  <?php echo wpautop('Sorry, there are no posts'); ?>
<?php endif; ?>

<?php get_footer(); ?>
```

We will now remove `get_template_part` in this code:

```php
<?php get_header(); ?>

<?php if(have_posts()) : ?>
  <?php while(have_posts()) : the_post(); ?>
  <?php endwhile; ?>

<?php else : ?>
  <?php echo wpautop('Sorry, there are no posts'); ?>
```

```
<?php endif; ?>

<?php get_footer(); ?>
```

And in place of the `while` loop, we will put our article, which we have created in our `single.html` file. Open the `single.html` file and copy the entire `<article>` section. Now paste this code in the `while` loop in the `single.php` file as show here:

```
<?php get_header(); ?>

<?php if(have_posts()) : ?>
  <?php while(have_posts()) : the_post(); ?>
    <article class="post">
      <p class="meta">
      Posted at 2:00pm on 03-29-2017 by Brad
      </p>

      <hr/>
      <img src="images/1.jpg" class="pic w3-animate-rigt">
      <div class="w3-row">
        <div class="w3-col l2">
          <br />
          <a href="index.html" class="w3-btn w3-red">Back</a>
        </div>
        <div class="w3-col l10">
        <h1>Photo Title</h1>
        <p>Lorem ipsum dolor sit amet, consectetur adipiscing elit.</p>
        </div>
      </div>
    </article>
```

Making metadata dynamic

Now we need to make the fields in the preceding code dynamic. We'll start with the `meta` class since that's at the top. Let's replace `2:00pm` with `<?php the_time ();?>` and `03-29-2017` with `<?php the_date (); ?>`, as shown here:

```
Posted at <?php the_time(); ?> on <?php the_date(); ?> by Brad
```

 One of the best things about WordPress is the ease of including dynamic content.

Now to replace the author name (Brad, in our case), we will grab the following code from the `content.php` file and add it in place of Brad:

```
<a href="<?php echo get_author_posts_url(get_the_author_meta('ID'));
?>"><?php the_author(); ?></a>
```

So this makes the metadata dynamic.

Changing the static image

Now, in the `single.php` file, we just have a static image:

```
<img src="images/1.jpg" class="pic w3-animate-right">
```

To change the static image, let's copy the `if` statement we have in the `content-gallery.php` file and paste that in place of the `<img>` tag as shown here:

```
      </p>

      <hr/>
      <?php if(has_post_thumbnail()) : ?>
        <div class="post-thumbnail">
          <?php
            $attr = array(
              'class' => 'w3-animate-opacity w3-hover-opacity'
            );
          ?>
          <a href="<?php echo the_permalink(); ?>">
            <?php echo get_the_post_thumbnail($id,
            'large', $attr);    ?>
          </a>
        </div>
      <?php endif; ?>
      <?php the_content(); ?>
    </div>
```

In this code, we will change `w3-animate-opacity` to `w3-animate-right` and remove `w3-hover-opacity` as shown here:

```
      <?php if(has_post_thumbnail()) : ?>
        <div class="post-thumbnail">
          <?php
            $attr = array(
              'class' => 'w3-animate-right'
            );
          ?>
```

Now, we don't need to have a link, so we'll remove the `permalink` statement:

```
<a href="<?php echo the_permalink(); ?>">
  <?php echo get_the_post_thumbnail($id,'large', $attr);  ?>
</a>
```

After removing the link, the code will look like the following:

```
<?php if(has_post_thumbnail()) : ?>
  <div class="post-thumbnail">
    <?php
      $attr = array(
        'class' => 'w3-animate-right'
      );
    ?>
    <?php echo get_the_post_thumbnail($id, 'large', $attr); ?>
  </div>
<?php endif; ?>
```

This looks good!

Changing the back button, title, and content

Now for the `Back` button we will change the `index.html` to `<?php echo site_url();
?>` as shown here:

```
<div class="w3-row">
  <div class="w3-col 12">
    <br />
    <a href="<?php echo site_url(); ?>"
    class="w3-btn w3-red">Back</a>
  </div>
```

This will take us back, and for a dynamic title we can simply replace the `Photo Title` with `<?php the_title();?>` as shown here:

```
</div>
<div class="w3-col l10>">
<h1><?php the_title(); ?></h1>
<p>Lorem ipsum dolor sit amet, consectetur adiposcing elit.</p>
</div>
```

Then for the dynamic content, we can replace the paragraph with `<?php the_content(); ?>`:

```
</div>
<div class="w3-col l10>">
<h1><?php the_title(); ?></h1>
<p><?php the_content(); ?></p>
</div>
```

With all the changes implemented in the code, let's take a look at the image in the WordPress:

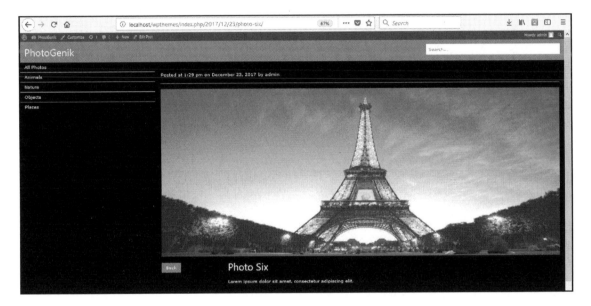

As shown in the preceding screenshot, this looks good. The **Back** button should also work. If you click on any one of the images, you can see it just slides right in.

I think that does it for our theme. It's very simple but I think it's pretty elegant, and of course, if you wanted to add widgets in the sidebar you could do that; if you want to create regular posts you can also do that, it doesn't have to be photos.

Summary

In this chapter, we worked on the project to create a WordPress theme for a photo gallery. We created the HTML and CSS for our home page. Next, we have implemented the animation using the built-in W3.CSS-animation.

After this, we have templated the HTML into a WordPress theme, created header and footer files separately, and included them in the `index.php` file. Next, we have worked on the main post area and added `if` and `while` loops for the different post formats. Then, we have worked on the content pages, both the regular and gallery post content. Once this was done, we worked on the categories widget. Last, we worked on the theme of the single page.

In the next chapter, we will build a Twitter Bootstrap WordPress theme.

4

Building a Twitter Bootstrap WordPress Theme

In this chapter, we'll integrate Bootstrap with WordPress. The look of the template that we created earlier was pretty simple. We didn't go for some spectacular design. The goal of this project is to get you to see how we can bring Bootstrap and WordPress together and use it to build more Bootstrap themes for WordPress in the future.

In this chapter, we'll cover the following topics:

- Building a Bootstrap theme
- Dealing with the post loop
- Implementing the Navbar
- Adding the search bar and single post page
- Exploring the comment functionality

So let's build a Twitter Bootstrap WordPress theme.

Building a Bootstrap theme

In our previously created template, we have a standard Bootstrap navbar up, and you can see that we have a drop down:

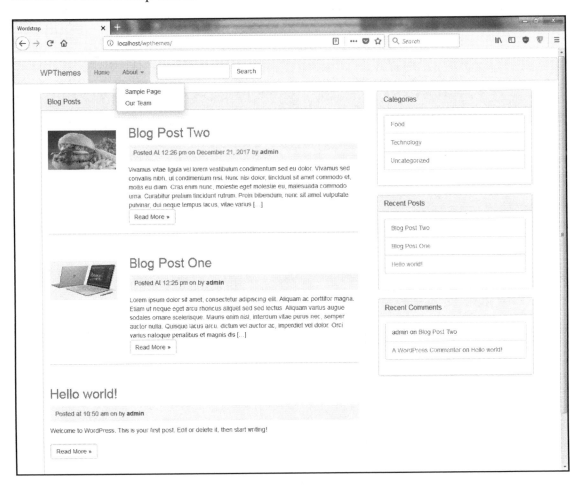

The way that we got to do the drop-down functionality was by using the `wp-bootstrap-navwalker` class at `www.github.com/twittem/wp-bootstrap-navwalker` shown in the following screenshot:

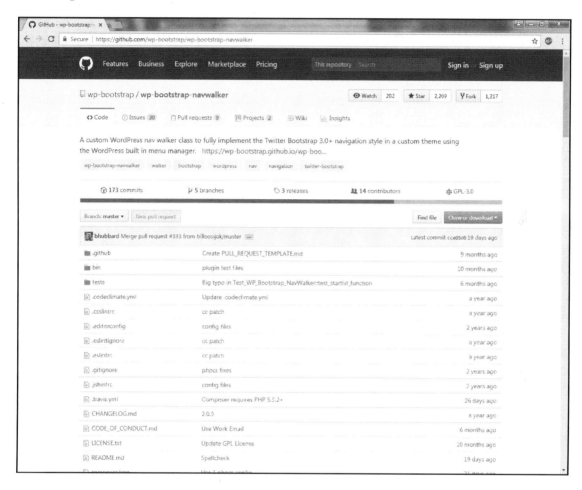

This is the most common and, probably, the easiest way to integrate a Bootstrap navbar with the drop-down functionality in WordPress. Let's implement that.

As seen earlier, we have the search box up on our WordPress page. We have some custom code in the `header` file that allows us to use the search box and have it work correctly, and this will work for posts and pages.

For instance, if I type `lorem` and hit the **Search** button, it's going to bring back everything that has the word *lorem* in it:

If we go to the backend, we can see we have some posts that we created earlier:

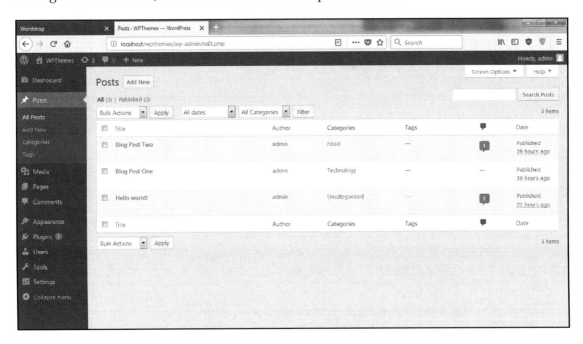

We also have the featured image for it on the main page:

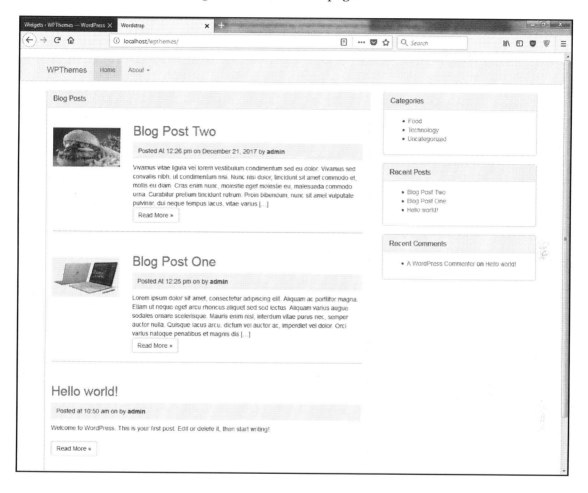

It is the same image we selected in the backend as the featured image:

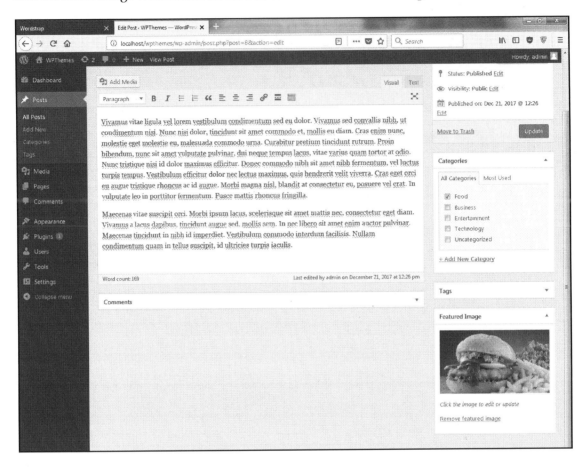

If we click on the title or the **Read More** button on the **Home** page, it takes us to an inner page with a larger image:

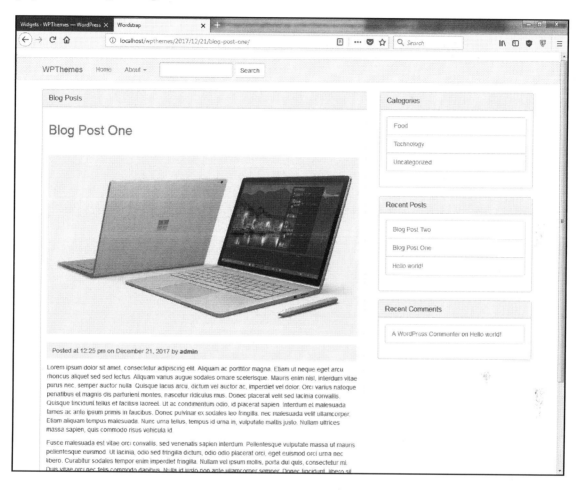

You will see that we have the comments down at the bottom of the page and the **Comment** form:

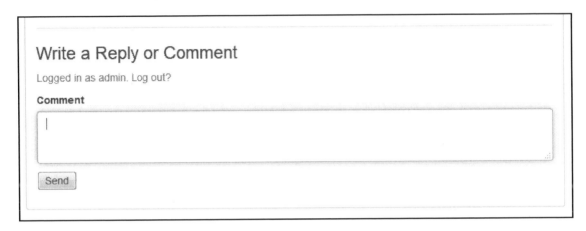

Now on the right-hand side, we have a widget sidebar shown as follows:

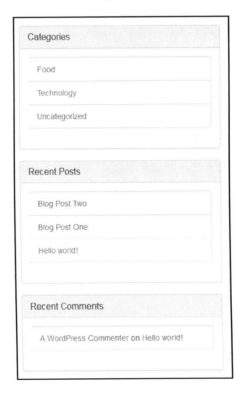

We actually took some of the core widgets and just tweaked them a little, so that we could use the Bootstrap list group. We'll tweak the following widgets: **Categories**, **Recent Posts**, and **Recent Comments**. This will be done to make them fit in with the Bootstrap theme.

Let's go ahead and get started on our Bootstrap theme for WordPress:

1. Go to `localhost/wpthemes/`.

   What we can see is just a default installation of WordPress without any posts. So we're starting from scratch.

2. In the Sublime Text editor, we have the sidebar where you can see WordPress project root directories, and in the `themes` folder, you can see that we have the default themes:

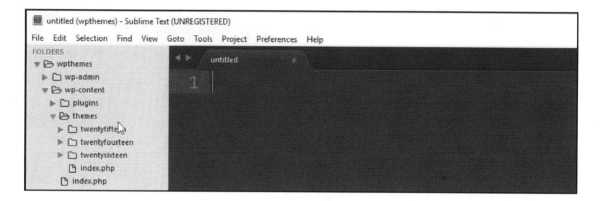

3. Now create a new folder in the `themes` folder called `wordstrap`:

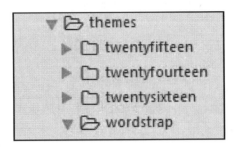

4. Next, we will create the `style.css` file for it. This file also acts like a manifest file.

5. We need to put in our comments and then add a `Theme Name` called `Wordstrap`. We then need to add the `Author` name, `Author URI`, `Description`, and `Version` as shown in the following code block:

```
/*
Theme Name: Wordstrap
Author: Brad Traversy
Author URI: http://eduonix.com
Description: Simple Bootstrap Theme For Wordpress
Version: 1.0
*/
```

6. Save that and then let's create an `index.php` file.

7. If we go to **Appearance** | **Themes**, you can see that we have this **wordstrap** theme now:

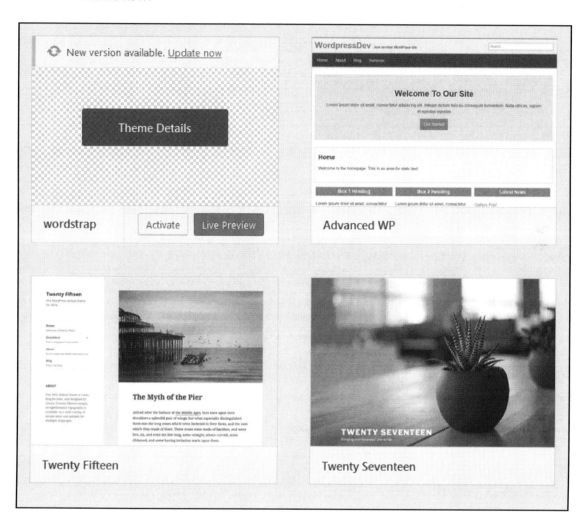

8. Now we will place an image file in the `theme` folder. You can take any image from your project files. Very simple, let's go ahead and reload. We have the **wordstrap** theme, which is very simple.

9. Now, let's go into `index.php` and put some base HTML tags: `<head>`, `<title>`, and `<body>`. We will add `Wordstrap` as the title:

```
<!DOCTYPE html>
<html>
<head>
    <title>Wordstrap</title>
</head>
<body>

</body>
</html>
```

10. Next, we need Bootstrap. Let's go ahead and get that. Go to `https://getbootstrap.com/` and let's download it:

Download

Bootstrap (currently v3.3.7) has a few easy ways to quickly get started, each one appealing to a different skill level and use case. Read through to see what suits your particular needs.

Bootstrap	Source code	Sass
Compiled and minified CSS, JavaScript, and fonts. No docs or original source files are included.	Source Less, JavaScript, and font files, along with our docs. **Requires a Less compiler and some setup.**	Bootstrap ported from Less to Sass for easy inclusion in Rails, Compass, or Sass-only projects.
Download Bootstrap	Download source	Download Sass

11. Open up the downloaded ZIP file and our `theme` folder.

12. Now create a `css` folder within the `wordstrap` folder. We'll now bring `bootstrap.css` over.

13. We'll then create a `js` folder and bring over `bootstrap.js`.

14. Now let's go back into the `index.php` file and include a couple of the `<link>` tags. For that, we will add the following code:

```
<!DOCTYPE html>
<html>
<head>
    <title>Wordstrap</title>
    <link rel="stylesheet" href="">
</head>
```

15. Now, we'll go into the `css` folder and `bootstrap.css`. Next, we also want to make sure we include the main stylesheet. To do that, Bootstrap gives us a function we can use. We'll add `stylesheet` and then `href`. We can also put in some php tags, add `bloginfo`, and here we just want to put in `stylesheet_url`. It'll now bring all the system stylesheets:

```
<!DOCTYPE html>
<html>
<head>
    <title>Wordstrap</title>
    <link rel="stylesheet" href="./css/bootstrap.css">
    <link rel="stylesheet" href="<?php
        bloginfo('stylesheet_url'); ?>">
</head>
<body>
```

16. Now we want to grab a navbar.

So on the Bootstrap website, let's go to **Components** and then **navbar**:

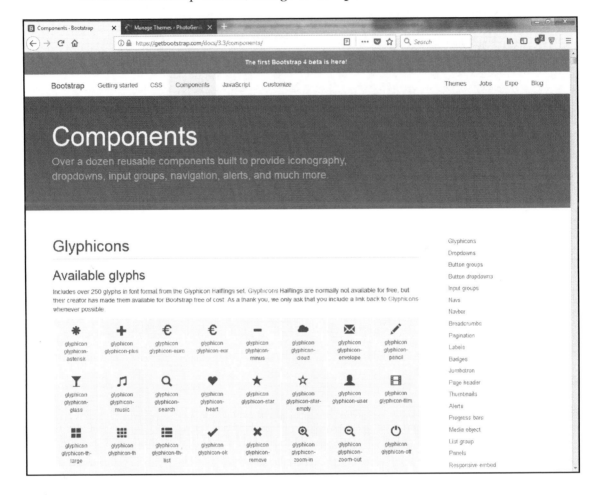

17. Let's copy the entire code example as shown in the following screenshot:

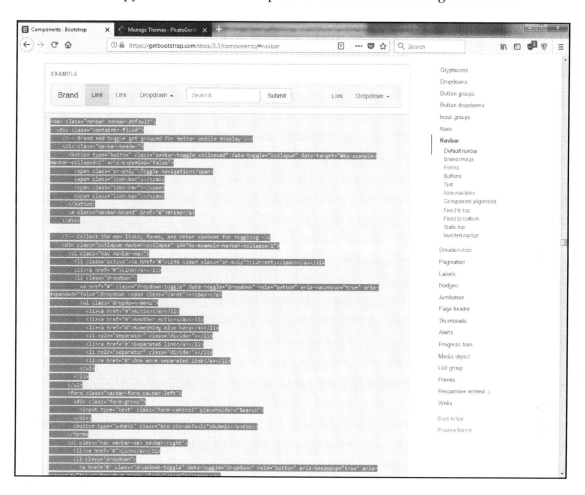

18. We will paste that in the `body` section of our `index.php` file.

19. Save it, and let's go ahead and activate the theme.

20. Now, let's go to the frontend and reload:

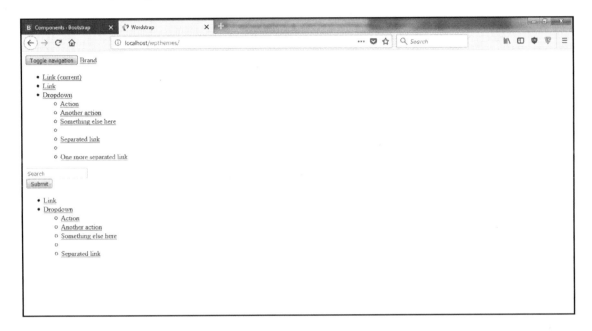

The reason that it looks like this is because it's not seeing the `bootstrap.css` file.

21. Let's look at the source code. You can see that the frontend is looking inside /css/bootstrap, but this file is actually in the themes folder:

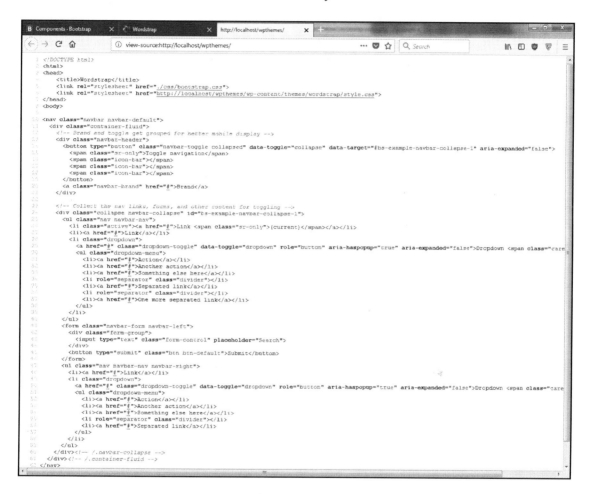

22. In order to fix this, we will go back to index.php. Let's go to the `<link>` tag and update the code as follows:

```
<link rel="stylesheet" href="<?php
    bloginfo('template_directory'); ?>/css/bootstrap.css">
<link rel="stylesheet" href="<?php
    bloginfo('stylesheet_url'); ?>">
```

23. We'll save that, go back, and see that it's working:

24. To change the navbar a little bit, we will indent the `<nav>` tag.

25. We'll now dump the code quite a bit. First, we will get rid of `fluid`; we want it to just be `container`:

```
<div class="container">
```

26. We'll get rid of the comments we don't need.

27. Then we have the `navbar-header` class. This button is for responsiveness. So when it's on a mobile or just a smaller screen in general, we'll have a button we can click on that will then show the menu, so we'll leave all that stuff:

```
<div class="navbar-header">
    <button type="button" class="navbar-toggle collapsed"
        data-toggle="collapse" data-target="#bs-example-navbar-
        collapse-1" aria-expanded="false">
```

28. For the brand, let's change the code a little bit. We want it to reflect whatever we have as the site name in WordPress. We will add `<?php bloginfo(); ?>` and then pass in `name`. For `href`, we will add the `<?php bloginfo(); ?>` link and put in `url`:

```
<a class="navbar-brand" href="<?php bloginfo('url'); ?>">
  <?php bloginfo('name'); ?></a>
```

29. We then have the `<ul>` tag where we'll implement the `wp-nav-walker` class. For that we will just get rid of this whole `<ul>`.

30. Then, we have our form that is the search form. It's going to be pretty much completely redone, so we will take out everything that's in the `<form>` tags.

31. We'll then take out the whole `<ul>` with the `nav navbar-nav navbar-right` class.

32. Here's the entire `nav`:

```
<nav class="navbar navbar-default">
<div class="container">

<div class="navbar-header">
<button type="button" class="navbar-toggle collapsed"
 data-toggle="collapse" data-target="#bs-example-navbar-
 collapse-1" aria-expanded="false">
    <span class="sr-only">Toggle navigation</span>
    <span class="icon-bar"></span>
    <span class="icon-bar"></span>
    <span class="icon-bar"></span>
</button>
<a class="navbar-brand" href="<?php bloginfo('url'); ?>">
<?php bloginfo('name'); ?>
</a>
</div>

<div class="collapse navbar-collapse"
 id="bs-example-navbar-collapse-1">

<form class="navbar-form navbar-left">

</form>

</div>
</div>
</nav>
```

33. We'll hold off just for now with that, let's see what that looks like:

As you can see it's very basic. We just have our branding, we'll implement the `walker-nav` or the `nav-walker` class later; but let's just continue with some of the base HTML.

34. We will create a `<div>` tag right below the ending `</nav>` tag and give it a class of `container`, and also add `index`. We will also add a row since we'll use Bootstrap's grid system. Inside the `row` class, we will add a column using `col-md-8`, so that will be an 8-column div, and we'll also have a 4-column div, which will be the sidebar:

```
<div class="container index">
    <div class="row">
        <div class="col-md-8">

        </div>
        <div class="col-md-4">

        </div>
    </div>
</div>
```

35. So inside the 8-column div, we will add a panel by using `class="panel"` and `panel-default`:

```
<div class="col-md-8">
    <div class="panel panel-default">

</div>
```

36. We will then add `panel-heading`, and in `panel-heading` we'll have an `<h3>` tag. We'll give it a class of `panel-title`, and we'll give it the title `Blog Posts`:

```
<div class="panel panel-default">
    <div class="panel-heading">
        <h3 class="panel-title">Blog Posts</h3>
    </div>
</div>
```

37. Now under the heading `</div>` we will add the `panel-body` div. For that, we want the `div class` called `panel-body`. We will then add the post loop, using `if(have_posts())`, and the shorthand syntax shown in the following code block:

```
    <h3 class="panel-title">Blog Posts</h3>
</div>
<div class="panel-body">
    <?php if(have_posts()): ?>

    <?php endif; ?>
</div>
```

38. Then we'll add the `while` loop as shown in the following code block:

```
<?php if(have_posts()): ?>
    <?php while(have_posts()) : the_post(); ?>

    <?php endwhile; ?>
<?php endif; ?>
```

39. Next we will add two columns, one for the image and another for all the data. So let's add a class called `row` and then we will add a `div class` whose value will be `col-md-3`. We will next add IMAGE HERE and then add nine columns by using `col-md-9`. We will then add in `the_title()` by using `<h2>`:

```
<?php while(have_posts()) : the_post(); ?>
    <div class="row">
    <div class="col-md-3">
        IMAGE HERE
    </div>
    <div class="col-md-9">
        <h2><?php echo the_title(); ?></h2>
    </div>
```

40. Let's save that:

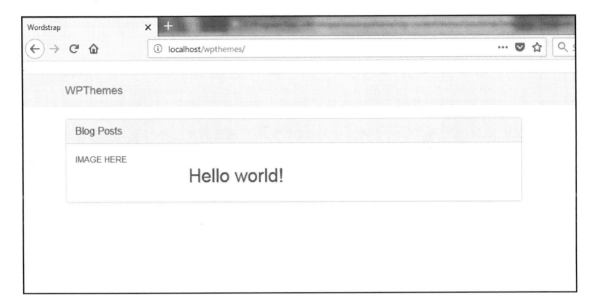

As you can see, we have our 3-column div where the image will go and then our nine-column with the content. We'll get back to adding all the content but let's continue and add the sidebar code first.

Adding the sidebar

This is going to be the widget area and for that, we'll need to do create a `functions.php` file first. We'll need to register the widgets we want which will be just the sidebar:

1. In the `index.php` file right under the `div class`, we'll add `<?php`. We'll then see if there's actually a widget active here using `if(is_active_sidebar)` and if we need the actual widget position (which will be `sidebar`):

```
<div class="col-md-4">
    <?php if(is_active_sidebar('sidebar')) : ?>
</div>
```

2. Next, we will add `<?php dynamic_sidebar(); ?>`. We also need the position, which is `sidebar`. It doesn't have to be called sidebar; you can call it whatever you'd like:

```php
<?php if(is_active_sidebar('sidebar')) : ?>
    <?php dynamic_sidebar('sidebar'); ?>
<?php endif; ?>
```

Now let's save that.

Adding the footer

Now let's quickly add the footer:

1. Right under the `container` div, we will create another container. We will put a horizontal rule in this container and the `<footer>` tags. Inside `<footer>` we'll have a paragraph and copyright:

```html
<div class="container">
    <hr>
    <footer>
        <p>&copy; 2017 WordStrap</p>
    </footer>
</div>
```

2. Now we also want to include two things: we want jQuery and the Bootstrap JavaScript files. We'll place JavaScript files right under the ending `</div>` as shown in the following code. We'll paste in the jQuery script, which is just going to be the **CDN (Content Delivery Network)**, and also `bootstrap.js`. We will also use `<?php bloginfo('template_directory'); ?>` just like we did with the `css` file:

```html
</div>
<script src="http://code.jquery.com/jquery-1.12.0.min.js">
</script>
<script src="<?php bloginfo('template_directory'); ?>
    /js/bootstrap.js">
</script>
</body>
</html>
```

3. Let's save that and reload:

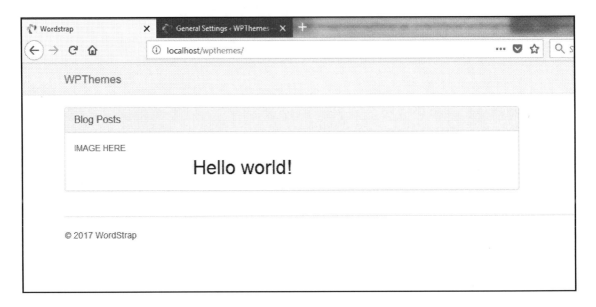

Header and footer

Now let's split this up into a header and a footer file in addition to `index.php`:

1. From the `index.php` file, we'll grab the code from the top down to the end of `</nav>`.

2. Let's create a new file called `header.php`. We will paste the code that we grabbed earlier and into this header file and save it.

3. In its place inside `index.php`, we'll open up a set of `php` tags using `get_header()`:

```
<?php get_header(); ?>
    <div class="container index">
```

Our page will look the exact same.

4. We'll then do the same thing with footer. We'll grab the code from this container down to the very bottom, from <div class="container"> till closing </html> tag:

```
<div class="container">
    <hr>
    <footer>
        <p>&copy; 2017 WordStrap</p>
    </footer>
</div>
<script src="http://code.jquery.com/jquery-1.12.0.min.js">
</script>
<script src="<?php bloginfo('template_directory'); ?>
    /js/bootstrap.js">
</script>
</body>
</html>
```

Create a footer file, paste the grabbed content, and save it.

5. In index.php we will add get_footer():

```
<?php get_footer(); ?>
```

6. OK, now that should look the exact same. That cleans things up a little bit.

The post loop

So until now we went ahead and set up our core template, core theme, with an index, a header, and a footer file. We have also implemented the main post loop, but we don't have anything else. We just have the title; we need to fix that.

But before we do that, we need to make it so that we can actually add images to our posts.

This is because right now if we go and we try to add a new post, we don't have a **Featured Image** area:

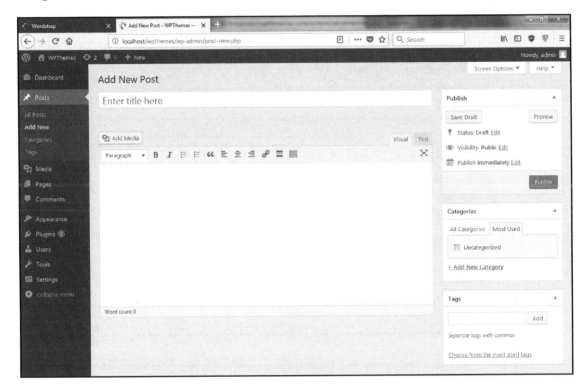

The Featured Image area

For the **Featured Image** area to show we need to create a `functions.php` file:

1. Let's create a new file and call it `functions.php`. Then let's create a function `theme_setup()`. Now, let's add a comment `Featured Image Support` and also add `add_theme_support()` with the value `post-thumbnails`:

```php
<?php

function theme_setup(){
    // Featured Image Support
    add_theme_support('post-thumbnails');
}
```

2. Underneath the function declaration, we will place `add_action()` and then pass in the hook that we want, which is going to be `after_setup_theme`. Then we will place the function that we want to use, which is `theme_setup`:

```
add_action('after_setup_theme', 'theme_setup');
```

3. Let's save that and reload:

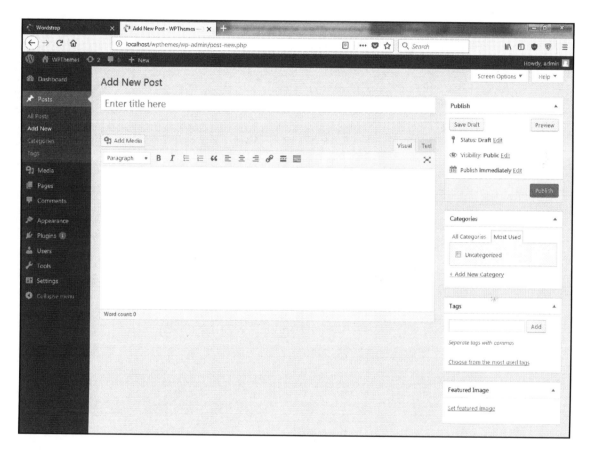

Now you can see that we have a **Featured Image** area.

Creating categories

1. So let's create a couple of categories first before we add a post. Let's add `Technology`, `Food`, `Entertainment`, and `Business` as shown in the following screenshot:

2. We will only select **Technology** for now and add the title as `Blog Post One`. We will copy some text from the Lorem Ipsum site as before and paste that in:

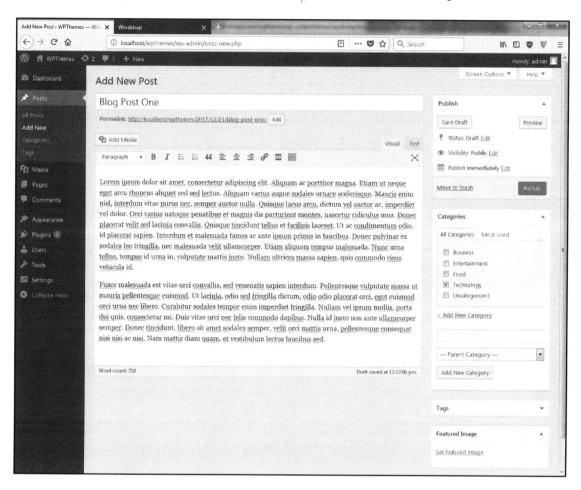

3. Now we need to select a featured image:

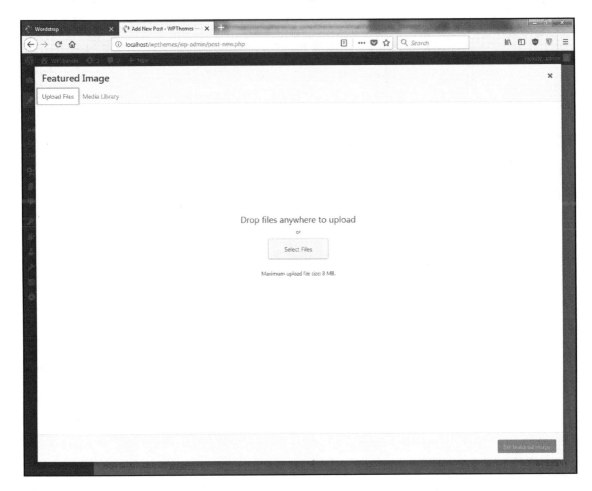

4. We can choose any image. In this case, I have selected an image of the Microsoft Surface. Click on **Set Featured Image** and then **Publish**:

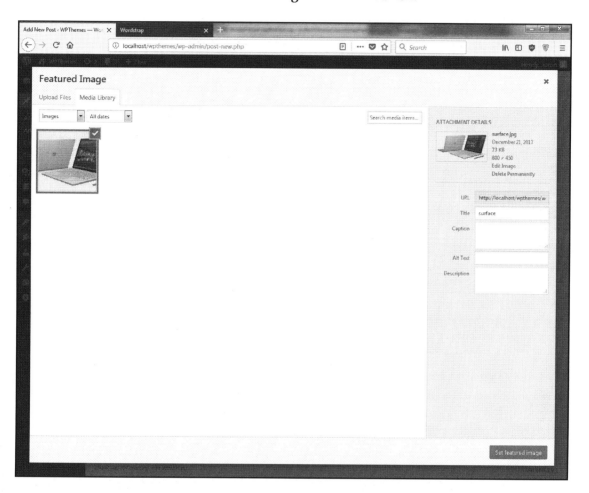

5. Go back and reload the page:

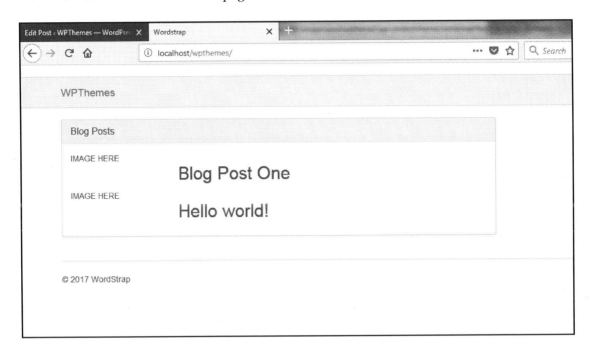

You can see the post but it doesn't look too good. So let's add one more.

6. Similarly, we will add `Blog Post Two`, paste some text in, let's choose **Food** for a category, and then upload an image. We'll choose the burger image and click on **Publish.**

7. We now have a couple of posts to work with:

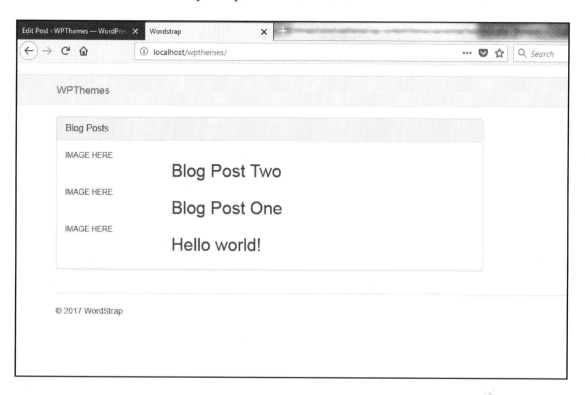

We have an issue here because we're putting the image in its own column inside the post, and some posts aren't going to have images. For instance, the **Hello world** post does not have an image. So we need to have some kind of a conditional statement, where we'll say if this post has an image, then format it in a certain way, and then we'll place an else statement; if it doesn't have an image, we'll format it differently.

Formatting the post

1. Let's go into our `index.php` file. You can see that we have our loop and a row:

```php
<?php while(have_posts()) : the_post(); ?>
    <div class="row">
        <div class="col-md-3">
            IMAGE HERE
        </div>
        <div class="col-md-9">
            <h2><?php echo the_title(); ?></h2>
        </div>
    </div>
<?php endwhile; ?>
```

2. Right after the `row` div is where we'll check to see if there is an image using `if(has_post_thumbnail())` and down where the `</div>` ends we'll add `<?php else : ?>` and `<?php endif; ?>`.

```php
<div class="row">
    <?php if(has_post_thumbnail()): ?>
    <div class="col-md-3">
        IMAGE HERE
    </div>
    <div class="col-md-9">
        <h2><?php echo the_title(); ?></h2>
    </div>
    <?php else : ?>

    <?php endif; ?>
```

3. If there is a thumbnail, then it's going to show a three-column and a nine-column, but if there is no thumbnail, then we want it to be a full twelve-column. For that we will use:

```php
<?php else: ?>
    <div class="col-md-12">
        IMAGE HERE
    </div>
<?php endif; ?>
```

4. We'll start with posts that have the thumbnail. We will get rid of the text `Image Here`. We will then create `div` with a class of `post-thumbnail` and then we can use `the_post_thumbnail()`:

```
<div class="col-md-3">
   <div class="post-thumbnail">
   <?php the_post_thumbnail(); ?>
   </div>
```

5. Let's take a look at that so far:

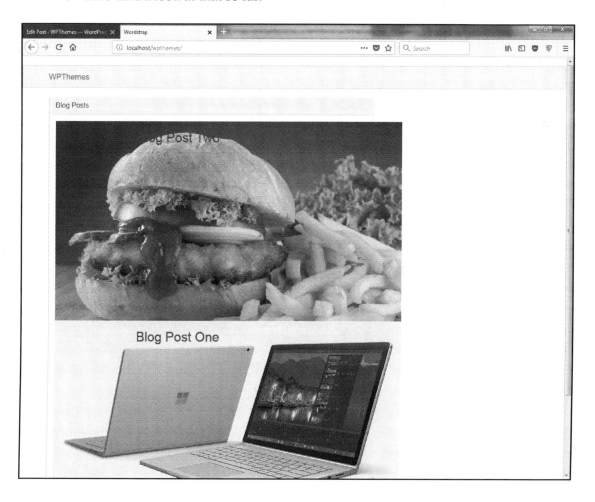

So it's showing the images, they're insanely big but that's alright, the functionality is there.

Wrapping the post in an article tag

Let's wrap the post in an `<article>` tag:

1. Right inside the `while` loop, we'll add `<article>`, give it a class of `post`, and end that just after we end `</div>`:

```
<article class="post">
   <div class="row">
      <?php if(has_post_thumbnail()): ?>
         <div class="col-md-3">
            <div class="post-thumbnail">
            <?php the_post_thumbnail(); ?>
            </div>
         </div>
         <div class="col-md-9">
            <h2><?php echo the_title(); ?></h2>
         </div>
      <?php else : ?>
         <div class="col-md-12">

         </div>
      <?php endif; ?>
   </div>
</article>
```

2. Now, open the `style.css` file and add `article.post img`. We'll set `width` to `100%`. It's going to be 100% of its container. We'll also set `height` to `auto` and let's use `margin-top:30px`.

```
article.post img{
    width:100%;
    height:auto;
    margin-top:30px;
}
```

3. Now if we reload the page, we get this:

This looks much better.

4. Now, let's go back to the `index.php` file. We want the title to be a link. Let's go right to the `<h2>` tag and let's put in an `<a>` tag using `echo the_permalink()`. And that should be a link to that post:

```
<h2>
    <a href="<?php echo the_permalink(); ?>">
        <?php echo the_title(); ?>
    </a>
</h2>
```

5. Now under the `<h2>` tag, we will place the metadata. We will add it in a paragraph and give it a class of `meta`. We will then add `Posted at` and get the time by using `the_time()` function. We will use `on` and then we'll add `the_date()`. We will open up some `<strong>` tags and add the author's name using `the_author()`, which should be a function:

```
</h2>

<p class="meta">
Posted At
<?php the_time(); ?> on
<?php the_date(); ?> by
<strong><?php the_author(); ?></strong>
</p>
```

6. Let's make sure that's working:

You can see it's telling us the time, the date, and also the author. Also, this is a link, so if I click on it, it takes us to that page or that post.

Adding content to the post

Now what we want is the excerpt or the content, but not all of it. We'll use an `excerpt` class instead of `content` because that'll truncate the content. Let's go!

1. We want to still be in the nine-column div, so we'll go under the paragraph tag and add `<div class="excerpt">`. We will then add `<?php echo get_the_excerpt(); ?>`:

   ```
   </p>
   ```

```
<div class="excerpt">
<?php echo get_the_excerpt(); ?>
</div>
```

2. Let's see if that works:

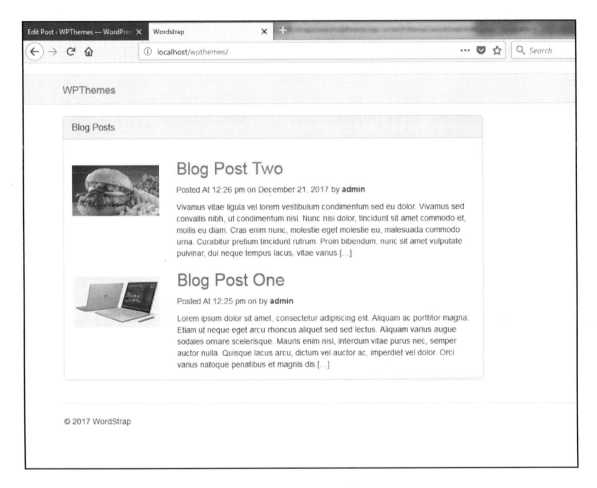

That looks good!

Adding a Read More button

Now we will also require a **Read More** button:

1. We'll go right under the excerpt class, and use bootstrap class's `btn` and then `btn-default`. We will then use `href` and set that to `the_permalink()`. For the text, we'll say `Read More` and for the arrow symbol we can use `&raquo;`. We will also add a line break above the class:

```
<br>
<a class="btn btn-default" href="<?php the_permalink(); ?>">
Read More &raquo;
</a>
```

2. Reload and let's take a look at that:

Dealing with post without an image

So now what we want to do is take care of the posts that don't have an image. Right now the **Hello World** post doesn't have one and it's not showing up because we haven't put any code in that yet. So let's check for the thumbnails now:

1. This `div` is where the code for the post without an image will go:

```
<div class="col-md-12">
    <h2>
        <a href="<?php echo the_permalink(); ?>">
        <?php echo the_title(); ?>
        </a>
    </h2>

    <p class="meta">
    Posted at
    <?php the_time(); ?> on
    <?php the_date(); ?> by
    <strong><?php the_author(); ?></strong>
    </p>

    <div class="excerpt">
    <?php echo get_the_excerpt(); ?>
    </div>
    <br>
    <a class="btn btn-default" href="<?php
       the_permalink(); ?>">
    Read More &raquo;
    </a>
```

2. Now we can have posts without images and not have just an empty space:

If we didn't use the conditional statement, then this would just have an empty space where the image was supposed to go.

Adding a bit of style

Now we will add a little bit of CSS to make the post look a little better:

1. Let's go to `style.css` and use the `article.post` with a border at the bottom of each post. The border will be gray, `solid` and 1px. Also, let's add some padding using `padding-bottom: 20px` and `margin-bottom: 30px`:

```
article.post{
    border-bottom: #ccc solid 1px;
    padding-bottom: 20px;
    margin-bottom: 30px;
}
```

2. Let's add the last article or post. We don't want to have a border for it. We will add `article.post` and use `last-child` to target that last one and we'll set `border-bottom` to none:

```
article.post:last-child{
    border-bottom:none;
}
```

3. For the metadata, we will add a little bit of style using `article.post .meta` and give it a light gray background. We will also add a little padding, `8px` and `12px`. Let's add a color; we'll use dark gray.

Let's save that and reload:

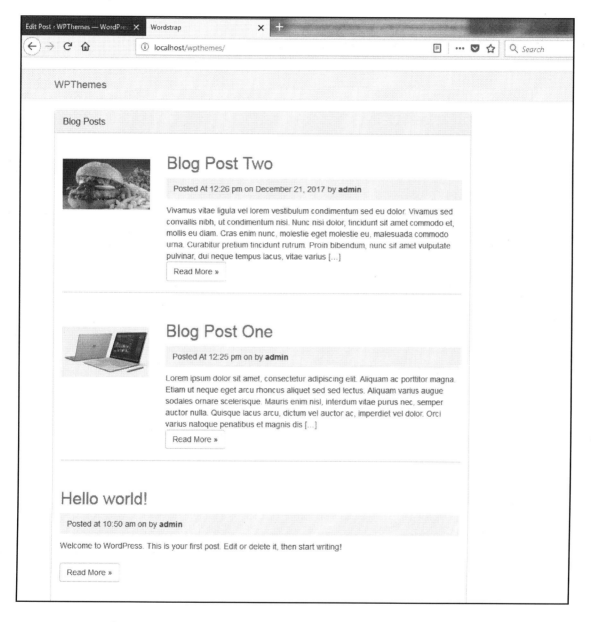

Now that looks a little better.

In the next section, we will see how to get the navbar set up with the `custom-walker` class.

Implementing Navbar

We will now see how to implement a Bootstrap navbar with a WordPress theme using `wp-bootstrap-navwalker`. This is a really popular script that will integrate your navbar so that you can create sub-items and things like that.

Displaying menu

1. Go to `www.github.com/twittem/wp-bootstrap-navwalker`, and we'll just go ahead and download the ZIP file. Open the ZIP file, and you'll see a folder with the PHP file inside it:

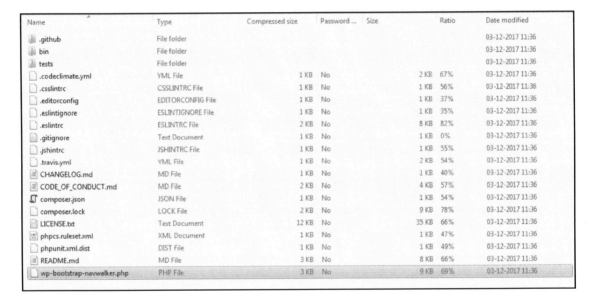

2. Let's open up our project folder. We will copy the PHP file into our folder.
3. Open the `functions.php` file and we want to include the `wp_bootstrap_navwalker.php` file as shown:

   ```php
   <?php

   require_once('wp-bootstrap-navwalker.php');

   function theme_setup(){
       // Featured Image Support
   ```

```
        add_theme_support('post-thumbnails');
    }

    add_action('after_setup_theme', 'theme_setup');
```

As you can see we have `require_once()` with `wp_bootstrap_navwalker.php`. Save it.

4. Go back to the GitHub page where we'll now deal with the usage. We want to use the `wp_nav_menu()` function inside of our navbar. For that, let's copy the highlighted part:

Update your `wp_nav_menu()` function in `header.php` to use the new walker by adding a "walker" item to the wp_nav_menu array.

```php
<?php
wp_nav_menu( array(
    'theme_location'    => 'primary',
    'depth'             => 2,
    'container'         => 'div',
    'container_class'   => 'collapse navbar-collapse',
    'container_id'      => 'bs-example-navbar-collapse-1',
    'menu_class'        => 'nav navbar-nav',
    'fallback_cb'       => 'WP_Bootstrap_Navwalker::fallback',
    'walker'            => new WP_Bootstrap_Navwalker(),
) );
```

5. Go into our `header` file where our navbar is, go down into the `div` where we have the `collapse` class, and we will paste the code as shown in the following code block:

```
<div class="collapse navbar-collapse"
  id="bs-example-navbar-collapse-1">
    <?php
        wp_nav_menu( array(
        'theme_location' => 'primary',
        'depth' => 2,
        'container' => 'div',
        'container_class' => 'collapse navbar-collapse',
        'container_id' => 'bs-example-navbar-collapse-1',
        'menu_class' => 'nav navbar-nav',
        'fallback_cb' => 'WP_Bootstrap_Navwalker::fallback',
        'walker' => new WP_Bootstrap_Navwalker(),
    ));
    ?>
    <form class="navbar-form navbar-left">
```

```
</form>
</div>
```

6. This basically defines a bunch of options for us. We don't need all of them. We will get rid of a few things. Here is the updated code:

```
wp_nav_menu( array(
    'theme_location' => 'primary',
    'depth'          => 2,
    'container'      => false,
    'menu_class'     => 'nav navbar-nav',
    'fallback_cb'    => 'wp_bootstrap_navwalker::fallback',
    'walker'         => new wp_bootstrap_navwalker())
);
```

We have the `theme_location`, which is `primary`, and `depth` is 2. We have set `container` to `false`. Get rid of the quotes, `container_class` or a `container_id`. Now save it.

7. Now go back to `functions.php`. Let's register our nav menus now by adding the following code:

```
// Nav Menus
register_nav_menus(array(
    'primary' => __('Primary Menu')
));
}

add_action('after_setup_theme', 'theme_setup');
```

Inside this `theme_setup`, we have `register_nav_menus()` and that's going to take in an array, which will be called `primary`. We'll then set that to `__()` and then the readable name will be `Primary Menu`. We'll save that.

8. Let's go back into the backend and go down to **Appearance**. You will see the **Menus** option:

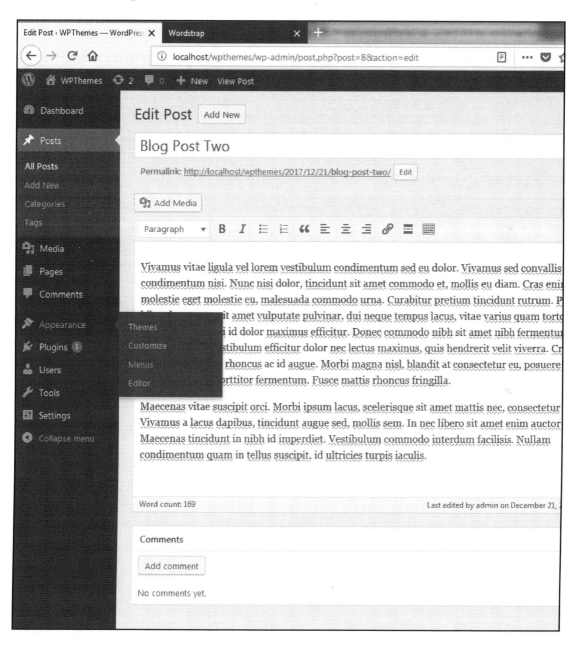

9. Now create an extra page called About and click on **Publish**. Let's create one more and we'll call this Our Team:

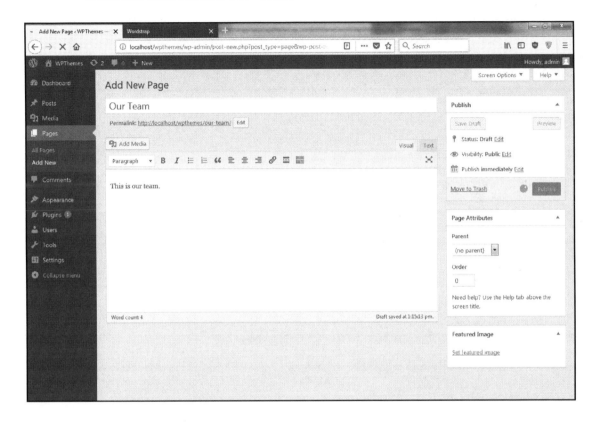

10. Go back to the **Menus** page and let's take a look at this menu. Let's go ahead and click on **Create Menu**:

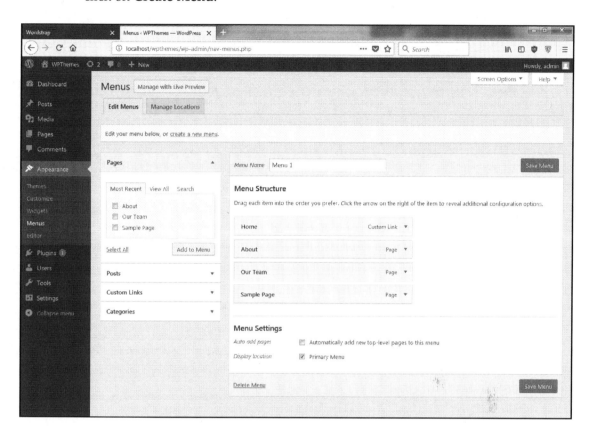

11. Ensure that you check the **Primary Menu** option and then save it:

Menu Settings

Auto add pages ☐ Automatically add new top-level pages to this menu

Display location ☑ Primary Menu

12. Go to our frontend and reload. You will now see we have our menu and it works:

13. Now let's test out the drop-down functionality. All we need to do is select **Sample Page** and **Our Team**, and place them right under **About** as shown in the following screenshot:

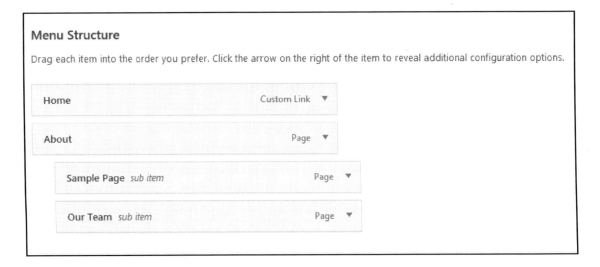

14. Save the menu, go back, and now we have a drop down:

So you can see how easy that was to implement a navbar, and this is definitely something that you could use in other projects as well, any Bootstrap WordPress theme.

Setting the sidebar

Let's now get the sidebar set up so that we can add sidebar widgets:

1. In the `functions.php` file underneath the `add_action()`, we will create a function called `init_widgets()` and that's going to take in an `id`. We will add `register_sidebar()` and that's going to take in an `array`. And then we have a bunch of options, so let's add `'name'` `=>` `'Sidebar'` and `'id'` `=>` `'sidebar'`.

    ```
    // Widget Locations
    function init_widgets($id){
        register_sidebar(array(
            'name' => 'Sidebar',
            'id'   => 'sidebar'
        ));
    }
    ```

    We can also include other things here; for instance, we can add `'before_widget'`:

    ```
    'id' => 'sidebar',
    'before_widget' => '<div class="panel panel-default">'
    ```

Now what this does is it allows us to insert code right before the widget renders. We'll need this because we want our widgets to render inside Bootstrap panels, so we need to include the panel classes. We can see we have a `div` with a class of `panel`, and also `panel-default`.

2. Let's then add `'after_widget'` and that's just going to be two ending div tags:

```
'after_widget' => '</div></div>',
```

We now also have the ability to add content before and after the title.

3. To use this, we'll use `'before_title'` and this is going to have a div with the class of `panel-heading`. We also want the `<h3>` tag, and we'll give that a class of `panel-title`:

```
'before_title' => '<div class="panel-heading">
  <h3 class="panel-title">',
```

4. Finally, we'll add `'after_title'` with ending `</h3>` and `</div>`, and then we also want the start of the `panel-body` class:

```
'after_title' => '</h3></div><div class="panel-body">'
```

5. Now we need to add an action, so we'll place `add_action()`. The hook will be `widgets_init` with the function `init_widgets`:

```
add_action('widgets_init', 'init_widgets');
```

6. Save it. If we now go to the backend and reload the page, you should now have a **Widgets** option under **Appearance**, and you should also see **Sidebar**:

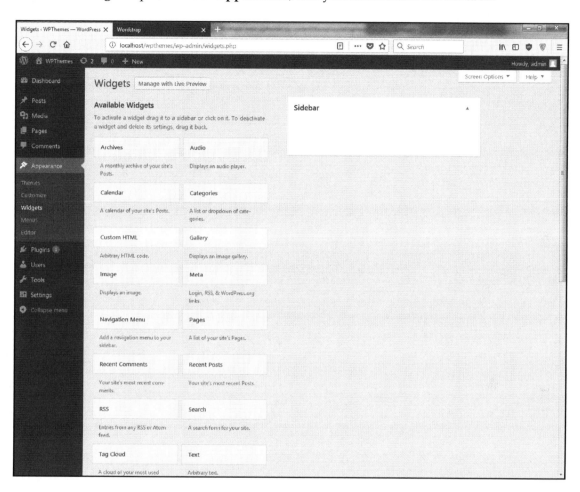

7. Now let's bring over **Categories**, and hit **Save**:

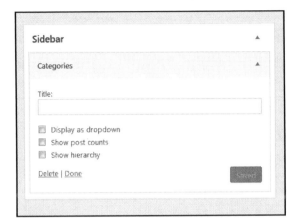

8. Let's see if those render:

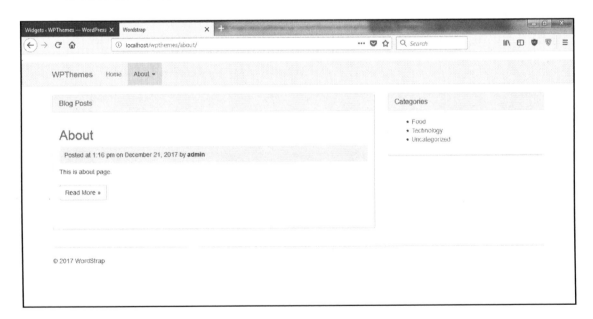

So now we have our categories and you can see that now we have the panel around it as well.

9. Let's also bring over **Recent Posts**, change **Number of posts to show** to 3, and bring over **Recent Comments**:

10. Let's take a look at our page now:

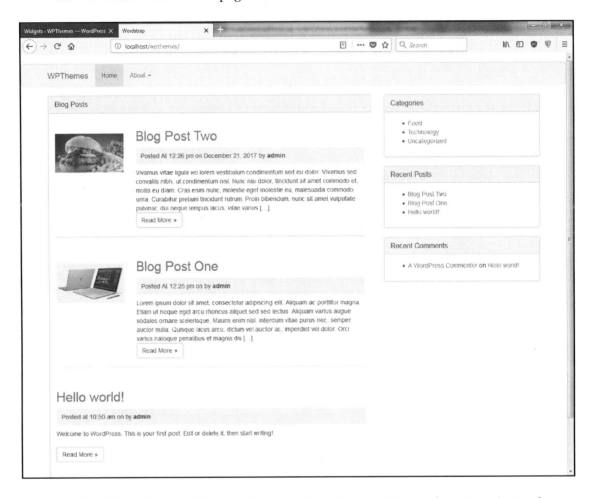

And there they are! Now we have an issue because I want the categories to show up as list groups, which are formatted better than this. They take away the bullets, add some padding, and add some borders. So what we'll need to do is create our own version of these widgets inside our theme folder.

11. Inside the `theme` folder, we'll create another folder called `widgets`. We'll go to this folder through the file manager. Now go to `wp-includes | widgets`. You'll see all of the core widget files here:

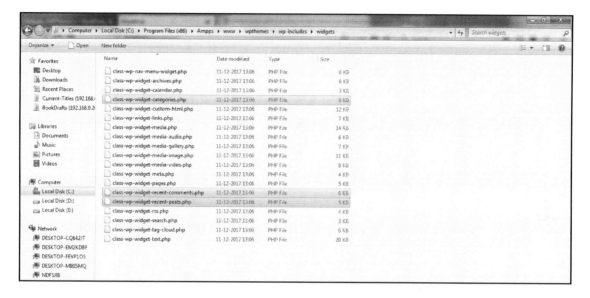

12. We want to grab the categories, the recent comments, and the recent posts. We'll copy (make sure you don't cut, but copy them) and paste them into our `widgets` folder.

13. Now let's start with the categories one. Let's open that up through Sublime Text. Here we will change the classname: put an _ and then `Custom`.

```
class WP_Widget_Categories_Custom extends WP_Widget {
```

14. Next, we will change the class names for the `<ul>` and `<li>` tags. We will add the Bootstrap classes. For this, we will add `class="list-group"` to the `<ul>` tag:

```
<ul class="list-group">
```

15. Now we also want the list items to have the class of `list-group-item` but the way that this is set up, we can't access the list item tags from within. So we need to do a little bit of customization in the `functions.php` file.

So let's open the `function.php` file, go to the very bottom, and add a comment first: Adds `'list-group-item'` to categories li, just so we know what it does. Then we add the function `add_new_class_list_categories()`:

```
// Adds 'list-group-item' to categories li
function add_new_class_list_categories(){
```

16. We will then pass in a variable by adding `$list = str_replace()`, and we'll add `cat-item`, which is the original class name, but we want to change that. Now we still want it to have the `cat-item` class because it needs that, but we also want to add on the `list-group-item class`. Then we just need to return the list.

```
function add_new_class_list_categories($list){
$list = str_replace('cat-item', 'cat-item list-group-item',
  $list);
return $list;
```

17. Now instead of adding an action, we will add `add_filter()`. Basically, an action is used when you want to add something, a filter is when you want to change something. So let's use `add_filter('wp_list_categories')` and then we place the name of our function:

```
add_filter('wp_list_categories',
  'add_new_class_list_categories');
```

18. We're not out of the woods yet with these widgets; we have to register them. So before we do that, we need to include them at the top or use `require`. So we will add `require_once()`. It's going to be the `widgets` folder, and then we just need to include each widget. We'll use `class-wp-widget-categories.php`:

```
require_once('widgets/class-wp-widget-categories.php');
```

19. We might as well include all of them. So we will get the recent posts and recent comments:

```
require_once('widgets/class-wp-widget-recent-posts.php');
require_once('widgets/class-wp-widget-recent-comments.php');
```

Now we need to register.

20. Down at the bottom, we'll add `function wordstrap_register_widgets()`. We need the classname as well, so we add `'WP_Widget_Recent_Posts_Custom'`. Next one will be `'WP_Widget_Recent_Comments_Custom'`. The last one will be to add `'WP_Widget_Categories_Custom'`:

```
//Register Widgets
function wordstrap_register_widgets(){
    register_widget('WP_Widget_Recent_Posts_Custom');
    register_widget('WP_Widget_Recent_Comments_Custom');
    register_widget('WP_Widget_Categories_Custom');
}
```

21. Now we add another `add_action()`, and this is going to be again on `'widgets_init'`, and then we just need the name of the function:

```
add_action('widgets_init', 'wordstrap_register_widgets');
```

22. Let's save that and reload the page:

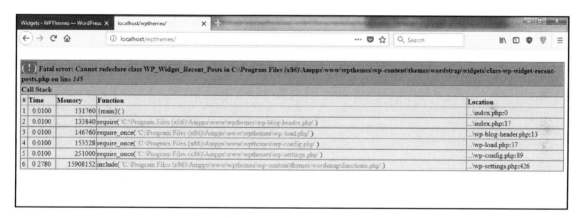

23. We get an error: **Cannot declare class Recent_Posts**. So let's verify our code:

```
class WP_Widgets_Recent_Posts_Customs extends WP_Widget {
class WP_Widgets_Recent_Comments_Customs extends WP_Widget {
```

So these should have _Custom as well. Now reload the page:

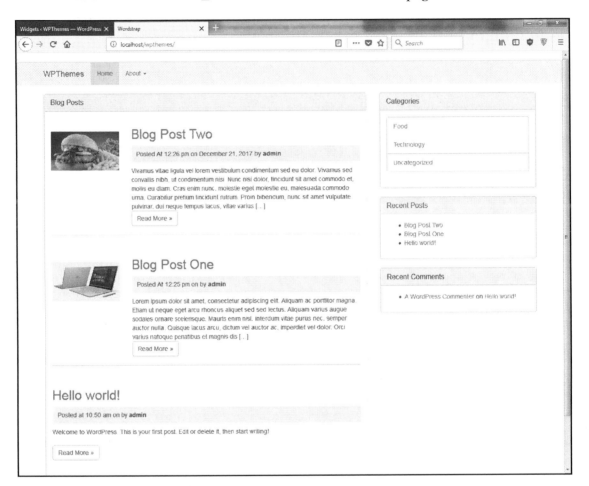

So we have all of our widgets registered and categories now has the list-item class, so that looks good. We also want to add these classes to recent posts and recent comments as well, so that instead of the bullet points we have it look like how categories look.

24. So let's go to our `class-wp-widget-recent-posts.php` widget file, and we want to go to the `<ul>` tag. We will just add a class of `list-group` and then the `<li>` tag will have a class of `list-group-item`:

```
<ul class="list-group">
<?php foreach ( $r->posts as $recent_post ) : ?>
    <li class="list-group-item">
```

Let's reload the page; that looks good!

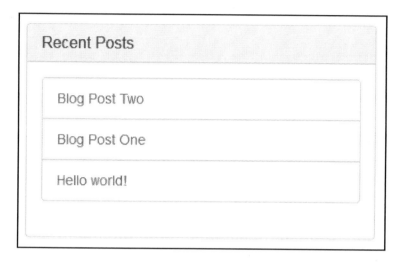

25. Now let's go to `class-wp-widget-recent-comments.php`. We will add a class to `<ul>` of `list-group` and then for the `<li>` tag, we'll add a class of `list-group-item`:

```
$output .= '<ul class="list-group" id="recentcomments">';
if(is_array($comments) && $comments){
$post_ids = array_unique(wp_list_pluck($comments,
'comment_post_ID'));
_prime_post_caches($post_ids,
strpos(get_option('permalink_structure'),
'%category'), false);
foreach((array) $comments as $comment){
    $output .= '<li class="list-group-item recentcomments">';
```

Save, reload, and there we go:

So now we have some custom widgets. You could make widgets look totally different if you want to, and it would only affect these widgets when your theme is loaded so that you're not editing any core WordPress code. We have our navbar set up as well as our sidebar widgets.

Adding a search bar and single post page

So let's get started.

Dealing with the search box

Go to our `header` file and go to the empty form down at the bottom of the file, and we will add some stuff to it. The first thing we'll do is adding a method and the method is going to be `get`. We can actually change the class from left to right. We also need to add an action. For that, we will use the `php` tags and add `echo esc_url()`.

This is because we want the URL checked and escaped. We will use `home_url` with a `/`:

```
<form method="get" class="navbar-form navbar-right"
  role="search" action="<?php echo esc_url(home_url('/')); ?>">
```

Basically, we're just submitting to the home URL.

1. Now as for the fields, we'll just want one field for **Search**, but let's add a label. So we will add `<label for ="navbar-search"` and give it a class of `sr-only`. Next let's add `<?php _e('Search')`, and this is just for localization of _e. And then we need a second parameter of `textdomain`. Let's then close up those the `php` tags and under the `</label>` tag, let's add `<div class="form-group">`. In the div class we'll have an input. We'll give it a type of `text` and give it a `class` of `form-control`, which is just a Bootstrap class. Let's add a name called s for search, and let's give it an `id` of `navbar-search`:

```
<label for="navbar-search" class="sr-only">
<?php _e('Search', 'textdomain'); ?></label>
<div class="form-group">
<input type="text" class="form-control" name="s"
  id="navbar-search">
</div>
```

2. We then need a submit. So we'll add a button with a type of `submit` and give it a class of `btn` and `btn-default`:

```
<button type="submit" class="btn btn-default">
<?php _e('Search', 'textdomain'); ?>
</button>
```

Let's save it.

Now let's do a search for `lorem`, and it gives us these results:

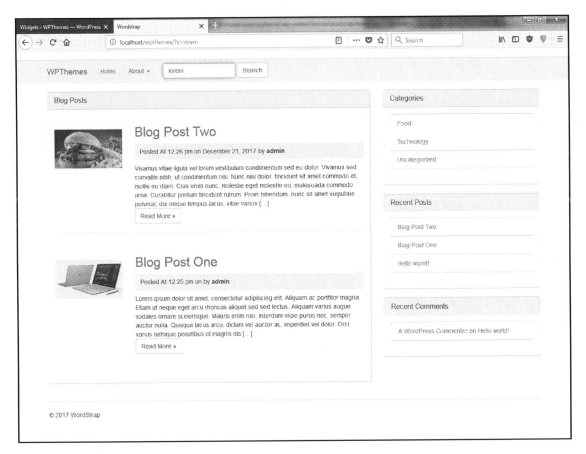

You can also try searching for the word `one` or `two`.

Now we have a search bar and the last thing that we need to do is the single post.

Dealing with the single post page

1. Let's create a file in our theme root and save the file as `single.php`.

2. Now while creating this file, if we go and click on one of these blog posts, it'll be completely blank because it's automatically looking at the `single.php` page.

3. We'll now copy everything that we have in the `index.php` file and paste it into the `single.php` file. Save it and reload the page; it looks exactly the same way as the index page:

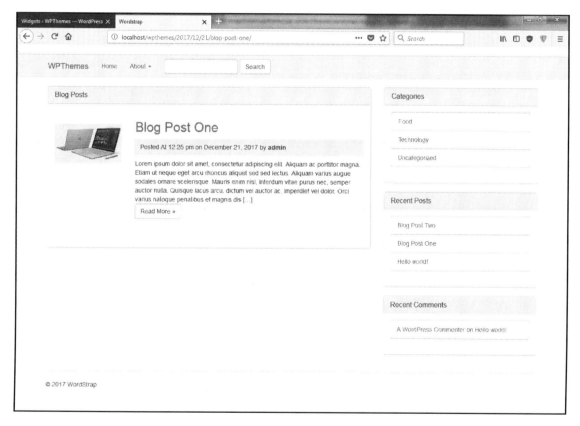

4. Let's go in and change some of that. First, let's remove `if(has_post_thumbnail())`. Now go down to where it says `else` and cut out from there up to the actual `if` statement.
   We will also get rid of `endif` because of the way we'll be formatting it irrespective of the image being present or not.

5. We want the image, though, so we'll put it. Let's put it right under the ending `</h2>`:

```php
<?php if(has_post_thumbnail()): ?>
    <div class="post-thumbnail">
        <?php the_post_thumbnail(); ?>
    </div>
<?php endif; ?>
```

6. We're putting in the thumbnail or the featured image, if there is one. Let's save that and see what that looks like:

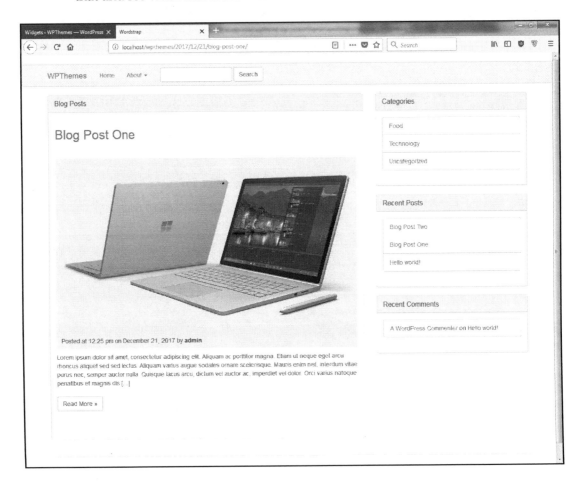

7. So we have our big image now, let's put a line break `<br>` underneath it as well.

```
<?php endif; ?>
<br>
```

We don't want **Read More** but we want the full content not the excerpt.

8. So let's get rid of **Read More**, and instead of `get_the_excerpt()` let's use `the_content()`. We will also get rid of `echo`. Let's also change the class to content:

```
<div class="content">
<?php the_content(); ?>
</div>
```

9. Save it and reload:

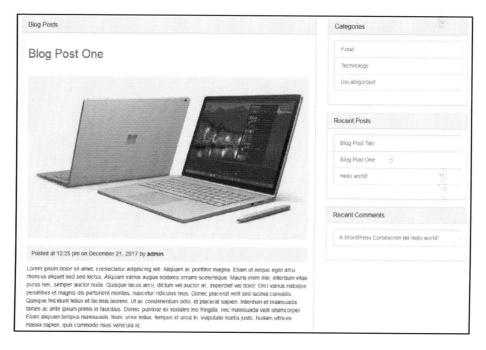

Now it renders the HTML as well. So that's the single page.

Next, we will deal with the comment functionality as well.

The comment functionality

The last thing we need to do is add some comment functionality to our single post page:

1. Let's go into `single.php` and go down. What we want to do is still within the panel body so that ends where it is shown.

2. Let's create a comment template and add `comments_template()`:

```
<?php endif; ?>
<?php comments_template(); ?>
</div>
```

3. We'll save that and create a new file. We'll save it as `comments.php`.

   That needs to be in your `theme` folder, and then if we go ahead and type something in here, we'll say `TEST`.

4. If we save and reload, and you can see we're getting **TEST**:

Vivamus vitae ligula vel lorem vestibulum condimentum sed eu dolor. Vivamus sed convallis nibh, ut condimentum nisi. Nunc nisi dolor, tincidunt sit amet commodo et, mollis eu diam. Cras enim nunc, molestie eget molestie eu, malesuada commodo urna. Curabitur pretium tincidunt rutrum. Proin bibendum, nunc sit amet vulputate pulvinar, dui neque tempus lacus, vitae varius quam tortor at odio. Nunc tristique nisi id dolor maximus efficitur. Donec commodo nibh sit amet nibh fermentum, vel luctus turpis tempus. Vestibulum efficitur dolor nec lectus maximus, quis hendrerit velit viverra. Cras eget orci eu augue tristique rhoncus ac id augue. Morbi magna nisl, blandit at consectetur eu, posuere vel erat. In vulputate leo in porttitor fermentum. Fusce mattis rhoncus fringilla.

Maecenas vitae suscipit orci. Morbi ipsum lacus, scelerisque sit amet mattis nec, consectetur eget diam. Vivamus a lacus dapibus, tincidunt augue sed, mollis sem. In nec libero sit amet enim auctor pulvinar. Maecenas tincidunt in nibh id imperdiet. Vestibulum commodo interdum facilisis. Nullam condimentum quam in tellus suscipit, id ultricies turpis iaculis.

TEST

Now let's create a div with a class of comments and add `<?php if(have_comments); ?>`.

5. We also add heading `<h3>` with class of comments_title. We will add `if(get_comments_number() == 1)`. We are doing this because if there's only one comment then we should get comment singular, if there's more than one then it should say comments.

6. So we're checking to see if there's one comment, if there is then we'll echo `get_comments_number()` and then just concatenate the word Comment. Then we'll put an `else` and just add an Comments to the end here:

```
<div class="comments">
<?php if(have_comments()): ?>
    <h3 class="comments-title">
    <?php
        if(get_comments_number() == 1){
            echo get_comments_number(). ' Comment';
        } else {
            echo get_comments_number(). ' Comments';
        }
    ?>
    </h3>
```

So that'll be the heading.

7. Then under the `</h3>` tag, we'll have a `<ul>` tag, give it a class of row and comment-list. We will add `wp_list_comments()` and that's going to get passed in an array. We will also use avatars so let's add avatar_size and set that to 90. We then have a callback, which we have to create as well.

For that, we will add add_theme_comments and this is going to go inside the functions.php file.

```
<ul class="row comment-list">
<?php
    wp_list_comments(array(
        'avatar_size' => 90,
        'callback'    => 'add_theme_comments'
    ));
?>
</ul>
```

8. Now, we have a few big blocks of code that we need to use:

```php
<?php if(!comments_open() && '0' != get_comments_number() &&
  post_type_supports(get_post_type(), 'comments')) : ?>
   <p class="no-comments"><?php _e('Comments are closed.',
    'dazzling'); ?>
   </p>
<?php endif; ?>
</div>
```

The preceding code is going to check if comments are closed, and if they are then we can leave a little note.

9. Now let's go under this `div` and we'll put a horizontal rule. We then need to create our comment arguments and then create the form:

```php
<hr>
<?php
    $comments_args = array(
    // change the title of send button
    'label_submit'=>'Send',
    // change the title of the reply section
    'title_reply'=>'Write a Reply or Comment',
    // remove "Text or HTML to be displayed after the set of comment
    //fields"
    'comment_notes_after'=>'',
    // redefine your own textarea (the comment body)
    'comment_field'=>'<p class="comment-form-comment">
    <label for="comment">' ._x('Comment', 'noun') . '</label><br/>
    <textarea class="form-control" id="comment" name="comment"
     aria-required="true">
    </textarea></p>',
    );
comment_form($comments_args);
```

We have a variable called `comment_args` and that's set to an array with a bunch of different values. You can have your submit button label, the title reply, notes, and things like that. Then down in the code file, we're also calling the `comment_form()` function and passing in those arguments.

10. Save it and reload. Now if we go and try to check it out now you can see that we have a form here. Let's try to add something:

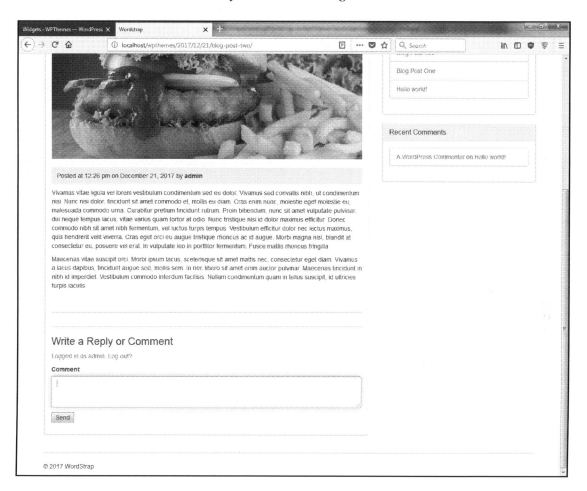

11. Click on **Send**:

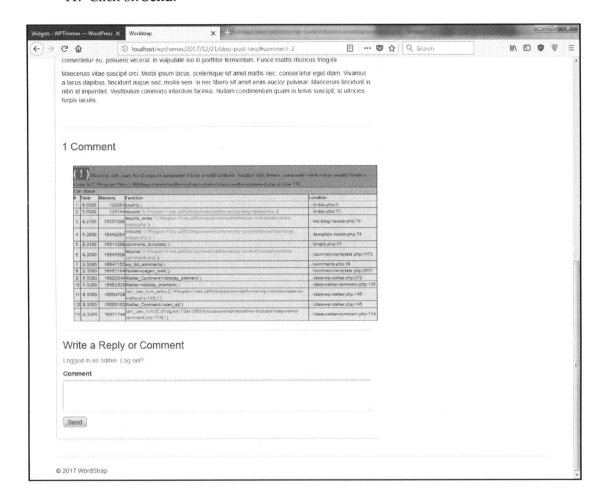

12. Now what's going on here is it's looking for the callback that we specified. It is up at `add_theme_comments` as shown:

```php
<?php
    wp_list_comments(array(
        'avatar_size' => 90,
        'callback' => 'add_theme_comments'
    ));
?>
```

It is looking for callback but not finding it. So let's go into `functions.php` and we'll fix that.

13. We'll go ahead and paste the code as shown:

```php
// Add Comments
function add_theme_comments($comment, $args, $depth){
    $GLOBALS['comment'] = $comment;
    extract($args, EXTR_SKIP);

    if('div' == $args['style']){
        $tag = 'div';
        $add_below = 'comment';
    } else {
        $tag = 'li class="well comment-item"';
        $add_below = 'div-comment';
    }
```

So we have a function called `add_theme_comments()` and that should match your callback. Then we pass in `comment`, `args`, and `depth`. As you can see we have added some tags and classes below so that we can style this.

14. Now we'll post some other stuff in as well. For that lets add the following code:

```php
<<?php echo $tag ?>
<?php comment_class(empty($args['has_children']) ? '' : 'parent') ?>
  id="comment-<?php comment_ID() ?>">
<?php if('div' != $args['style']) : ?>
<div id="div-comment-<?php comment_ID() ?>" class="comment-body">
<?php endif; ?>
```

```php
        <div class="col-md-2">
        <div class="comment-author vcard">
        <?php if($args['avatar_size'] != 0)
          echo get_avatar($comment, $args['avatar_size']); ?>
        <?php printf(__('<cite class="fn">%s</cite>'),
           get_comment_author_link()); ?>
        </div>
        </div>

        <div class="col-md-10">
        <?php if($comment->comment_approved =='0') : ?>
        <em class="comment-awaiting-moderation">
        <?php _e('Your comment is awaiting moderation.'); ?></em>
        <br/>
        <?php endif; ?>

        <div class="comment-meta commentmetadata">
        <a href="<?php echo htmlspecialchars(get_comment_link
           ($comment->comment_ID)); ?>">
        <?php
           printf(__('%1$s at %2$s'), get_comment_date(),
get_comment_time()); ?></a>
        <?php edit_comment_link(__('(Edit)'), ' ', ''); ?>
        </div>
        <?php comment_text(); ?>

        <div class="reply">
        <?php comment_reply_link(array_merge($args, array
          ( 'add_below' => $add_below, 'depth' =>
           $depth, 'max_depth' => $args['max_depth'] )));
        ?>
        </div>
        </div>

    <?php if('div' != $args['style']) : ?>
    </div>
    <?php endif; ?>
    <?php
    }
```

You can get the code from the WordPress documentation (`https://codex.`
`wordpress.org/Function_Reference/wp_list_comments`).

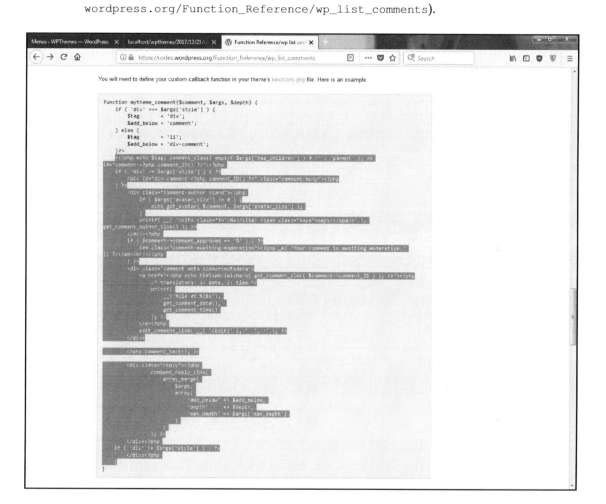

So this code will give you correct functionality.

15. Let's go ahead and save the code and see what happens:

16. Now let's open up `style.css` and the class called `comment-item`. So in the code we add `.comment-item` and set `overflow` to `auto`. We will also add `comment-list`, and set `list-style` to `none` and `margin` to 0. We then mark that as important and set `padding` to 0:

```
.comment-list{
    list-style: none;
    margin:0 !important;
    padding:0 !important;
}

.comment-item{
    overflow:auto;
}
```

That looks pretty good. We can reply and leave comments, and that's really awesome. So that's it, we are done. We now have a WordPress theme with Bootstrap, and you could use this as a base theme to create other Bootstrap themes. You can use the `navbar-walker`, which is really helpful.

Summary

Awesome!! In this chapter we saw how to build a Twitter Bootstrap WordPress theme. We dealt with widgets such as **Categories**, **Recent Posts**, and **Recent Comments** to make them fit in with the Bootstrap theme.

We also worked on the posts loop and included the metadata for it. We saw how to get the navbar set up as well as our sidebar widgets. We also added a Search box and built the single pages. We also dealt with comment functionality – the comments section and form. I hope you enjoyed this chapter.

5
The Foundation E-Commerce Theme

In this chapter, we'll build an e-commerce theme or an online shop theme. We'll not have full functionality to buy products, but just the theme, and we'll look at how to format it so that the posts look more like product pages.

The following screenshot is of the home page we'll create. We have a header (**MyShop**), a spot for a custom image (this is going to be available through the theme customizer, so you can upload that), our menu over the top-right corner of the page, a showcase widget (which is the big rectangular space right below the header, **MyShop** with a heading—Discount Clothing, some texts, and **Read more**), and we'll see where we can actually edit that content. If we scroll down the page (below the showcase widget rectangle) we have the main post loop, but we have it formatted so that it looks more like an e-commerce site.

Lastly, we have some side widgets which is to right-hand side of the page:

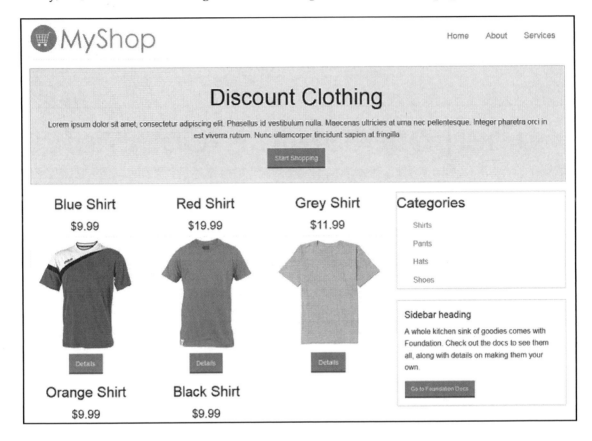

Now, if we click on **Details** for one of the products, for example, **Black Shirt**, it's going to take us to the product page (as shown in the following screenshot). It has the image, title, text, price, and then a **Buy Now** button. Also, we have the tags below the **Buy Now** button as shown in the following screenshot:

Black Shirt

Lorem ipsum dolor sit amet, consectetur adipiscing elit. Aliquam aliquet turpis dui, sit amet vestibulum tellus aliquet sit amet. Praesent viverra lorem at ipsum dignissim, dictum pellentesque enim finibus. Curabitur et turpis id elit vehicula auctor et vel ante. Nunc at erat dictum, porta nibh vitae, egestas augue.

$9.99

Buy Now

Tags: Black, Clothing, Shirt

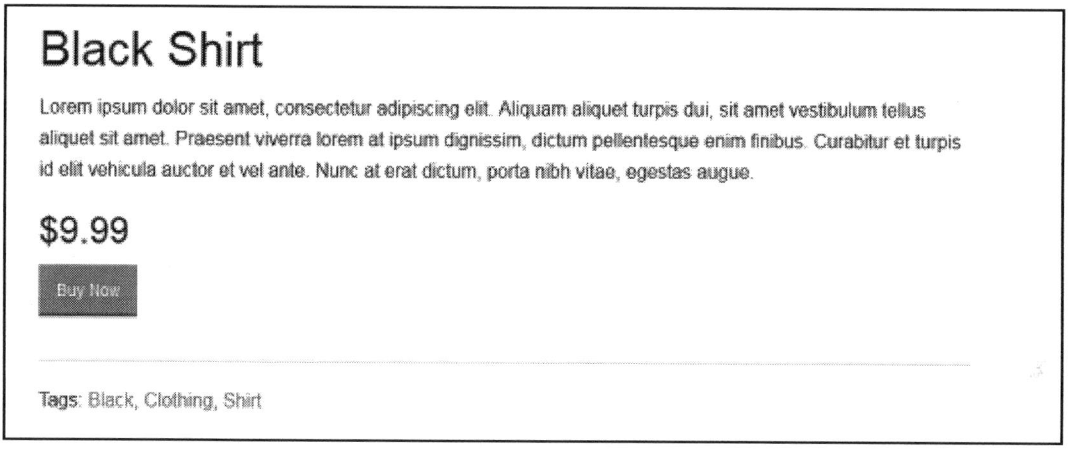

Also, if we go to **Blue & White Shirt** we can see we have some images, so we can include an image gallery as well, and we will see how to do that:

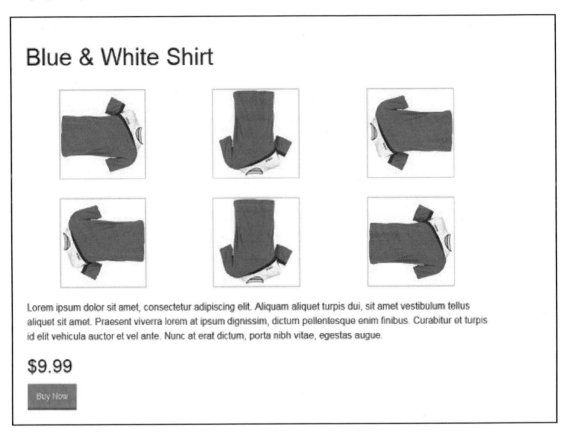

The pages themselves are very simple. We just have an **About** page with a title and heading, and it's the same with **Sample Page**. If we go to the backend of the page and go to **Posts**, we can see the different products we have. Click on the **Pink Shirt** product; we have included the text, the price, and the button. If we scroll down, on the bottom-right corner we can see we're using the featured image.

For the showcase, if we go to **Appearance** | **Widgets**, we can see in **Showcase** we have a **Showcase widget**, which is actually a custom widget that we'll create and use it in the theme. We also have our **Sidebar** at the right-hand side of the page with the **Categories** and then the **Text widget**. Now for the gallery, if we go to the **Blue Shirt** product and click on **Add Media,** we can go to **Create Gallery** and choose a bunch of images, go ahead, and upload that gallery. If we click on **Visual**, you can see that and we can edit it as a whole by clicking on the Edit icon as seen in the following screenshot:

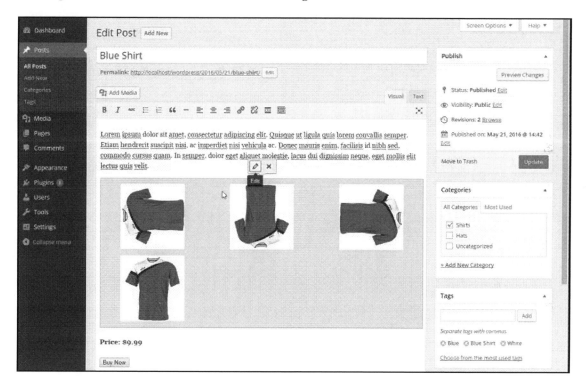

That's pretty simple. It's not the best looking online shop you've ever seen, but it does have some features that are really important. For the logo, what we can do to switch that is go to **Appearance** | **Customize** | **Site Identity** and then you will see the **Logo** option from where we can remove it. We can also change it and update our title and tagline.

E-commerce HTML template – Part A

We'll first build a flat-out HTML template and then move on to integrating it and making it a WordPress theme. Let's go ahead and create a folder for this template, and we will call this `myshop_html`. Now let us download Foundation from `foundation.zurb.com`. Click on the **Download Foundation 6** button which will take you to the downloads page. Now, click on **Download Everything** under **Complete**:

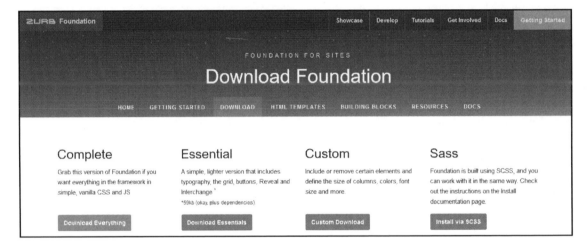

We'll now open up the downloaded ZIP file and let's just take everything out and move it to our `myshop_html` folder:

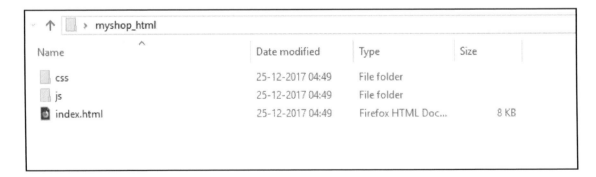

Now if we open up `index.html` with our desired web browser, we will see that we pretty much have a boilerplate:

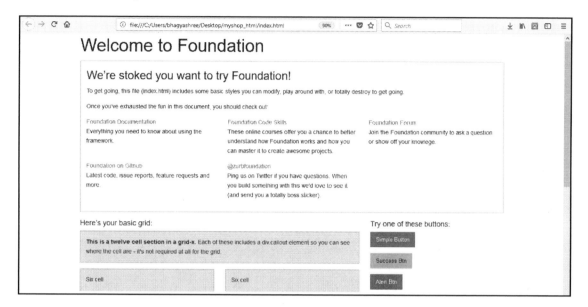

The CSS is implemented and the JavaScript should be implemented, so let's go ahead and open up `index.html` in our editor. We will work through this code of `index.html` and replace what we need. Let's open up our CSS file, `app.css`, inside the CSS folder in the `myshop_html` folder that we have created. There's nothing inside our CSS file; the only styles are the core foundation styles.

We also have some images that we need to upload (you will get these images along with the code bundle), so we will create a new folder called `img` and paste these images inside the `img` folder. If we take a look at the images, we have our `logo.jpg` and a bunch of clothes.

We have a bunch of shirts and a hat. The blue shirt has multiple images because we'll implement a mini gallery, so these are all the images that we'll be needing:

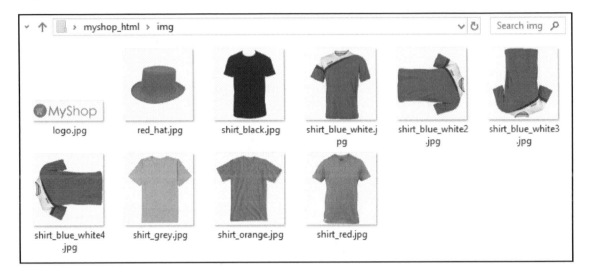

Let's go back to the `index.html` file. The head can stay how it is; we're linking our CSS files and our viewport is already set. In the `<body>` tag, you will see that we are using the XY grid system. The first `<div>` tag has a class of `grid-container`. The grid will default to the full width of the available space. To contain it we use the `grid-container` class. Below this, we have a `<div>` tag with two classes—`grid-x` and `grid-padding-x`:

```
<body>
  <div class="grid-container">
    <div class="grid-x grid-padding-x">
      <div class="large-12 cell">
        <h1>Welcome to Foundation</h1>
      </div>
    </div>
```

We will change this `<div>` to `<header>` and change the `large-12` div to `large-6` div, as shown in the following code snippet:

```
<body>
  <div class="grid-container">
    <header class="grid-x grid-padding-x">
      <div class="large-6 cell">
        <img src="./img/logo.jpg">
      </div>
    </header>
```

Reload the `index.html` page and you will see our logo:

Next, add a second `<div>` tag. This will have our navigation menu:

```
<header class="grid-x grid-padding-x">
  <div class="large-6 cell">
    <img src="./img/logo.jpg">
  </div>
  <div class="large-6 cell">
    <ul class="menu simple main-nav">
      <li><a href="index.html">Home</a></li>
      <li><a href="about.html">About</a></li>
      <li><a href="index.html">Services</a></li>
    </ul>
  </div>
</header>
```

Let's save that and reload the web page:

The style that the menu has is coming from the core foundation file. We'll add some other styles; for instance, we push it down, we push it over, but we'll get into the CSS after the HTML.

Next, we have the showcase area which is going to change quite a bit. We'll add the `showcase` class to the `<div>` tag with the `grid-x` and `grid-padding-x` classes. We'll leave the 12-cells and `callout` div as it is, but we will add a class called `secondary`, which will make it gray. Get rid of everything inside that. Inside the `secondary` class div we'll have an h1, and this will say `Discount Clothing`, and then we will paste in a paragraph and a `button` as seen in the following code:

```
  </header>
    <div class="grid-x grid-padding-x showcase">
      <div class="large-12 cell">
        <div class="callout secondary">
          <h1>Discount Clothing</h1>
            <p>Lorem ipsum dolor sit amet, consectetur adipiscing elit.
            Phasellus id vestibulum nulla. Maecenas ultricies
            at urna nec pellentesque.
            Integer pharetra orci in est viverra rutrum.
            Nunc ullamcorper tincidunt sapien at fringilla</p>
          <button class="button">Start Shopping</button>
        </div>
      </div>
    </div>
```

Now, you will see the showcase area which appears in the web page under the **MyShop** logo:

We'll add some more styles to the paragraph afterwards so don't worry about it. If we scroll down in our editor, we have another `grid-x grid-padding-x` div, this has an 8-cells `div`, which is the main area:

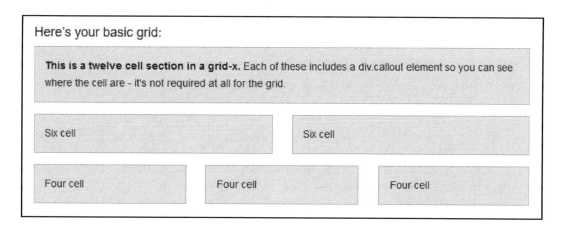

Then, way down at the bottom there's a 4-cells `div`, which is the sidebar:

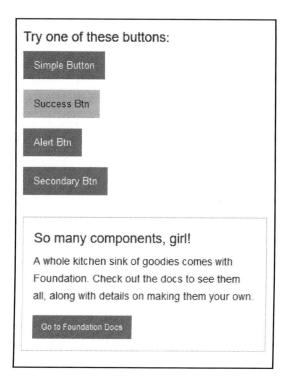

We will clear these divs out completely. Now we have a cleared out 8-cells div and a sidebar of 4-cells div. Next, for the products we'll add a `<div>` tag inside the 8-cells div and give it a class of `products`.

Inside this div, we will add 4-cell divs and give them a class of `large-4 medium-4 small-12 columns product end`. We will add the title, price, and image and then we'll put in a button. Here's how our first product's div looks like:

```
<div class="grid-x grid-padding-x">
  <div class="large-8 medium-8 cell">
    <div class="grid-x grid-padding-x">
      <div class="products">
        <div class="large-4 medium-4 small-12 cell product end">
          <h3>Blue Shirt</h3>
          <h4>$9.99</h4>
          <img src="./img/shirt_blue_white.jpg">
          <button class="button">Details</button>
        </div>
      </div>
    </div>
  </div>
</div>
```

 When we do the WordPress theme things might look a little different than the HTML theme because there's some limitation to where we can put the content. So just remember that there may be some minor differences.

Now, let's grab the 4-cell div and paste it in a bunch of times. We will just change the content a little bit to add all the shirts:

```
<div class="grid-x grid-padding-x">
  <div class="large-8 medium-8 cell">
    <div class="grid-x grid-padding-x">
      <div class="products">
        <div class="large-4 medium-4 small-12 cell product">
          <h3>Blue Shirt</h3>
          <h4>$9.99</h4>
          <img src="./img/shirt_blue_white.jpg">
          <button class="button">Details</button>
        </div>
        <div class="large-4 medium-4 small-12 cell product">
          <h3>Red Shirt</h3>
          <h4>$19.99</h4>
          <img src="./img/shirt_red.jpg">
          <button class="button">Details</button>
        </div>
        <div class="large-4 medium-4 small-12 cell product end">
          <h3>Grey Shirt</h3>
          <h4>$11.99</h4>
          <img src="./img/shirt_grey.jpg">
          <button class="button">Details</button>
```

```
      </div>
      <div class="large-4 medium-4 small-12 cell product end">
        <h3>Orange Shirt</h3>
        <h4>$9.99</h4>
        <img src="./img/shirt_orange.jpg">
        <button class="button">Details</button>
      </div>
      <div class="large-4 medium-4 small-12 cell product end">
        <h3>Black Shirt</h3>
        <h4>$9.99</h4>
        <img src="./img/shirt_black.jpg">
        <button class="button">Details</button>
      </div>
    </div>
   </div>
  </div>
 </div>
```

Now reload the `index.html` page:

Now for the sidebar we'll go down to the 4-cell div and add the following code:

```
<div class="large-4 medium-4 cell">
  <div class="callout">
    <h3>Categories</h3>
    <ul class="menu vertical">
      <li><a href="#">Shirts</a></li>
      <li><a href="#">Pants</a></li>
      <li><a href="#">Hats</a></li>
      <li><a href="#">Shoes</a></li>
    </ul>
  </div>
  <br>
  <div class="callout">
    <h5>Sidebar heading</h5>
    <p>A whole kitchen sink of goodies comes with Foundation.
       Check out the docs to see them all, along with details on
       making them your own.</p>
    <a href="http://foundation.zurb.com/sites/docs/" class="small button">
    Go to Foundation Docs</a>
  </div>
</div>
```

We have given the div a class of callout that gives it a border and some padding. We have also added the Categories heading and the <ul> tag with the class of menu and vertical. We will have one more sidebar widget right below it with a heading and some text. This is how our sidebar will look like:

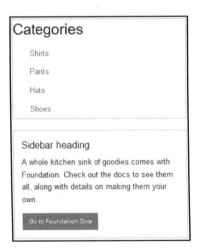

Now we'll go down to the very bottom, right above the script tags, and create our footer. Our footer is just going to be a paragraph, we'll put our copyright. The code for the footer is:

```
<footer>
  <p>&copy; 2017, MyShop</p>
</footer>
```

That's it for the index.html page! Now we will move on to the details page, and obviously we'll fix rest of the index and details page in the second part where we'll do the CSS.

Let's go back to our myshop_html folder and create a new file called details.html. Copy the code of index.html and paste it in the details.html file. Now go to the main area, the 8-cell div. We will change the products class to single-product, remove all the products, and change the 4-cell div to 12-cell div:

```
<div class="large-8 medium-8 cell">
  <div class="grid-x grid-padding-x">
    <div class="single-product">
      <div class="large-12 medium-12 small-12 cell product end">
      </div>
    </div>
  </div>
</div>
```

Now inside the 12-cell div that we just updated, we'll have two more columns. Here's the new code after some changes to the 12-column div:

```
<div class="large-8 medium-8 cell">
  <div class="grid-x grid-padding-x">
    <div class="single-product">
      <div class="large-12 medium-12 small-12 cell product end">
        <div class="large-5 medium-5 small-5 cell product end">
        </div>
        <div class="large-7 medium-7 small-7 cell product end">
        </div>
      </div>
    </div>
  </div>
</div>
```

As shown in the preceding code, we have a 5-cell div in which we will add the image and a 7-cell div which will contain the content. Here is how our final code will look like:

```
<div class="large-8 medium-8 cell">
  <div class="grid-x grid-padding-x">
    <div class="single-product">
      <div class="large-12 medium-12 small-12 cell product end">
        <div class="grid-x grid-padding-x">
          <div class="large-5 medium-5 small-5 cell product end">
            <a href="index.html">Go Back</a>
            <img src="./img/shirt_blue_white.jpg">
          </div>
          <div class="large-7 medium-7 small-7 cell product end">
            <h2>Blue & Shirt</h2>
            <h4>Price: $9.99</h4>
            <p>Lorem ipsum dolor sit amet, consectetur adipiscing elit.
                Phasellus id vestibulum nulla. Maecenas ultricies at
                urna nec pellentesque. Integer pharetra orci in est viverra
                rutrum. Nunc ullamcorper tincidunt sapien at fringilla</p>
            <button class="button">Buy Now</button>
            <hr>
            <div class="tags"><strong>Tags:</strong>Shirt, Blue Shirt,
                White Shirt</div>
          </div>
        </div>
      </div>
    </div>
  </div>
</div>
```

As we want the 5-cell and 7-cell div in a single row, we have added a div of classes grid-x and grid-padding-x in the 12-cell div.

Now, let's reload the details.html page:

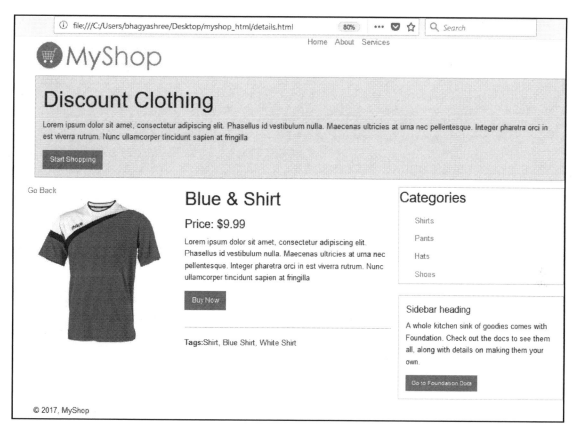

That looks good so far in our web page.

Now we're also going to create an **About** page just to represent a normal page that's not a product page. Let's go to our myshop_html folder again and create a new file, and we'll name it about.html. Open that up in our editor, and now we are going to copy everything that we have in the details.html file. Then we will go to the main area and instead of having a 5-cell and a 7-cell, we'll just have the one 12-cell div. The code for the about section is:

```
<div class="large-12 medium-12 small-12 cell product end">
  <h2>About Us</h2>
  <p>Lorem ipsum dolor sit amet, consectetur adipiscing elit,
     sed do eiusmod tempor incididunt ut labore et dolore magna aliqua.
     Ut enim ad minim veniam, quis nostrud exercitation ullamco laboris
     nisi ut aliquip ex ea commodo consequat. Duis aute irure dolor in
     reprehenderit in voluptate velit esse cillum dolore eu
     fugiat nulla pariatur. Excepteur sint occaecat cupidatat non
```

```
        proident, sunt in culpa qui officia deserunt mollit anim id est
        laborum.</p>

    <p>Ex soleat habemus usu, te nec eligendi deserunt vituperata.
        Natum consulatu vel ea, duo cetero repudiare efficiendi cu. Has at
        quas nonumy facilisis, enim percipitur mei ad.
        Mazim possim adipisci sea ei, omnium aeterno platonem mei no.
        Consectetur adipiscing elit, sed do eiusmod tempor incididunt
        ut labore et dolore magna aliqua. Ut enim ad minim veniam,
        quis nostrud exercitation ullamco laboris nisi ut aliquip ex
        ea commodo consequat.</p>
</div>
```

Let's go to **About** section in our web page, and there we go, just some text and a heading:

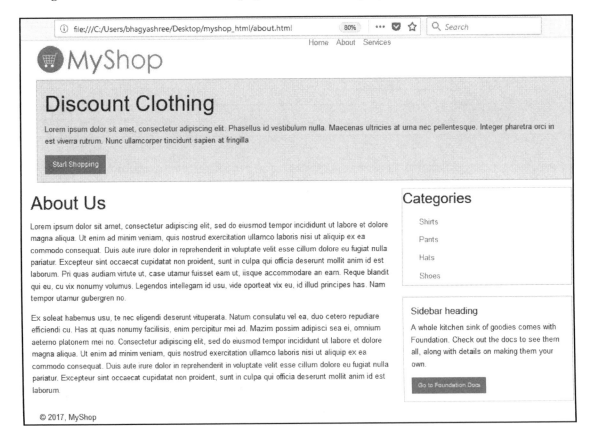

E-commerce HTML template – Part B

We have the HTML done, but we need to do the CSS bit. Let's go ahead and open up `app.css` and if we take a look at the template, we'll have to start with the core styles.

Now we will notice that by default, the buttons and the links are blue. We actually want to change that to red. We'll put `a` tag, let's write `color` and that's going to be a value of `ec2c2f`, which will give it the red color. Now we also want the buttons to have a background color of red. Let's say, we also want to give the buttons a little border at the bottom. So, we'll use `border-bottom: 3px #333solid;`.

Now when we hover over the buttons, you'll see it turns blue, same thing with the links:

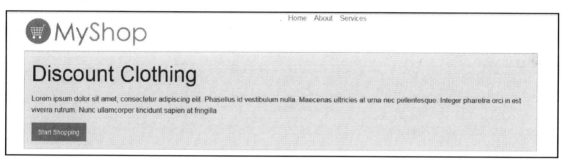

To fix this, let's use the following code:

```
a{
    color: #ec2c2f;
}

a:hover{
    color: #333;
}

.button{
    background:#ec2c2f;
    border-bottom: 3px #333 solid;
}

.button:hover{
    background:#333;
}
```

Let's save the file and reload the page. This is what you will now see with the buttons and links in red even when you hover over them:

Let's now take care of the positions of the **Home**, **About**, and **Services** links. We want them to be at the top-right of the page. Here's the code to do this with some font size modifications:

```
header .main-nav{
    float:right;
    margin-top: 30px;
    font-size: 18px;
}

header .main-nav li{
    padding-right:20px;
}
```

Let's reload the page and see the changes:

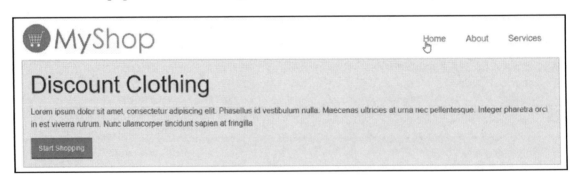

Let's also give a little margin to the header on the bottom:

```
header{
    margin-bottom: 20px;
}
```

Reload the page and this is what you should see:

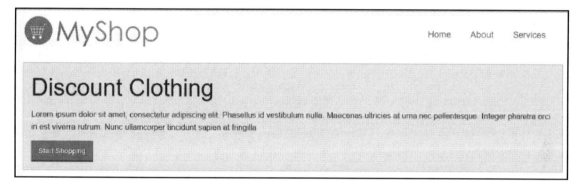

Next, let's do the showcase area. For this, use the following code:

```
.showcase .callout{
    text-align: center;
    padding: 30px;
    margin-bottom: 20px;
}
```

Here's what you will see now:

Now for the products area, we'll write `products .columns`, we're just going to add a `margin-bottom` and let's do `product`, singular, and for that we want to `text-align` to the center. Let's see, so for the button we want to add a little margin to the top, so let's write `product .button` `margin-top` and let's use `10px`:

```
.products .columns{
    margin-bottom: 40px;
}

.product{
    text-align: center;
}

.product .button{
    margin-top: 10px;
}
```

Let's save that and reload the page:

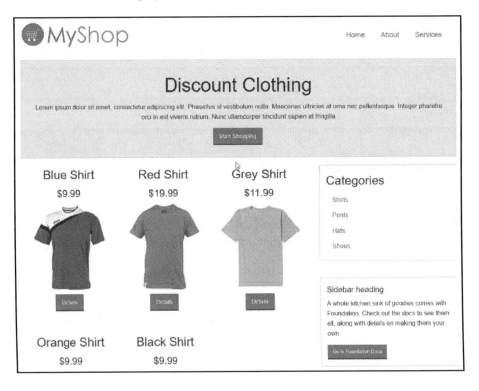

Now for the menu on the right-hand side of our webpage (**Categories**), we will add a border underneath each list item. However, we don't want to have a border for the last list item. Type the following code to execute this:

```
.vertical li{
    border-bottom: 1px #ccc solid;
}

.vertical li:last-child{
    border-bottom: none;
}
```

Save that and reload the page:

Lastly, let's add the footer. We'll set some properties and display the footer on the page using the following code:

```
footer{
    background: #333;
    color: #fff;
    text-align: center;
    margin-top: 30px;
    padding-top: 20px;
    height: 70px;
}
```

Save that and reload the page:

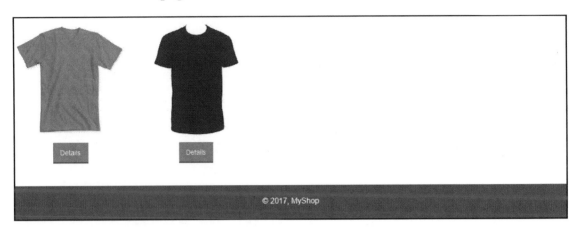

Let's take a look at **Details** and **About** page on our webpage. You will see that the **Details** page looks good; however, the **About** page has the content center-aligned. To fix this, go to the `about.html` file and remove `product end` from the 12-column div. Reload the page, and the **About** page should look perfectly fine.

In the next section, we'll jump into WordPress and we'll start to create a WordPress theme based on this design.

Theme setup, logo, and navigation

Now that the HTML template is done, we can now start to convert it into a WordPress theme.

We have a default installation of WordPress. Let's create a new theme folder. We will go to `wp-content | themes` and create a new folder, `MyShop`. Inside `MyShop`, we'll create an `index.php` file and a `style.css` file. Let's go ahead and put our declaration in our `style.css` file as shown in the following snippet:

```
/*
    Theme name: MyShop
    Author: Brad Traversy
    Author URI: http://eduonix.com
    Description: Simple ecommerce theme
    Version: 1.0.0
*/
```

Let's save that. Now if we go to the backend in our webpage and go to **Appearance** | **Themes**, we'll see **MyShop** as seen in the following screenshot:

We have a screenshot that we can pop above the **MyShop** preview image in our project files. Paste this inside the MyShop folder. So now we have **MyShop**, let's go ahead and activate it. Obviously, right now if we go and reload the frontend, it'll just be blank.

We'll open the MyShop and myshop_html folders, which is the HTML template that we created, and bring over the css and the js folders into the MyShop folder. Now we have a style.css in our WordPress site. We'll take everything out of the app.css file from our template, cut that out, put it into style.css, and save it. Then we can completely delete the app.css.

We'll now put everything from our `index.html` folder into `index.php`. Let's save that, and if we go to our website and reload the page, we can see all of our HTML there. The CSS isn't connected yet so we're not seeing that, but you can see the HTML:

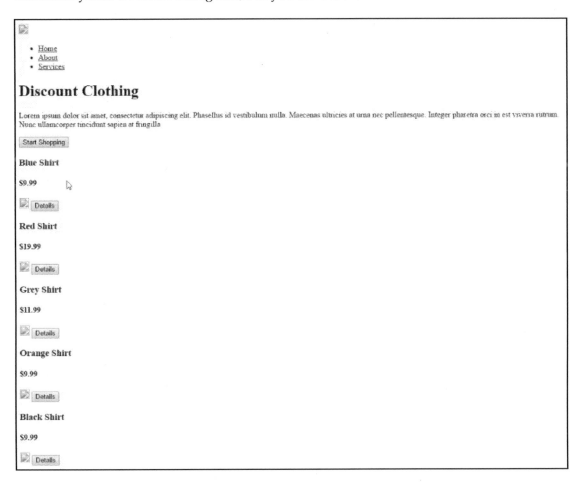

Let's go to the top of the file. We will add our title and fix the stylesheet declarations:

```
<title><?php bloginfo('name'); ?></title>
<link rel="stylesheet" href="<?php echo bloginfo('template_url');
?>/css/foundation.css">
<link rel="stylesheet" href="<?php echo bloginfo('stylesheet_url'); ?>">
<?php wp_head(); ?>
</head>
```

Let's save that, reload our webpage, and now we can see that our CSS is in effect:

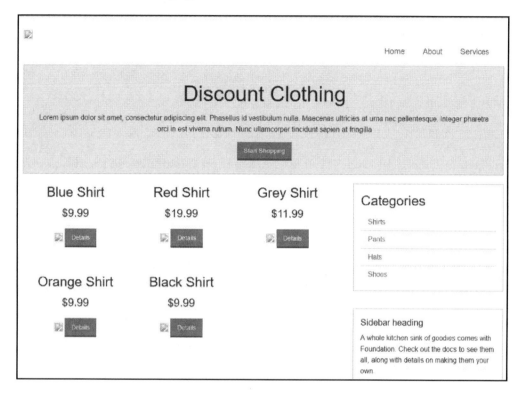

We're just going to work from the top down. So next is the body! We also want to add our body class. So beside our `body` tag, let's add `<?php echo body_class() ?>`.

Now for the logo, we'll do something that we haven't done yet; we'll implement an image, a logo upload from the theme customizer. In order to do that, we need to create a `functions.php` file. So in our `themes` folder, let's create a file called `functions.php` and create a function for `Theme Support`. Here's what the code should look like inside `functions.php`:

```php
<?php
    // Theme Support
    function ms_theme_setup(){
        add_theme_support('custom-logo');
    }

    add_action('after_setup_theme', 'ms_theme_setup');
```

Save that and let's now go to the `index.php` file. Let's remove `<img src="./img/logo.jpg">` and replace it with the following code snippet:

```
<header class="grid-x grid-padding-x">
    <div class="large-6 cell">
        <?php
           if(function_exists('the_custom_logo')){
               the_custom_logo();
           }
        ?>
    </div>
```

We now go to our backend. In the **Themes** we'll click on **Customize**, go to **Site Identity**, and now you should have the area as seen in the following screenshot for a logo:

We are going to click on **Select Logo** and we'll upload the `logo.jpg` file from the `myshop_html` folder, crop the image as per your preference, and click on **Save** and then **Publish**. Now let's go to our frontend and reload, and we now have a logo:

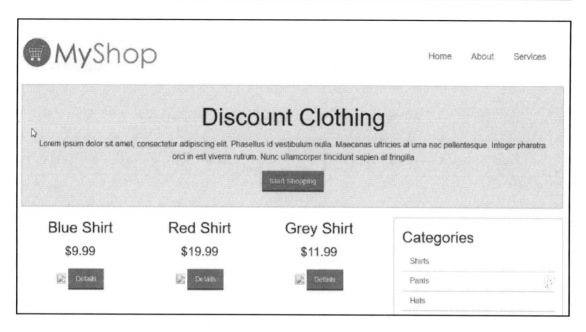

Now let's do the menu. We'll go to the `functions.php` file and add the following code for Nav Menus:

```
register_nav_menus(array(
    'primary' => __('Primary Menu')
));
```

Next we will go to `index.php` and we have our menu. We'll get rid of it completely and add the following code:

```
<div class="large-6 cell">
    <?php wp_nav_menu(array(
      'theme_location' => 'primary',
      'container_class' => 'menu simple main-nav'
    ));
    ?>
</div>
```

Now let's go to our backend. First of all we'll reload, click on the **Menus** option, and we will keep **Sample Page**. Make sure that we have the **Primary Menu** option checked:

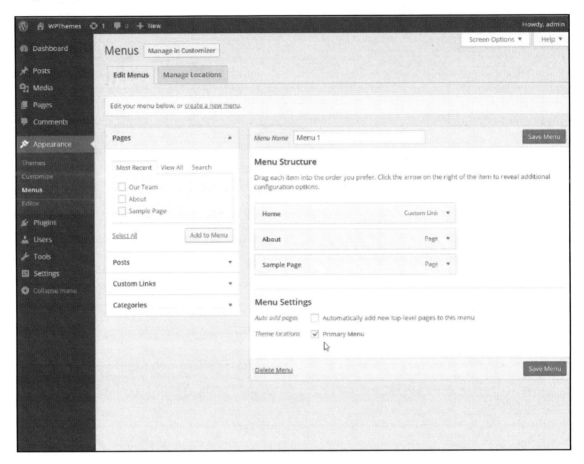

We'll click on **Save Menu** and reload our page. We can see that, now we have our menu and if we click on it we can see the link has changed. You won't see it in the main area of the web page because we don't have that area of the theme set up yet; it's just static content for now, but the menu is working and the logo is there:

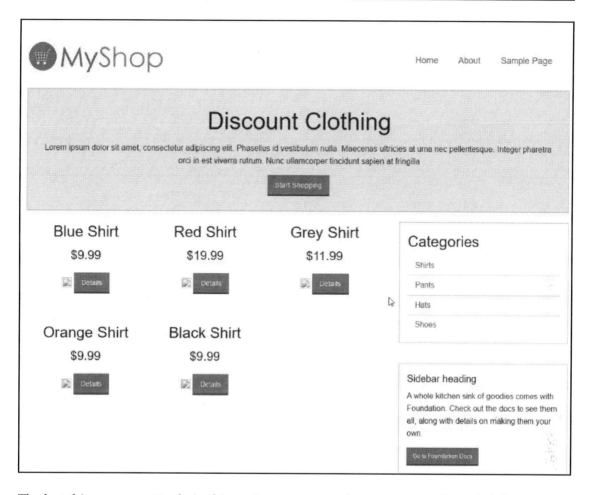

The last thing we want to do in this section is to go to the `index.php` file and right underneath the `footer` tags, we'll put `wp_footer` as shown in the following code snippet:

```
<footer>
<p>&copy; 2017, MyShop</p>
</footer>
<?php wp_footer(); ?>
```

That should give us the admin menu at the top of the web page:

In the next section we'll work with widgets. We will see how to create a custom widget for our showcase area.

The custom showcase widget plugin

In this section we'll create a custom widget for our theme. We have the showcase area on our web page and we will create a widget that can take in a title and some text, and will spit it out right in the widget position.

If we look at the documentation page at `https://codex.wordpress.org/Widgets_API` for the Widgets API, what we need to do basically is create a class that extends `WP_Widget`, and it's going to have a few different methods. It'll have a constructor to call the constructor of the parent class and also set up the title and description, the `widget` method that will output the content of the widget, the `form` method that will output the admin form, and `update` that will take care of updating any fields.

We'll go into the `wp-content | plugins` folder and create a new folder there, `showcase-widget` (although it is a plugin, it's also a widget). Let's go ahead and create a new file in this folder, `showcase-widget.php`, and then one more file, which is going to be the class file, `class.showcase-widget.php`. The `showcase-widget.php` file is going to be the main file but the class file is going to be where we'll do most of the functionality.

We'll now add some code to the `showcase-widget.php` file:

```php
<?php
/*
 * Plugin Name: Showcase Widget
 * Description: Simple showcase area
 * Version: 1.0
 * Author: Brad Traversy
 */

// Include class
include('class.showcase-widget.php');

// Register Widget
function register_showcase_widget(){
    register_widget('Showcase_Widget');
}

add_action('widgets_init', 'register_showcase_widget');
```

 `Showcase_Widget` in the `register_widget('Showcase_Widget');` is our class name. This, in general, needs to be your class name, whatever you choose.

Let's go into the `class.showcase-widget.php` file now. We'll grab the **Default Usage** code from the documentation page (`https://codex.wordpress.org/Widgets_API`) and we'll paste that in our editor with `php` tags. First of all we will have to change the name of the class from `My_Widget` to `Showcase_Widget`, and then let's take a look at the constructor and replace our code in there:

```php
public function __construct() {
    parent::__construct(
        'showcase_widget',
        __('Showcase Widget', 'text_domain'),
        array('description' => __('A widget to display showcase content',
            'text_domain'),)
    );
}
```

The widget method will display the frontend of the widget, so we basically need three things which are as follows:

- We need the title of the widget
- We need the heading
- We need a field for the text

We are going to paste the following code:

```
public function widget( $args, $instance ) {
    $title = apply_filters('widget_title', $instance['title']);
    $heading = $instance['heading'];
    $text = $instance['text'];
}
```

We'll stay in the same method and paste some other stuff in:

```
public function widget( $args, $instance ) {
    $title = apply_filters('widget_title', $instance['title']);
    $heading = $instance['heading'];
    $text = $instance['text'];

    echo $args['before_title'];
    if(!empty($title))
      echo $args['before_title'] . $title . $args['after_title'];

    //Display Content
    echo $this->getContent($heading, $text);
    echo $args['after_widget'];
}
```

Before we move on to these let's create `getContent`, which takes in the heading and text. Let's use the following code snippet:

```
public function getContent($heading, $text){
  $output = '<h1>'.$heading.'</h1><p>'
            .$text.'</p><button class="button">
            Start Shopping</button>';

  return $output;
}
```

Now, we have a variable called `output` that we're sending it to a template with the `h1` and the text. Then we have a button and we are returning the output. So this `getContent` is actually going to display content's `echo $this->getContent($headng, $text);` where we're calling it.

Next, let's scroll down to `function form`. This represents the backend form where we can actually put the heading and the text and stuff like that. We will paste the following code in this function:

```php
public function form( $instance ) {
    if(isset($instance['title'])){
        $title = $instance['title'];
    }
    else{
        $title = __('Showcase Widget', 'text_domain');
    }
}
```

We're checking to see if there's a title, and if there is we'll set it to the variable to whatever is in the instance. If there's not, then we're just going to set it to `Showcase_Widget`. Then we also need to get the heading and the text, which we're pulling from the instances as well:

```php
public function form( $instance ) {
    if(isset($instance['title'])){
        $title = $instance['title'];
    }
    else{
        $title = __('Showcase Widget', 'text_domain');
    }
    $heading = $instance['heading'];
    $text = $instance['text'];
}
```

Now for the actual backend form it's a lot of HTML. We will end the `php` tag after `$text = $instance` and start the `php` tag on the next line. We will then put all the HTML between these opening and closing `phg` tags. Let's paste the following HTML code:

```html
<p>
<label for="<?php echo $this->get_field_id('title'); ?>">
    <?php _e('Title:'); ?>
</label>
<input class="widefat" id="<?php echo $this->
  get_field_id('title'); ?>" name="<?php echo $this->
  get_field_name('title'); ?>" type="text"
  value="<?php echo esc_attr($title); ?>">
 </p>

<p>
<label for="<?php echo $this->get_field_id('heading'); ?>">
    <?php _e('Heading:'); ?>
</label>
<input class="widefat" id="<?php echo $this->
```

```
    get_field_id('heading'); ?>" name="<?php echo $this->
    get_field_name('heading'); ?>" type="text"
    value="<?php echo esc_attr($heading); ?>">
</p>

<p>
<label for="<?php echo $this->get_field_id('text'); ?>">
    <?php _e('Text:'); ?>
</label>
<input class="widefat" id="<?php echo $this->
    get_field_id('text'); ?>" name="<?php echo $this->
    get_field_name('text'); ?>" type="text"
    value="<?php echo esc_attr($text); ?>">
</p>
```

Basically, we have a couple of paragraphs and they contain a label for each field and then the input. We can see for the label we can echo out $this->get_field_id and then what we want is the title. Then for the input we have an id, get_field_id, and then the name of the field which is title. Then for the name we have get_field_name('title'), and for the value we'll use the title variable. We'll escape it with the escape attribute, escape_attr. We'll do the same thing for the heading and for the text. It's really quite simple even although it looks like a lot of code.

Next we want to go to the update method, when we add a heading and text in the backend and we click save, the update method is what saves it. Let us grab some code:

```
public function update( $new_instance, $old_instance ) {
    $instance = array();
    $instance['title'] = (!empty($new_instance['title'])) ?
        strip_tags($new_instance['title']) : '';
    $instance['heading'] = (!empty($new_instance['heading'])) ?
        strip_tags($new_instance['heading']) : '';
    $instance['text'] = (!empty($new_instance[$text])) ?
        strip_tags($new_instance['text']) : '';

    return $instance;
}
```

We have an instance that equals an empty array. We'll say instance['title'] equals whatever is in the new instance saved as the title. It's the same thing with the heading; we'll set it to the new instance heading, and the same with the text, and we'll return that instance. This will update whatever we put in for the fields in the backend widget form.

We'll make sure both files are saved and then we'll go in the backend and let's reload the webpage. Go to **Plugins**, and we can see in the following screenshot the **Showcase Widget** option; it has the description, version, and name, and we'll click on **Activate**.

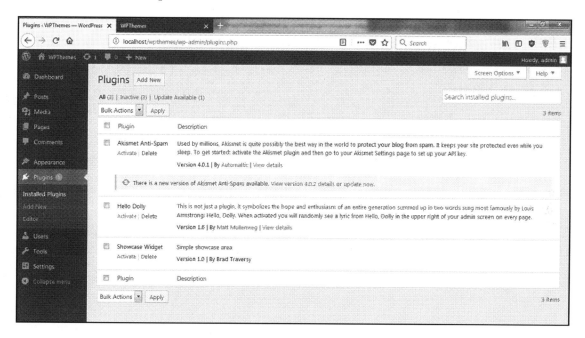

Let's set up a widget position by going into `functions.php` in our `themes` folder. We'll set up our widget locations. So we'll scroll down to the bottom of the file and paste the following code:

```
// Widget Locations
function ms_init_widgets($id){
    register_sidebar(array(
    'name' => 'Sidebar',
    'id' => 'sidebar',
    'before_widget' => '<div class="callout">',
    'after_widget' => '</div>',
    'before_title' => '<h3>',
    'after_title' => '</h3>'
));

register_sidebar(array(
    'name' => 'Showcase',
    'id' => 'showcase',
    'before_widget' => '',
    'after_widget' => '',
```

```
        'before_title' => '',
        'after_title' =>''
    ));
    }


    add_action('widgets_init', 'ms_init_widgets');
```

So we have a function called `ms_init_widgets` and we have two places where we want widgets: one is on the sidebar and the other in the showcase for the widget we just created. In our sidebar we want `div class="callout"` to wrap around the whole widget, we want the title to be an h3. At the end, we'll call our action on `widgets_init` and input the name of our function, `ms_init_widgets`.

Let's save that, go back to the backend, and reload. Now under **Appearance** we can now see **Widgets**. If we click on that, we can see we have the **Sidebar** and the **Showcase** available, and if we scroll down the same page, we can see our **Showcase Widget**, which is the plugin we just created:

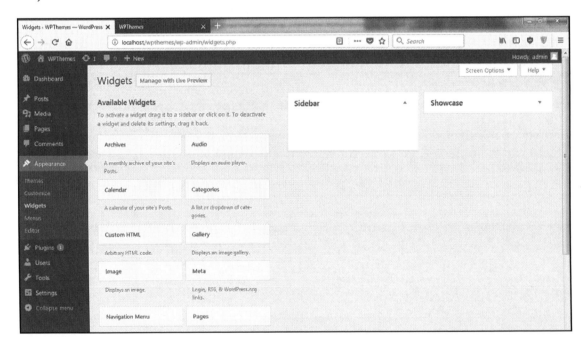

So let's go ahead and add the **Showcase Widget** to the showcase area. Here, we have our title, which we'll get rid of. For the heading we'll type `Discount Clothing`, and for the text we'll put some random text in there. Save that, go back. Well actually, the frontend is not going to change yet because we didn't implement it in the template, but we can see that the content has saved.

What we need to do now is go into our `index.php` file and scroll down to where we have this showcase area. Before we actually show it we want to check to make sure that it's enabled. So we'll modify and put the following code:

```php
<?php if(is_active_sidebar('showcase')) : ?>
    <div class="grid-x grid-padding-x showcase">
        <div class="large-12 cell">
            <div class="callout secondary">
                <?php dynamic_sidebar('showcase'); ?>
            </div>
        </div>
    </div>
<?php endif; ?>
```

Save that, let's go check out the frontend, and we see **Discount Clothing** on the web page, which is our title. Just to make sure that it's actually reading our widget, let's go and change the title to `Discount Clothings` and save it. Go to the frontend, reload, and we get **Discount Clothings**. So you know that this is coming from our custom plugin.

We created a plugin wherein we'll not only able to use it on this theme, but we can use it anywhere. Alright, so in the next section we'll take care of the sidebar widgets. We want the Categories section to actually come from WordPress categories.

The sidebar widget setup

In the last section, we made a custom widget plugin for our showcase area. We'll now implement the sidebar.

We've already done half the work. If we look at `functions.php`, we already have registered our sidebar area.

So what we need to do now is go to `index.php` and go down to where we have our sidebar. Before I get rid of this, let's make sure that we create our widgets.

So we already have the Categories one; we don't have to worry too much about that. But let's create the sidebar heading:

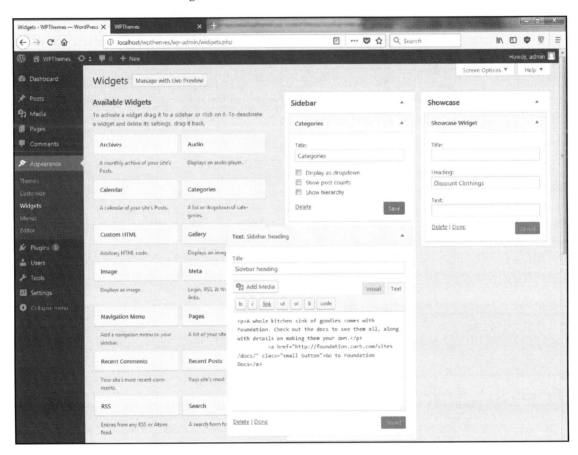

OK, so if we go to our backend, we have **Categories**, we can bring that over to the sidebar at the right, enter the title as **Categories** and save that. Then we also want the custom text present at the bottom-left of the window; we'll put that right under **Categories**. Paste in our heading, `Sidebar heading`, and then our text and the button from the code. We'll save and now we can go ahead and replace this stuff. We remove both the `callout` divs.

We'll then check to see if the sidebar is active, so we'll put `if(is_active_sidebar)` and the position is also called sidebar:

```
<div class="large-4 medium-4 cell">
    <?php if(is_active_sidebar('sidebar')) : ?>
        <?php dynamic_sidebar('sidebar'); ?>
    <?php endif; ?>
</div>
```

In the preceding code, we'll type in `php dynamic_sidebar` and save that. Let's go to the frontend and reload. So there are our widgets, and these are coming from the backend:

Now for the categories let's create some. By default, it's only going to show categories that have posts in them:

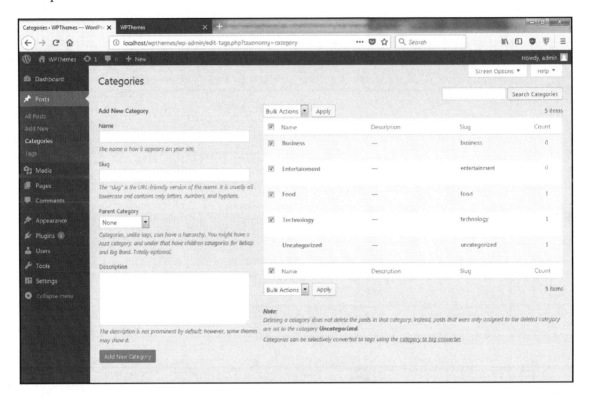

Now these aren't the ones we want at all. So we'll get rid of these and then add **Shirts**, **Hats**, and **Shoes**:

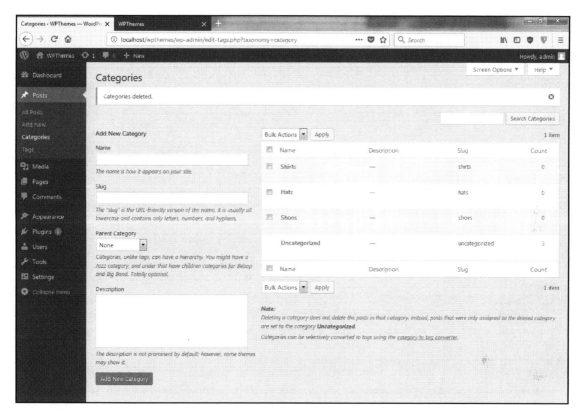

If we go and reload, you still don't see them because we don't have anything in them.

Now just to make sure that the categories will show up, we'll add this `Hello world` to all of the categories and reload them:

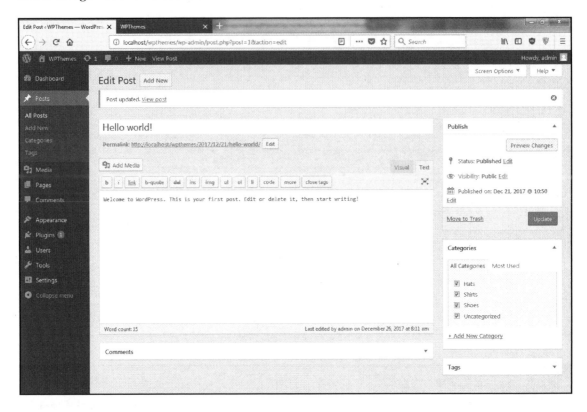

So now you can see they're showing up. That doesn't look great, so we want it to use some custom classes, Foundation classes. We'll create a `widgets` folder in the `themes` folder, and let's grab the `widgets` folder. We'll go to `wp-includes` | `widgets`, and grab the `class-wp-widget-categories.php` file, so we'll copy that and then bring it to the `widgets` in the `themes` folder.

Then we can open that from within Sublime Text. We'll add `Custom` to the end of the class name and search for the `ul` tag. We will add some classes. OK, so `class="menu vertical"` and save it. Then we have to include that file in our `functions.php` file. We'll go to the top and let's type in `require_once` and then we'll pass in `widgets/class-wp-widget-categories.php`.

```
require_once('widgets/class-wp-widget-categories.php');
```

We'll include that file now. Now we'll have to register it. So, let's go down to the bottom and create a function called `ms_register_widgets`. We will pass in the class name, `WP_Widget_Categories_Custom`. We'll then add an action:

```
//Register Widgets
function ms_register_widgets(){
    register_widget('WP_Widget_Categories_Custom');
}

add_action('widgets_init', 'ms_register_widgets');
```

Save it, and let's just go and look at the frontend now. You can see that **Categories** has changed and looks a little better:

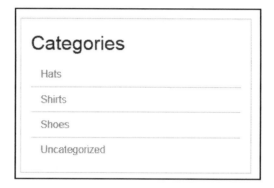

Now the next big thing we have to do is the main content area. We'll do that in the next section, but before we go there, we just want to split up the `index.php` file into our header and footer files. So we'll go from the very top of the file to the end of the `header` tag. We'll cut the code and in its place, we'll say `<?php get_header(); ?>`. We'll then create a file called `header.php` and paste that in there. We should see no change.

So we'll do the same thing with the footer. So in `index.php` we'll go from the bottom up to, let's see, till the `footer` tag, cut that out, and then we'll put in `get_footer`. We'll then create a file called `footer`, and paste that in, go back to the frontend, reload and everything's fine.

The main product post page

In this section, we'll work on this main content area, the area where the posts show up. Right now it's just a bunch of static HTML, so we'll go ahead and fix that.

So let's go into the `index.php` file in the `MyShop` folder in themes. Let's go to `div class="products"` where we have 4-column divs to represent each product. We'll add a class of row on this `products` div and then get rid of all but one of these 4-column divs. We'll preserve the `div` tag with the black shirt details. We'll get rid of all the div tags and then inside the 4-column div we'll go right above it and create our `while` loop.

Before we do the `while` loop, though, let's make sure that there are some posts. So we'll say `if(have_posts)` and then we'll end it. Also, if there are some posts then we want our `while` loop:

```
<div class="grid-x grid-padding-x products">
    <?php if(have_posts()) : ?>
        <?php while(have_posts()) : the_post(); ?>
            <div class="large-4 medium-4 cell product end">
                <h3><?php the_title(); ?></h3>
                <?php if(has_post_thumbnail()) : ?>
                    <?php the_post_thumbnail(); ?>
                <?php endif; ?>

                <a class="button" href="<?php echo
                    the_permalink(); ?>">Details</a>
            </div>
        <?php endwhile; ?>
    <?php endif; ?>
</div>
```

So we'll say `php while`, and we'll say `while(have_posts)` and then we have to just add the `_post`. Then we'll do the `endwhile` on the bottom of this div. So we'll say `php endwhile`. Now inside the `div` tag, we'll have an `h3` and that's going to be the title. So we can say `php the_title`. We're also going to have the thumbnail, so let's do `php` and check for the thumbnail first. We'll say `if(has_post_thumbnail)`. If there's a thumbnail, then we'll say `php the_post_thumbnail`. Then, we'll go right under the `endif` and we need our button, so it's going to actually be a link formatted as a button. We'll give is a class of button, and then this is going to go to `php echo the_permalink`. The text will just say `Details`. So let's save that and let's take a look:

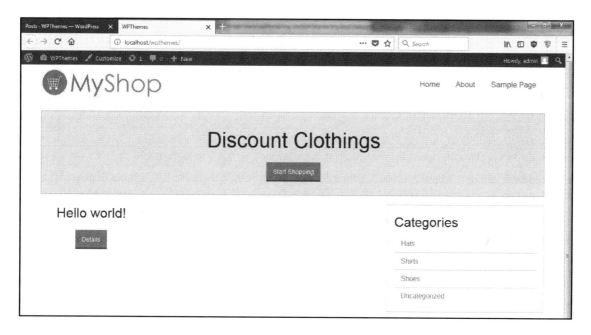

The reason we don't see anything here except for **Hello world** is that's the only post we have. So we'll go in and create some posts. Let us just log back in real quick. We'll go to **All Posts** and you can see we only have **Hello world**. So let's go ahead and click on **Add New**:

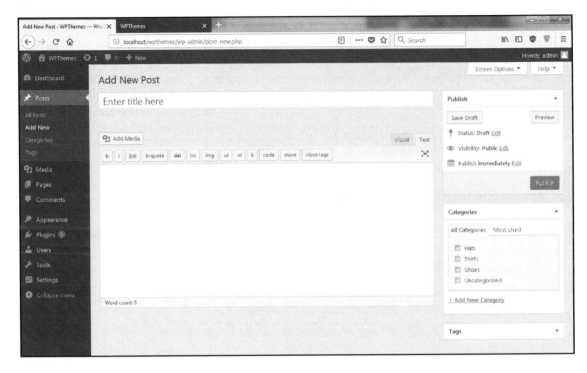

Now notice that there's no area for the featured image down here, so we'll have to make changes in `functions.php` file:

```
function ms_theme_setup(){
    add_theme_support('custom-logo');

    // Featured Image Support
    add_theme_support('post-thumbnails');

    // Nav Menus
    register_nav_menus(array(
        'primary' => __('Primary Menu')
    ));
}
```

To add that, let's go to `functions.php` and go into the `ms_theme_setup` function. We'll type in `add_theme_support`, and we want `post-thumbnails`. Let us now check the output.

You can now see the **Featured Image** box at the bottom-right. So let's go ahead and click on the **Featured Image** box and upload a file.

We have all these shirts. We'll choose the blue and white one and set that as a featured image. Let's call this `Blue & White Shirt`. For the description, we'll get some sample text real quick:

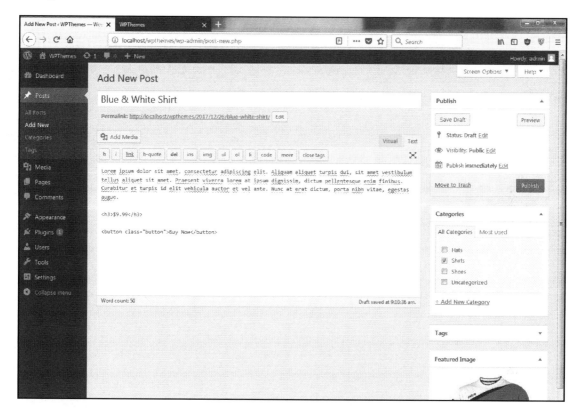

We'll copy a couple of random sentences for the description and paste that in. We want the price as well. So we'll put that in an `h3` and say `$9.99`. We also want the button, so we'll give that a class of `button` and we'll just say `Buy Now`. It's not going to have actual e-commerce functionality. So this is what pretty much all of our product descriptions are going to look like. Let's copy that, and then let's choose the **Shirts** category. We can add some tags; we'll say `blue shirt`, `white shirt`, and `clothes`. We added those and that looks good, so let's go ahead and publish.

We'll go back to the home page and there's our shirt. We'll disable the **Hello world** post in the **Posts** by moving it to **Trash**. For the black shirt, we'll go ahead an upload the image. We'll grab the `shirt_black.jpg` image file, say `Black Shirt`, and then paste in what we had for the other one:

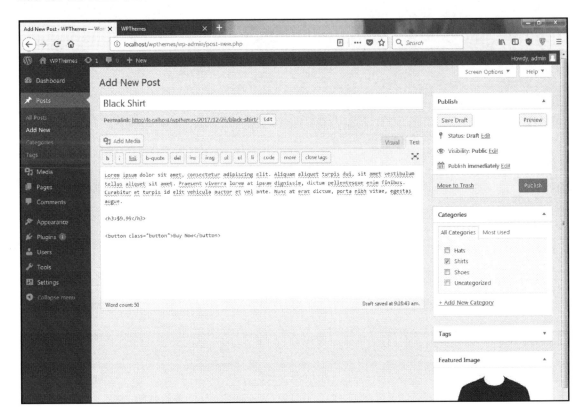

We'll publish that and go ahead and add the rest of them. We went ahead and added the rest of the products. Let's go to the frontend and reload, and there we go! It's starting to look like a real shopping cart:

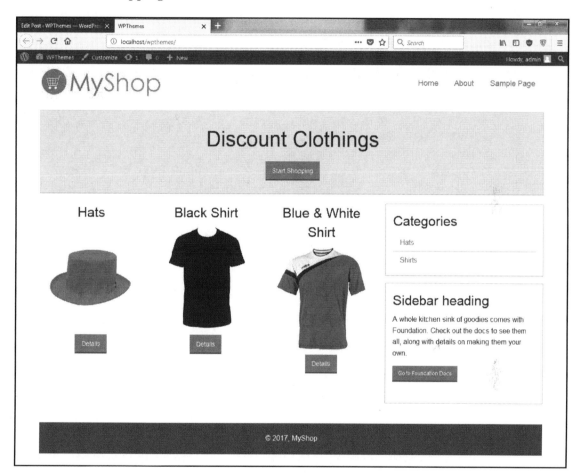

Now if we go and click on one of the **Details** buttons, it takes us to the correct place, to the right product, but this isn't how we want to set it up. We want to have the description and look like a real shopping cart page.

Another issue if we go to a regular page and not a post, like say the **About** page, is that it's formatted the same way as the main post page. So we don't want that either. So in the next section, we'll take care of that and get these pages looking correctly.

Single product and single page

Up to this point we've done pretty well. We have our main post page or our homepage done, but if I click on one of these and we go to the single product page, it doesn't look too good. We're also missing a bunch of information.

So we'll now create a new file inside the `MyShop` theme folder and save it as `single.php`. After creating this file if we go back to the single view and reload, it'll be blank because it's looking at the single file. So what we'll do is copy everything we have in the `index` page.

So we'll grab all of it, we'll paste it in, and get rid of the `showcase` part because we don't want that. We want the showcase on the homepage only. We'll put an `hr` tag in there.

We'll do the same thing as far as checking for posts and looping through the post even though it's a single post as we did in the previous section. But we'll get rid of everything that's in between the `while` loop:

```
<?php while(have_posts()) : the_post(); ?>
    <div class="row single-product">
        <div class="large-5 columns">
            <a href="#">Go Back</a>
            <br>
            <?php if(has_post_thumbnail()) : ?>
                <?php the_post_thumbnail(); ?>
            <?php endif; ?>
        </div>
    </div>
<?php endwhile; ?>
```

We're just going to get that out and then we'll create a new `div` with a class. Let's create a div with the class of `row` and also `single-product`. Inside that, we'll have a 5-column div. Within this div, we'll have our `Go Back` link, and let's put a line break. Then we'll check for the featured image or the thumbnail. So we'll copy from the `index.php` file. We just want to check to see if it's there, and if it is then we'll display it. Then that should be it for the 5-column div. So that's just going to be the image.

After that, we'll have a 7-column div. This is going to have the title, which we'll put in an h2. So we'll say `php the_title` and right under that, we'll put `the_content`. We'll then put an `hr` tag. We want the tags and the following code snippet. We're just checking for the tags, see if the function exists, and then spit them out:

```
<div class="large-7 columns">
    <h2><?php the_title(); ?></h2>
    <?php the_content(); ?>
```

```
<hr>
<?php if(the_tags()): ?>
    <?php if(function_exist('the_tags')) { ?>
        <strong>Tags: </strong>
        <?php the_content_tags('', ',',''); ?><br/><?php } ?>
    <?php endif; ?>
</div>
```

Let's go ahead and save this. We'll go back to our page and reload, and now we have a product page:

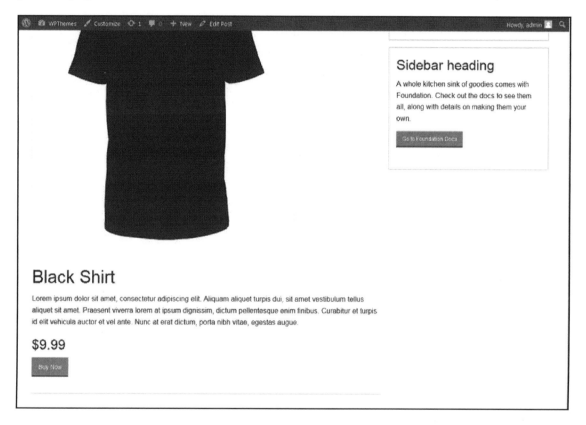

As for **Go Back**, right now it won't do anything. Let's have it go to the home page. We'll say php and we should be able to say echo site_url:

```
<div class="row single-product">
    <div class="large-5 columns">
    <a href="<?php echo site_url(); ?>">Go Back</a>
    <br>
```

Click on **Go Back**, and it brings us back to our homepage. So that looks good.

Adding multiple images

Now we also want to be able to have multiple images in here as well. Let's go to our **Posts** in the backend, and let's go to **Blue & White Shirt**. Click on **Add Media** and then **Create Gallery**. We'll upload a couple more files. We have files in the folder as shown in the following screenshot. We'll use those and create a new gallery:

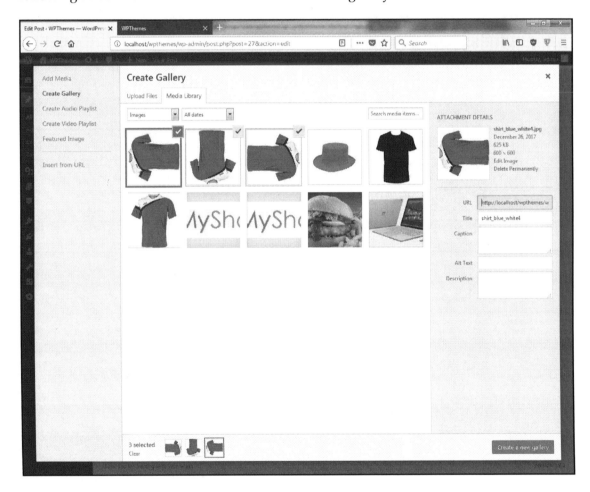

For the link, we'll just say **Media File** and **Insert gallery**. Let's update, go back to the frontend, reload, and now we have some images for that product. That looks pretty much like a like a standard shopping cart details page!

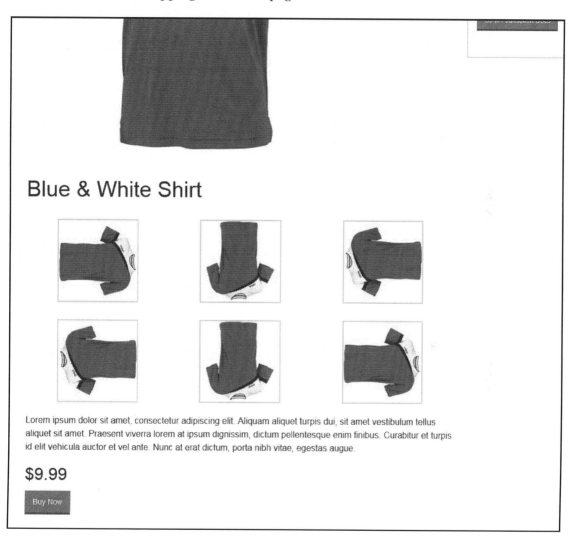

We're getting there! Now for the regular pages such as **About**, we obviously don't want this. We'll go into our folder and create a new file, page.php. Then if we go back and reload, it's going to be blank. Let's grab what we have in the index page, paste it right in there, and then we want to go down to where the post loop is.

Let's just take everything out from within the `while` loop and create a `div` and this will be a 12-column div, `large-12 columns`. Let's then add an `h3`, which will have `the_title`. Under `the_title` let's add the whole thumbnail thing. We'll grab it from `single.php`. So if there's an image it'll show it, and then we just need `the_content`:

```php
<?php while(have_posts()) : the_post(); ?>
    <div class="large-12 columns"></h3>
        <h3><?php the_title(); ?></h3>
        <?php if(has_post_thumbnail()): ?>
            <?php the_post_thumbnail(); ?>
        <?php endif; ?>

        <?php the_content(); ?>
    </div>
<?php endwhile; ?>
```

Let's save it, go back to **About**, and now we have just a standard page with a title and the body. It's the same thing for **Sample Page**. We look pretty good at the moment:

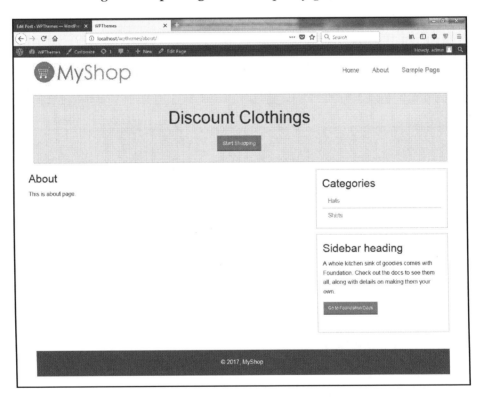

Now if you want to have comments on your product or post pages, you could do that. We could go to `single.php`, go after the `div` tag, and just say php `comments_template` and save it. Go back, reload, and now we have our comments:

```php
<?php comments_template(); ?>
```

Let's say `This is a test comment`. It will then leave comments:

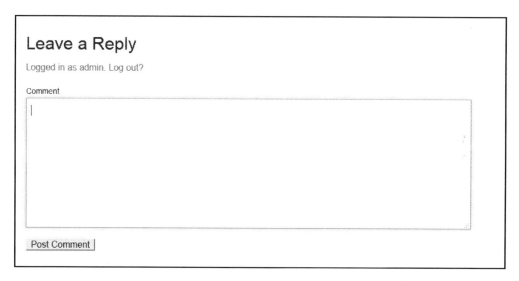

> You could make your comments template look better as we have done it previously.

You may even re-brand it as reviews (product review).

Summary

We introduced a few new aspects of WordPress theme development in this project, such as creating your own plugin widget and implementing the image, the logo, and the customizer, and so on.

Conclusion

That's the end of the book, and we have created five amazing WordPress-based themes. We hope that you liked the journey this book has taken you through to create them. We wish you all the success and hope that you continue to better your WordPress themes.

Index

Made in the USA
Lexington, KY
28 August 2018